Invested in the Common Good

Susan Meeker-Lowry

New Society Publishers
Philadelphia, PA   Gabriola Island, BC

Library of Congress Cataloging-in-Publication Data
Meeker-Lowry, Susan.
   Invested in the common good / Susan Meeker-Lowry.
     p.   cm.
   Includes biblographical references and index.
   ISBN 0-86571-291-3 (hard). -- ISBN 0-86571-292-1 (pbk.)
   1. Investments--Moral and ethical aspects. 2. Economics--Moral and ethical
aspects. 3. Common good. 4. Social responsibility of business. I. Title.
HG4528.M44 1995   332.6--dc20   95-11866

Inquiries regarding requests to reprint all or part of *Invested in the Common Good*
should be addressed to New Society Publishers, 4527 Springfield Avenue,
Philadelphia, PA, 19143, USA; or New Society Publishers, P.O. Box 189, Gabriola
Island, BC V0R 1X0, Canada.

   ISBN Hardcover   USA 0-86571-291-3   CAN 1-55092-242-4
   ISBN Paperback   USA 0-86571-292-1   CAN 1-55092-243-2

Cover design by Jodi Forlizzi of Inks Studio. Book design by Martin Kelley. Index
by DoMi Stauber. Printed on partially-recycled paper using soy-based ink by
Capital City Press of Montpelier, Vermont.

To order directly from the publisher, add $3.00 to the price for the first copy, and
add 75¢ for each additional copy. Send check or money order to:
   In the United States: *In Canada:*
   New Society Publishers   New Society Publishers
   4527 Springfield Avenue   PO Box 189
   Philadelphia, PA 19143   Gabriola Island, BC V0R 1XO

NEW SOCIETY PUBLISHERS is a project of the New Society Educational
Foundation, a nonprofit, tax-exempt, public foundation in the United States, and
of the Catalyst Education Society, a nonprofit society in Canada. Opinions
expressed in this book do not necessarily represent positions of the New Society
Educational Foundation, nor the Catalyst Education Society.

Dedication

TO DADDY, WHO UNDERSTANDS

Table of Contents

Acknowledgments

THIS BOOK HAS been several years in the making, so I want to apologize immediately to anyone who should be listed here and isn't. The pieces in Part Three: "Breaking the Corporate Grip," were compiled in 1992 and 1993 to be included in a book of that name. That book didn't happen, so these articles were incorporated into *Invested in the Common Good*, adding an important activist component. Of course the pieces were updated before being published here. I am grateful to Richard Grossman, Janice Mantell, Theresa Freeman, and Brian Tokar for their contributions and patience.

A special thanks to Thomas Berry for writing the foreword. I am grateful for his support of my work and greatly indebted to him, for his influence on my thinking and understanding of the world. I consider Thomas to be one of the great persons of our times and feel so honored to know him.

My gratitude also to the other writers whose articles add so much to this book: Joel Russ, John Mohawk, Susan Witt, Paul Glover, Todd Punam, Michael Kinsley, Paddy Garrett-McCarthy, Stephen Wheeler, Patti Wheeler, and Kenneth A. Dahlberg. Many thanks to Roger Pritchard, Paul Terry, Christopher Mogil, and Anne Slepian for their help and collaboration in Chapter Five: Investing Within the System. In addition, thanks to *The Boycott Quarterly*, *Neighborhood Works*, *Akwe:kon*, the Institute for Community Economics and the E. F. Schumacher Society for permission to reprint articles.

So much has happened in my own life since I began this book. Close friends have moved away (but aren't forgotten) and new energy is coming in. Through all these changes my family and small, close circle of friends have remained constant and supportive. I want to acknowledge these people here: My father who shared his love of the woods with me from the time I was a baby; my grandmother whose love, wisdom, and prayers have kept me going throughout my life, especially the hard times; my sister whose strength and courage are unmatched; and my mother whose love is as present and real to me today as when she lived. And my sons Jason, Ethan, and Colin deserve a medal for their patience, especially Colin who just wanted me to *do* something with him. Gratitude also to my friends Robin, Joe (see, I told you I'd put you in!), Cathy and Kathy and the folks at The Forest Partnership, Richard, Berne, Tris, and Charles (who always understood when I needed to hole up by myself for days to work on the book even when they needed me in the office).

I am indebted to Lorraine and Dana for their friendship and teachings, and to the circle for being there no matter what.

I want to acknowledge my dear friends Patty and Scott Manning who know what it is like to fight the system with courage and hope in the face of incredible odds. Patty and Scott are an inspiration to me and many others here. And when I think things are too tough, I remember what they have been through and know I can make it too. I love you guys!

Finally, much love and kisses (and thanks, too) to Brian Tokar for his support, encouragement, ideas, and for all the conversations about the book "stuff" and help with computer weirdnesses above and beyond the call of duty.

Foreword

THE TRANSITION FROM our present situation to a more viable mode of human presence I consider "The Great Work" of our times. It is the comprehensive answer to the supreme peril confronting the human community in this final decade of the twentieth century. The entire future of the planet and of every living and nonliving being on the planet will depend on our success in bringing about this transition.

This new era of a "mutually enhancing" human presence upon the Earth could be referred to as the Ecozoic Era. We need such a designation since, through our industrial plundering of the planet, we are terminating the Cenozoic Era in the geo-biological story of the Earth, a period which has lasted for the last 65 million years.

The danger is not precisely the extinction of life on the planet since that is not likely. The issue is the extent of degradation that is taking place, how this continued deteriorating can be terminated and a healing process initiated—how the Integral Ecozoic Community can be established.

The highly differentiated range of ecological efforts at the present time can be considered among the most encouraging aspects of the present situation. These efforts range from extensive studies of the more profound cultural causes of our present cultural pathologies, to statistical information of where the main difficulties are, to practical solutions in all the various phases of our society.

Among the most promising of recent human ventures is the increase in the number of community-supported agricultural projects. Generally in these projects a group of families each contributes a certain amount to a common fund to support an agriculturalist or knowledgeable person who will preside over the planting, tending, and harvesting of the crops, generally vegetables and fruits, that are chosen by the group before the planting season.

The associates in the projects may assist in the cultivation, although they are usually under no obligation to do so. The food is harvested each week, generally from May through December or throughout the year, and is made available to be picked up by the members whenever they wish.

Since the cultivation is carried out in accord with the organic processes of the local region, a bonding is established between the humans and the region and between the humans themselves. The immediacy of this bonding is easily carried over into more extensive relationships. A community life is begun.

The full significance of this relationship needs to be appreciated. The more this can be appreciated as carrying a sacred dimension in itself, the more effective it could be in the future. We need civic activities based on a profound sense of meaning inherent in the universe and in the life process. This is the beginning of a new realization that the human and the natural world form a single interdependent community of existence.

Fundamental to this project is the commitment of its members to the integrity of the food that is grown. It is grown in accord with the inner life of the soil and the natural biorhythms of the region. It represents a withdrawal from the efforts of industrial farming to impose arbitrary human patterns on the natural processes of the region. It represents, in its more profound meaning, a new sensitivity in our relations with the natural world. This new mode finds expression in a recent book by E. O. Wilson entitled *Biophilia*, a term that indicates the tendency of living beings to interact with each other in the intimacies of a single community of existence.

While I have mentioned here the formation of local communities in their expression through agricultural projects, this is only one of the multitude of ways in which the new era of human presence on the planet in a mutually enhancing manner is beginning to take shape. Community ventures emerging everywhere are withdrawing from the devastation that humans have been inflicting on the planet in recent centuries.

We are gradually shaping programs for the bioregional restructuring of the human communities in the various regions of the planet. This includes practical information concerning organic agriculture, local economic reforms, the use of solar energy, and a multitude of other movements toward a new mode of human-Earth relationships.

Through Wes Jackson and Wendell Berry and John Todd and so many others, we now know how to deal with the genetic basis of our food supply, how the local community functions, how to purify our waste water. Through Amory Lovins we know how to deal with our energy needs. Through the proposals of Peter Berg and the designs of Richard Register, we know how to design our cities so that we can diminish our dependence on the automobile and how we can bring about a renewal of the woodlands and streams and meadows and wildlife within an urban setting.

Through Brian Swimme we know the story of the universe throughout the total course of its emergence. We can experience our integral relationship not only with the planet Earth but also with the entire universe. The story of the universe is the story of every being in the universe. In a special manner the story of the universe and the story of the Earth are at the same time the story of the human. This identity that we experience with the Earth deepens our awareness that we prosper and decline together. We cannot long have a rising gross human product and a declining gross Earth product. We cannot have well humans on a sick planet.

Yet while we now experience some of more comprehensive contexts of our historical situation, we are, here in the United States, in urgent need of establishing the basic life communities through which we might create a profound bonding with each other and with the natural world. This bonding in sustainable local communities is a primary concern.

The first aspect of this bonding is to establish a viable habitat, that is, a context in which we attain our nourishment in as independent a manner as can be achieved. This includes shelter and food supply and basic life security. It also includes a limitation in numbers since the human has rights only to a certain limited area as habitat. The human must not intrude excessively on the habitat needed by other species. Our community habitat includes not only the human species but other species as well.

The second need is community education. None of us is sufficiently knowledgeable in every aspect of what is needed for sustainable living. We need to educate ourselves now in a special manner since we are entering into new areas of understanding. We need new skills in survival that we have neglected for so long due to our excessive dependence on the technologies of a plundering industrial society.

There is also the need to educate our children. So many things that they must learn are not being taught in the educational system such as now exists. Home schooling and group family schooling are increasingly needed. Local community schools need to be transformed under the guidance and with the encouragement of the local community.

Another need is the skill to participate in the governance of the civic communities to which we belong. We need to participate in the zoning boards of our local communities. If we do not participate more extensively, then developers will continue to take possession of what should be community land, land that should be saved from exploitation. A part of this community effort is also to establish local security. Members of communities must become responsible for each other and for the common well-being.

An increasing need for local communities is health care for everyone. For women, first of all, since upon the women of a society so much depends. They are most immediately in care of the children. Even with all the assistance given by men and with all possible help from public resources, the responsibilities that are assumed by women still tend to be disproportionate to the responsibilities assumed by men.

Most significant for the community is a realization that for the community, as for the individual and for the universe generally, the basic meaning of existence is celebration. The universe by definition is a celebratory reality. The birds sing, the flowers bloom, the rivers flow. The great natural phonomena of the day and the night, the dawn and the sunset, the spring and fall, the drought and the coming of the rains: all these constitute the Great Liturgy of the universe.

Humans throughout the planet establish their own rituals in relation to these grand transformational moments. These are the moments of Grace. These experiences provide the psychic energy that we need to endure the difficulties of life and to enter on to the creativity needed to achieve the destiny that is before us.

Poetry and art and music and dance, the stories told, the crafts in their creativity, our wedding rituals and family life, the entire range of human activities, all these are the forms in which human celebration expresses itself. We will bring about a fulfillment of the Great Work in proportion as we articulate our community celebrations with some true exaltation. We will have begun the Ecozoic Era.

The work of Susan Meeker-Lowry has, over the course of recent years, been among the most helpful in guiding us into this new era. Here in this book we find a clear understanding of the three aspects in any extensive program concerned with bringing about a profound adjustment or renewal of human affairs. There are the Principles Involved, the Guiding Strategy, and the Immediate Tactics; Meeker-Lowry emphasizes the Guiding Strategy and the Immediate Tactics that we need.

—Thomas Berry
July, 1994

Part I

TOWARD AN EARTH-CENTERED ECONOMY

ONE

The Earth is My/Our Source

ONE THING THAT has not changed in the years since *Economics as If the Earth Really Mattered* was published is my love of Earth and my belief—indeed, my knowing—that we can work consciously in partnership with Earth for healing, for growth, and for change. I grew up in the White Mountains of New Hampshire, before it was discovered by the multitudes. The woods were my playground. I knew all the special places: waterfalls, deep swimming holes, caves, secret paths to magical groves, berry patches, rare flowers, neat rocks, the best views. My father, to whom this book is dedicated, taught my sister and me about the plants and animals and how to treat the woods with care and respect. His love for the woods and everything that lives there was his greatest lesson to me and his greatest gift.

In my own life, I continue to find comfort and healing in the woods, although I don't spend nearly enough time there these days. I am grateful to carry nature in my heart wherever I happen to be. The knowledge that the life force running through trees, rivers, animals, insects, and plants is the same life force running though me gives me hope and adds meaning to my daily activities. The power and the connection this implies makes my heart sing. Beyond this, it brings home the fact that we, as humans, are not alone in our struggle. What more can we ask than a partnership with the Earth, with Creation herself?

If there is one "message" I want to share with you by writing this book, it is this: We are not separate from Earth—we are a part of Earth. We belong here. Earth is our home. The place we live on the Earth shapes and nourishes us, and this relationship needs to be reciprocal. When we become grounded in place, we know who we are, and we can take a stand for what we believe, for what we love. Becoming whole, then, means deepening our connection with the place we live and allowing ourselves to experience the implications this brings to our lives willingly and without reservation.

For me, today, this means writing about the importance of working in conscious partnership with the Earth for our mutual healing. I have spent the past several years willingly labeling myself an "activist." I have attempted to organize movements and events to catalyze changes I felt were necessary. Always I found myself grappling with linear problems, answering the "What about?" questions. These questions usually involve the incredibly powerful opposition. Or they deal with the supposed benefits associated with the status quo.

For example, in fighting Hydro-Quebec's plans for dams in Quebec that would destroy James Bay and the lives of indigenous peoples, we needed to deal with questions about future sources of "necessary" electricity. The assumption was that the energy needs projected into the future were true, and that they were valid. Those of us opposing Hydro-Quebec had to justify our opposition in the context of these assumptions. When we disagreed with the assumptions, we were labeled "unrealistic" and risked losing our credibility. In another example, the crisis in the old-growth forests in Pacific Northwest, the questions revolve around jobs and the political and economic power of the timber industry.

As an activist, I attempt to answer each of these concerns in a logical, linear fashion. Unfortunately, there is no end to these questions, and I eventually feel powerless and unable to make any headway. For me, the return to sanity—and to feeling powerful—comes when I let go of this level of inquiry and move to the place in my heart where Earth resides.

The crux of the problem, I feel, is our mistaken perception of being separated from nature. This perception is carried to an unfortunate extreme by some of the most well-meaning activists I know in their disdain for, and what sometimes feels like active hate of, human beings. Yes, I know people are responsible for all the destruction and exploitation of the Earth and Earth-based peoples. I know the quest for power and money is distinctly human. I know we are different from other species in many ways. So I understand where this hate comes from, and I think I understand the logic behind it.

But Earth does not hate. Earth does not judge. Earth simply is. She does what is necessary each moment to support life. There is no distinction: This is human life, this is nonhuman life. We, on the other hand, make judgments all the time—and our frame of reference isn't life, it is us. We ask, "How important is this insect? Can we afford to save these ancient trees? Can we relocate these Indians so we can mine these ores?" We develop elaborate, "balanced" methods of skewing the answers to these kinds of questions to give us what we want while making it look "right." You know what? It doesn't work. And the reason it doesn't work, ultimately, is we cannot realistically separate ourselves from the larger whole of the Earth, even if we think we can do it on paper.

It has been years since I became aware of my own personal connection with the Earth. Of course, in my childhood my relationship with the outdoors was unquestioned. I thought of certain trees, rocks, groupings of wildflowers (especially lady slippers) and places as special friends, but I didn't talk about it. I guess I took them for granted. When I was about twelve, things changed. I remember sitting at the kitchen table with my mother, telling her that "the magic is gone." I can still see the hurt look in her eyes. She had no idea what I was talking about—and I really didn't either. But she could see that I was in pain, and she assured me that more magic would come into my life as I got older. I wasn't so sure.

Then, when I was in my early twenties, I discovered the Findhorn community and the magical relationship its members had with plants growing in their vegetable garden. This relationship started when Dorothy Maclean, a community member, heeded her inner voice that told her to "harmonize with the essence of nature." At the time, her primary concern was growing food in the garden's poor soil. She writes, "I began to understand that these beings I was communicating with were actually the manifestations of an intelligent forcefield that had been interpreted in different ways by different cultures through the ages." People listened to the messages from the "devas," as Maclean called them, and Findhorn's garden became legendary. Here was the magic of my childhood!

Years have passed since those early days when Findhorn's garden produced twenty-pound cabbages. I hear that the garden is now relatively normal as the community concentrates on other aspects of its growth. But the early lessons of working consciously with nature have not been forgotten and, in fact, serve as a touchstone for many people and communities around the world seeking a healing and renewing relationship with nature and each other. Maclean believes, "There is a part of each of us that is of the same essense as the devas. We might call that the soul level, or the spirit. Thus any of us can 'listen to' and 'talk' with the angelic world, because we share the same worlds within us. Love and appreciation are the bridges between us."

Science itself is revealing to us a rather magical universe. The saying "Everything is connected" is being proven true on an actual, physical level. In fact, the emerging view of the universe is closer to that described by mystics of the past than by science of just twenty years ago. There are many books available today that can help us explore and understand the nature of the universe. These include my favorites such as *The Universe is a Green Dragon*, by Brian Swimme; *The Universe Story*, by Thomas Berry and Brian Swimme; and *The Breathing Cathedral*, by Martha Heyneman, as well as more technical books for those with a scientific bent. The film *Mindwalk* (based on Fritjof Capra's book *Turning Point*) addresses some of these issues in an interesting and thought-provoking manner. While I personally don't feel a need to use science to justify my own experiences, it is satisfying to discover that science is beginning to explain the universe in the way I've intuited things for as long as I can remember.

So how can we bring the Earth's messages into our decision-making processes? How can our oneness with all of life be a "practical" tool for creative, evolutionary change?

We need to open our minds and hearts to "hear" what the Earth tells us. In order to do this we need to

Believe it is possible. This is essential. Without belief, your heart and your inner ear will be blocked.

Desire that it happen. The place in your body this is felt is in your heart. Don't put stuff on this feeling, just let it be, close your eyes if you like and breathe into and out of your heart. Relax. What comes, comes.

Let the love flow. Love is what connects us to each other and to the Earth. It is the most powerful force in the universe.

Drop preconceived ideas. Don't get it into your head that you will "hear" a voice with a deep message. You might. But it is more likely you will get a sense of something. You might feel peaceful or experience a feeling of everything being in its place, a message of constancy over time, or of resilience. You might come away with a "knowing" that you can't explain—it just is. Whatever your experience, accept it and be grateful for it.

Give thanks and honor your experience. Saying "thank you" gives back energy and completes the circle. Honor your experience by allowing it a place in your life.

Again, let go of any doubt that creeps in. You might question your feelings and your inner knowing of what's real. When these doubts come (and they will), recognize them for what they are and gently let them go. The doubts represent the logical, rational mind, which is already overdeveloped in most of us anyway. The intuitive, open mind has gifts for us. Let them in.

Act. Find a way of integrating your experiences with your everyday living.

Share your experiences. This is important. In my experience, many people are open to deep communication with Earth and many more have had experiences (especially when they were children) they simply don't talk about. Sometimes this reluctance occurs because they don't want to look strange to others, but more often it is because they simply don't have a language for their experiences. And sometimes they have forgotten, and your story helps them remember.

Do I practice this in my own life? You bet! I believe we are in a constant and ever-changing relationship with all of life. There are no accidents or coincidences. Rather, life is a dance, a flowing of energy, a give and take. What comes into our life in any given moment has meaning, even if we are unable to understand it. If we can lose sight of this, our lives can become chaotic and painful. Remember, this is our perception, not how things really are. I have to remind myself of this often!

There is a small bird that sings to me on summer afternoons. I know this bird and I are connected and that both of us are very conscious of this connection. Sometimes she gets impatient with me. She sings and sings until finally I pay attention. When she knows I'm listening, her song changes and the frantic energy of my day fades away. I am always grateful for her song.

In my backyard, there is a tall spruce tree that, in the early morning before the dew has evaporated, literally vibrates with glowing, green, life energy. Every time I see this phenomenon I am blown away. That "ordinary" spruce tree has kept me sane many days, reminding me when I need it most that there is more to life than what appears on the surface.

Rainbows are also magical symbols of life. Their appearance is never an accident or coincidence—they always have meaning for me. In my life they appear in moments of joy or despair, bringing confirmation or the promise of hope and deliverance. A couple of years ago, I flew over clearcuts in Washington state with Michael Stewartt, then director of Lighthawk. (Lighthawk is a forest conservation organization based in Santa Fe, New Mexico that takes people—including Congresspersons and others in places of influence—on flights over degraded and clearcut forests to show what's really going on. The organization's flights and photos have had a major impact on public awareness of the damage caused by industrial forestry.) A major aspect of my work over the past several years has been doing what I can to awaken people to the majesty and wisdom of old growth. The love I feel for ancient forests is beyond words. That day was windy and rainy. In fact, until the actual moment of departure, we weren't sure we could even make the flight. While flying over the most devastated land, scarred by roads, denuded of trees, rivers clouded by silt from erosion, I looked to my left and saw a brilliant rainbow—and we flew right through it! Will there be deliverance from devastation and exploitation for the ancient trees, for all of us? I have to believe the answer is Yes!

I thought long and hard about including this section here. I often talk about my personal relationship with the Earth (specifically trees) with my friends, and even include it in my presentations at times. This is the first time I have put my own way of "talking with the Earth" in such detail, so I shared this section with a trusted friend for his feedback. My friend challenged me to take "listening to the Earth" into the realm of activism: How does my relationship with the Earth feed my work? How can we listen and act powerfully? How can we take Earth's messages into the streets? How can we become Earth's voice and Earth's hands? What moves us from quietly listening and giving thanks to outward action? His main concern was that too many people already have given up trying to change the system, focusing instead on personal change as a way of changing the world, a kind of narcissism. While it's true that "as we change, so changes the world," it is also true that we need to work together to do it. And changing the systems of repression takes more than good thoughts—we need to act powerfully and with compassion, and we need to take risks.

My immediate response is simple—love. Love leads to action on behalf of the beloved. For example, I love my sons, so I find myself going to bat for them, being their advocate in the schools, helping them understand how the system works, how to question it, how to take action that can change what they feel is unjust. When my sister was in the hospital after an accident, and all during the long months of her rehabilitation, I was her advocate with a whole range of professionals who worked with her—the neurologists, physical therapists, speech therapists, nurses and doctors. Love makes us strong; it gives us courage we never knew we had. Love that leads to action is a tangible thing—it is felt by others who find themselves doing what you ask, listening to you, respecting you almost in spite of themselves. Passion touches people; it is irresistible and strong.

Thanks to the magical nature of the universe, as I was pondering how to communicate my thoughts on this subject, I came across an article by Stephanie Kaza in *ReVision* (Winter 1993) entitled "Conversations with Trees: Toward an Ecologically Engaged Spirituality." Kaza is an assistant professor in the Environmental Program at the University of Vermont, where she teaches environmental and feminist ethics. She is also the author of *The Attentive Heart: Conversations with Trees* (Ballantine Books, 1993).

Kaza describes her own experience communicating with the Earth. She writes,

> My premise and experience is that ecological relationships are a critical aspect of social reality. By this I do not mean the many ways in which human life is supported by "ecological services" such as oxygen production by plants, groundwater recharge, and soil fertility. I refer instead to a view of "social" which reflects an expanded sense of ecological self.... The ecological self is experienced as one node in a web of relationships where one's actions reverberate throughout the causal web. The relational self... responds not only to human actions but also to the actions of plants, animals, stones, rivers, and mountains. These nonhuman members of the ecological web are themselves relational and influential. To the extent that one engages in developing relationships with spiders, snakes, and fir trees, for example, one is socially engaged with the nonhuman world.

For Kaza, the first steps in relating to nonhumans is to "acknowledge the existence of the Other" which, in a practical sense, means learning about local flora and fauna and the Earth's cycles and seasons. "With experience over time, one begins to actively participate in relationships with local life forms—the fence lizard on the deck, the towhees by the compost, the alders along the creek."

How does this lead to social action? Each person is different, of course. I found it interesting that Kaza and I have both identified similar specific actions that can be directly traced to "listening to the Earth:"

Speaking for those not included in human decision-making. Here in Vermont we did this rather memorably during a hearing in Burlington about the fate of the northern forests. Members of the Vermont All Species Project, wearing masks and costumes of their chosen species, spoke for wolf, bear and owl. Nothing like this had ever happened—and you can bet people paid attention. We even made the front page of local newspapers. I would like to see this kind of activism take place more often. It really gets people thinking and making important connections. (Plus it is nonthreatening and fun.)

Changing our language to include nonhumans more fully. I like to use the phrase "whole Earth community," which includes people as well as mountains, rivers, trees, and animals. I get frustrated with the need to say "people and the Earth" as if somehow people were separate from the Earth. To me, Earth includes all life. To most, it is still necessary to list us separately. I hope someday this separation in our minds no longer exists. Paying careful attention to our language, and changing it where necessary to be inclusive of all species, will help bring this about.

Cultivating moment-to-moment awareness, or mindfulness as an important arena of ecologically engaged social action. "Observing one's thoughts, emotions, and sense perceptions is a means to reduce activity and develop the capacity for restraint. This ability to stop habitual patterns and consider them in depth is fundamental to an ethical appraisal of human activities in the environment. If this mindfulness practice is extended to ecological relationships, one gains greater awareness of the myriad links of interdependence," Kaza writes.

Living a simpler lifestyle. According to Kaza, "A simple lifestyle of reduced consumption allows more time for interaction with living, dynamic beings, more opportunity for meeting the Other more fully and unencumbered. It is also a quiet but powerful political statement that rejects the manipulative nature of advertising or manufactured need."

Entering into a deep relationship with the Earth will inevitably cause you pain, perhaps even intense pain, because the history of our human relationship with the Earth, especially in past two hundred years, has been so destructive. We cannot feel the beauty and joy without also being willing to feel the pain.

When I traveled to the Pacific Northwest for the first time, I remember the pain of seeing my first clearcut. I could not believe what I was seeing. I felt as if someone had punched me hard. I could not breathe. It was beyond my comprehension that anyone could do such a thing! The Earth was raw, open, exposed, bleeding. The Earth had been raped, and I felt as if I had been raped, too. I have since seen many clearcuts, and familiarity has not led to numbness. I am grateful, however, that I can feel the Earth's pain, literally in my body. I feel somehow this is a gift I can give—a gift of love. It is such a small thing, but it is mine to give. When we face pain, allow it in, come through it, we become stronger, more whole, and more aware of who we are.

Each one of us is powerful. Our power is multiplied as our numbers increase. No action, good or bad, occurs in a vacuum. Just as our neglect and lack of understanding cause fouled air, water, and land, so will our love, care, and attention allow positive changes. These changes will need to be local and global. But since true learning seems to happen through personal experience, it makes the most sense to start making changes, trying new approaches, and developing new systems at home, with the people and places around us. As we develop more communitarian and responsive systems, we can apply the principles on the national and global levels. A good model can be replicated many times so long as it is tailored to local needs.

The Earth speaks in many languages. In North America, which Native people call Turtle Island, she speaks differently than in Africa or Southeast Asia. The rich cultures and traditions of indigenous peoples reflect Earth's diversity. Our culture, and therefore our politics and our economics, should ideally by guided by our listening and active participation in the life of the whole Earth community in the place we live. We have a long way to go. I do believe it is possible, however. It will take patience, understanding, compassion, a sense of humor, fearlessness, determination and the ability to "go with the flow," to work with what is here and to take one step a time. And we need to take some risks:

Wake up! See—and feel—what is here. Give thanks for the beauty and for what's working and allow the pain of what's not working to enter your heart. Don't hide from any of it. One of the most important things we can do is to see what we are doing.

Acknowledge your fear—don't deny it. Understand that fear is an emotion based on what might be, not on what is. Often, however, fears are very rational. For example, if we speak up at our job about an irresponsible practice or unreported violation, we fear we will be out of work. And the reality is we could lose our job. Therefore, taking action requires forethought and planning to minimize the risks and protect, as much as possible, those who depend on us. It would be irresponsible to do otherwise. Still, the times demand that we raise the stakes. Facing our fears is a step in this direction.

Take action. In my experience, doing something concrete not only takes our minds off of our fears and insecurities, it actually dissolves them. Taking action is empowering, energizing, and brings us together with others, thereby helping to create community. Some of the actions called for in this book seem small. But remember, all steps are important, regardless of how tiny they seem. Each one leads to a more powerful place than we are now.

Moving beyond our walls and our alienation from each other and the Earth is like slowly waking from a dream. It is hard and sometimes painful, but it is also exhilarating. As we discover our connections to other people and places around the world, we find we can no longer turn away from pain and suffering. But we also find the love and beauty inherent in life on Earth. Each day offers us new opportunities to participate in healing the Earth and creating a more humane culture. We share the life of all creation. If we open our hearts to the life around us, we can begin to discover how it feels to participate with life.

Imagine: You are walking in the woods or in a park—or even on a familiar street. It is a beautiful, clear day. Bright sun, blue sky, a few wispy clouds. A slight breeze stirs the leaves in your path. Your thoughts drift. First to work, unfinished business, the kids, the traffic. Then, suddenly, the thoughts fall away. You feel the warmth of the sun and the incredible deep blue of the sky. How beautiful it all is! You realize you are blessed and, in your own way, give thanks. And then, just at that moment, an especially large and gorgeous leaf falls right at your feet. You pick it up, knowing somehow it is a gift.

This is the partnership we have with life. All possibilities, all opportunity, are contained within it. We can accept the gift of life and meaning—and the responsibility that comes with it—or we can deny its existence and ignore it. The choice is up to each of us, each moment of our lives.

TWO

An Economy for the Living Earth

T HERE'S A SMALL, human-made pond I know of located by a brook on the edge of a small wood. Dug years ago, it has long since been integrated fully into its surroundings. What an idyllic spot! One can hear the brook, the rise and fall of the wind, the buzzing of myriad insects, a truck in the distance, a fish jumping. One can feel the wind and sun, an occasional insect, the firmness of the Earth. There are cattails across the pond, flanked by silvery birches and dark-green hemlock. The trees bend to the wind, an insect lands on the water, and a fish sucks it down.

I do not know what this place was like before some human created the pond. Nor do I know how much time has passed to allow such peace and contentment to be present now, as if the pond were always here. More than anything, I am struck by the harmony and abundance here, what the cooperation of all life has wrought. There are no expectations. There is simply acknowledgment and acceptance of the pattern, a pattern that smoothed the rough edges, placed the grasses and the cattails and restored the natural balance.

To me, this scene reveals the essential life force, an unknowable essence felt as love—the energy, wisdom, and desire of all living forms to be themselves. All living things—rocks (yes, rocks), plants, stars, animals, trees, fungi, insects—know themselves, are themselves. They are not necessarily self-conscious, but rather they live; in themselves alone and as part of a whole, they have a purpose. The challenge is to sense life's essence and to learn, perhaps relearn, our oneness, our place in the web, our purpose.

11

As we have struggled to understand the "laws of nature," we have come to assume that life can be explained in material and technical terms. While much can be understood this way, our reliance on this approach has drastically limited our ability to be conscious and present in life and to create from within that consciousness and presence. Looking out at the world with reductionistic eyes, we feel separate from all other life on Earth. On the surface our lives are full, but deeper down we feel a nagging doubt. Deeper down, our separating minds and reductionistic systems make us feel alone and afraid. This fear drives our manic systems. This fear drives us to accumulate more and more. In our search for security we create weapons of death, and rape and plunder the Earth. Our economy has institutionalized our fear-driven greed.

Money was once a tool, one way to facilitate the exchange of goods. Gradually, though, money has become a commodity, one of our main measures of worth. Success means accumulating more; ruin means being left destitute. In search of money, many of us forego special interests or talents that do not pay. Worse, we trade webs of relationships with communities, places, and the Earth for the search for the dollar. Seduced by the pleasures money can buy, or forced by economic circumstance, we trade self-reliance for dependence on our employers. We become commodities to be bought and sold. If we lose whatever money we have, we truly are destitute; we have nothing to fall back on.

If we can open ourselves again to the essence of life—to love—if we can relearn our place and purpose, we can begin to assuage our fear and to see new possibilities. One of our gifts is our self-awareness. We do not just live; we perceive our living.

As we become more aware of life and more aware of and present with ourselves, it is possible to envision a cooperative, patterned economy full of harmony and abundance. We can envision an economy that fits the Earth as well as the human-made pond fits its spot. An economy for the living Earth would be whole, organic, and synergetic; it would flow with the natural process of change.

One place to start our envisioning is with the processes that underlie all life. As we look carefully at the web of life around us, as we begin to trace its strands and the process of connection, we find values essential to creation, values that lead to principles that can guide us in our attempt to create an economy for the living Earth.

Respect and Cooperation

Awareness of the connections we are part of is central to respect. Each living thing has a place and purpose on Earth. Respect means paying attention to the web of life, to the processes of connection. Respect means taking the time to learn and value what each can offer and what role each can play. Respect means searching to find our own special gifts and then sharing them. When we do not respect life (or the Earth) we trample ahead, destroying the web and ultimately ourselves. When we do not respect others, we encourage defensiveness and rigidity. When we do not respect ourselves, we despair.

An economy built upon respect would mean cooperating for the life of the whole. Cooperation for the whole requires a real balance between self-interest and service. It requires letting go of the "me" that wants and wants. It requires learning to dance with life.

Our current economy fosters a ruthless "winner-take-all" competitiveness. We do not consider the results of this greedy consumption. We disregard our depletion of Earth's resources—her gifts to us—our exploitation of other people, and the impact of our individual and corporate actions on our societies and cultures. Our competitive economy has contributed to our living with little creativity and individuality in a faceless monoculture.

Building a cooperative economy means working together to develop resilient social structures, organizations, and relationships that provide for our needs as part of a living Earth. We must start our practical search for solutions now, and we must work together. Together, we are more powerful, more creative, more effective, and more supported. This book is full of resources that will enable you to connect with other groups and projects that are striving to create a humane, sustainable economy.

One example is Co-op America, a Washington, D.C.-based, national, nonprofit organization promoting responsibility, self-reliance, environmental and economic sustainability, cooperation, and workplace democracy. Businesses, organizations, and individuals who support these values make up the membership. Members' products are marketed in a quarterly catalog. The businesses, Co-op America, and the individuals who buy all benefit. Traditional marketing competition is replaced by cooperation, and the results are high-quality products, reasonable prices, and the commitment to providing these with respect for the Earth's limitations and resources.

Of course, some of these businesses may still fail. They may have less than adequate cash flow, suffer from inexperienced management, or be pushed out by other, more experienced producers of similar products. Cooperation for the whole provides the opportunity to develop strength, but does not guarantee success. Sometimes the interactions in and around the pond seem harsh and competitive, yet each is part of a larger dance of life that goes on.

Relationship and a Sense of Place

As important as the parts of the web of life are the dynamic relationships between the parts. We must pay attention to our roles in the web, to how what we give and take affects the processes. In and around the pond, the various parts of the whole are interwoven into a complex, changing pattern of relationships and cycles.

One characteristic of the pattern is that everything is interconnected. The trees bend in the wind, but they also lessen the wind's effect on the pond and its bank. In their shelter, tiny plants, bacteria, and insects compost the needles and leaves, enriching the soil for the trees. Although we can draw temporary boundaries around specific ecosystems, they overlap and the boundaries are permeable; the web of relationships reaches everywhere.

Another characteristic of the pattern is that the relationships and cycles are always changing. Each part reacts to its environment, and the whole environment, the whole web, changes over time. As the temperature of the water changes, so does the mixture of creatures living in it. As the plants die off and rot, they contribute to the silt and, over time, make the pond shallower and warmer. There is always change here, including life and death, and the change is what keeps the pond living.

If we are to build an economy for the living Earth, we must build one that is flexible, that changes with times and conditions. Each place, each community, each time is unique. To create a humane, sustainable economy, we must begin by studying where and when we live. Are we in New York City, Appalachia, the desert? What is the history of our place? How are things changing? How does what our neighbors, even our distant neighbors, do affect us and vice versa? As we look for the many answers to these questions, we will begin to find some of the many appropriate solutions for our place.

As we learn more about the complex interactions that characterize our place, we will find it harder to make decisions based on only one or two criteria (such as the number of new jobs, effect on the schools, or an increase in the tax base). By insisting on knowing beforehand what we are compromising, we may find ourselves willing to sacrifice some short-term gains in favor of longer term ones (e.g., fewer immediate jobs in exchange for those jobs having less impact on the environment and which are more creative and secure). Or we may find ourselves paying more attention to the appropriate timing of a decision (e.g., a park we badly want now might be more enjoyable if we take some time to plan it and perhaps scout several sites). And we will increasingly learn to think about the larger web of relationships that affect and are affected by our decisions (e.g., slopping our wastes into the river does not help us much if we buy our vegetables from the community downstream).

Diversity and Self-Reliance

One of the most important elements of creative response to changing conditions is diversity. Diversity is key to the sustainability of the web. At our pond, the essential processes—such as turning dead organisms into usable chemicals—are accomplished through several pathways. If one is blocked for some reason, the others take its place. On a larger, longer scale, this human-made pond fits its spot as well as it does only because enough different organisms with flexible requirements could adapt to this human change to the environment.

Without diversity, an ecosystem—or an economy—is much less flexible in the face of dramatic changes. If a community is dependent on a single major employer and that company closes down or moves, all facets of the community suffer. Workers lose jobs and cannot feed their families or patronize local businesses. Property taxes go uncollected and school budgets are slashed. Compounding the problem, if the company moves where wages are lower and environmental controls fewer, the second community risks becoming dependent on the same unreliable source of work, while general wage levels suffer and pollution increases.

In a community with a diverse economy, the loss of even a major employer would not be so devastating. For the most part, the community's needs could be met by the remaining businesses and organizations. At the same time, these other businesses and organizations supply the community with the resources to help those hurt by one company shutting down. Similarly, communities with diverse economies are more likely to control the actions of companies that try to move in. After all, they have less to lose if a company goes elsewhere.

Clearly, an important ingredient of diversity is self-reliance. I am not talking about old-fashioned isolationism. If the isolated community providing all basic needs of its members ever existed, it is certainly gone now. Furthermore, so many of Earth's problems are so large that we need each other to deal with them. But for there to be diversity, and thus flexibility and creativity, we need to have reasonably independent (albeit interdependent) communities, each adding its own originality to the mix.

Imagine a community totally dependent on outside resources for jobs, goods, services, support systems; Indian reservations are a good example. All the stores are owned by major chains. Although Native Americans are employed in the stores (usually at minimum wage), the money they earn is sucked out of the community by the same stores. Any other money that comes into the community—for instance, from the federal government— pours right out, destructively, like torrential rain running down a parched hill. And with the flood go the youth. Seeing that traditional values no longer appear to work and finding no other opportunities on the reservation, they leave for the cities, for the monoculture and the isolation of corporate or "traditional" capitalism.

But imagine these same communities with locally owned businesses and stores. Combine this with members creating their own support systems of bartered goods, shared skills, and friendship, allowing the community to maintain its identity and to respond to changing conditions. Now money entering the system is caught and used and reused, like rain falling in a rain forest, which recycles the moisture as its own rain. (Seeds of this exist on some reservations; see chapter 11.)

A warning: Self-reliance can harden into selfishness. Changes that eat away at the interconnections of the web, that fragment diversity into so many unrelated pieces, can eventually ruin Earth's ability to heal. This is the danger we face if self-reliance is viewed separately from the other principles of an economy for the living Earth.

Harmony and Appropriate Scale

Ultimately, the web of interconnected, diverse, essential parts must be balanced in some sort of harmony. Harmony is the heart of life. Harmony is the appropriate, dynamic balance of the many cycles and systems, the local and the global, life and death. For us to survive and prosper, we must align all our activities, including our economy, with the natural cycles of the Earth. We must listen to each other and to the Earth, to our place and to our communities. We must, I think, spend time in wild places where we can learn to be present and to listen deeply.

Perhaps the most important lesson of harmony for economics is attention to scale. This Earth sustains both incredibly large and incredibly small life forms. The question for us must always be, What is appropriate? For this function, what is the most productive, sustainable balance between large and small, short term and long term, local and global?

In our present economy, growth is automatically seen as a good thing. Whether or not it really is depends on the social and environmental effects of that growth. Likewise, a certain amount of algae in the pond provides food and oxygen, while an uncontrolled bloom ends with a pond devoid of oxygen and most life.

An economy for the living Earth would include great diversity with none operating at the expense of another, especially the Earth. There would be many small- and medium-sized organizations and a few larger ones, where appropriate size really does increase effectiveness. Scale would be a function of our area's maximum capacity, the available resources, the needs of the community, the influence of our global interconnections, and the economics of production.

As varied as its elements would be, the core of an Earth-conscious economy would be a web of strong local economies. To be strong, the local economies must be diverse, use local resources and talents well, and be able to recycle money rather than letting it leak out. For this to happen, local economies must be controlled by local people, by the people affected by their decisions.

In developing an Earth-conscious economy, our primary criterion must always be the integrity of life. If the web is threatened, if interconnections are ignored or severed, we must change our practices. Looking around today, we can see we must change. We are destroying ecosystems and diversity at an alarming rate. With our pollution and our monoculture, we are breaking the interconnections that keep our world alive and flexible. The "economy" we hear about on the evening news consists largely of various indices that once measured and now define the system. We know from our own experience that the Gross National Product (GNP), the "official" unemployment rate, and the inflation rate tell us little about what is going on in our economic lives. They tell us little about the dangerous working conditions, part-time work, increasing spirals of debt, and the informal economy that are so important to most of us.

Perhaps the most important thing to remember is that our economic system is not a shell built elsewhere and imposed upon us and our transactions by politicians and businessmen. While some individuals, corporations, and institutions have tremendous power, we are all active participants in the economy at some level. In a very real sense, we are the economy. The economy depends on the work we do, the products we buy, and the often unpaid, "informal" productive work—child care, housecleaning, and bartering, and other forms of sweat equity—we do. We can begin to change our economy by taking more responsibility for our choices and their impact and by consciously choosing how we invest our time, skills, and money. We can work to make existing institutions more responsible and accountable. And we can gather the power to really change things by working together to create new economic structures. If we wait for "experts" to come up with brilliant one-time solutions, we will simply watch—and help—our planet, ourselves, die.

In this book I try to give a sense of the vast number of efforts to transform our economy that already exist. Some people are helping investors influence the actions of corporations. Some are finding ways to invest time and money in local businesses and organizations. And many more are developing entirely new models for communities striving to provide food, housing, skills, capital, and various products to their members. Many of the most innovative projects are fully or partially in the "informal" (nonmonetary) sector of our present economy. This is the sector where we can find the space to create an economy where the bottom line is not purely financial.

The projects in this book are only a beginning. The transformation to a humane, sustainable economy will be difficult, fraught with confrontation, and slow. Just as we have participated in creating a nuclear nightmare, starving children, and toxic chemicals oozing into our basements, we can participate in creating a living economy. Despite all the horror stories and pain, I see incredible opportunity for us to remember what it means to be truly human and alive on this beautiful planet.

We must open to the life force that breathes through the Earth, join with it, nurture it, and grow with it. As we awaken from our illusion of separation, we will know that we, too, are an integral part of Creation. As we awaken, we can dance and create. Join in the dance; we need you all!

THREE

Empowerment for Change

THE WORLD FEELS like a very different place than when I wrote *Economics as If the Earth Really Mattered* in 1986. Many things have changed, on many levels. At that time, few people wanted to try to understand or even talk about economics. It was, indeed, the "dismal science." Today, conversations about economics are commonplace and more people than ever want to understand economics and learn what they can do to make their own lives more secure.

It is obvious the old system isn't working, leading people to actively seek solutions. Even President Bill Clinton acknowledged that the economy must change during his Economic Summit held shortly after his election. He and Vice President Al Gore listened to people who advocate investing in local communities, who support the creation of women- and minority-owned businesses, and who understand the importance of strong local economies. I was inspired that some of the organizations represented included those I have worked with and written about over the past few years.

People need to have a reason to change and, for many, the reason has to directly benefit them. The patterns of our daily lives, the perspectives we bring to each activity in which we are involved, our level of hope and our ability (or inability) to suspend doubt for a time in order to engage in something outside of our normal experience—all support or limit our willingness and ability to change. This is why it so often takes a catastrophic event to force us to reevaluate our lives and make positive

18

changes. Today's social, economic, and ecological upheavals are providing many with the needed stimulous for change. These events don't change us so much as they bring out aspects of ourselves that were hidden, sometimes even from ourselves.

My sister's car accident twelve years ago put me in touch with my own strength and inner knowing. It was early summer, and I was pregnant with my third son, Colin. A friend called to tell me that MaryJean (we call her MJ) had been very badly hurt in a car accident. As we sped to the hospital, I prayed, over and over, "Hang in there, MJ." It became my mantra.

We arrived to find my mother looking awful and my father incredibly, unspeakably sad. My mother had been undergoing chemotherapy for cancer for about a year but had been doing fine; she was cheerful and never missed work. But when my parents heard about MJ's accident, my mother asked for a painkiller for the first time and aged ten years in a week. I could see that this accident might kill my mother, or speed up the cancer's killing her. I was not at all ready for my mother to die.

MJ was in a deep coma with severe brain injuries, and the doctors were convinced that she would die or, at best, end up a vegetable. But my grandmother's wisdom buoyed me. She used to tell me, "Love is the most powerful force in the universe. Love can overcome all obstacles, both physical and mental." So I knew without any doubt that love is the greatest healer and that nothing is impossible in love. And I knew my sister's strong, stubborn spirit. If she were to live, she would not be a vegetable.

I concentrated all my love and being on my sister's spirit. On my first night home after the accident, I felt her with me and repeated my mantra, "Hang in there, MJ." And I heard her reply, "I will." From that moment on, I cradled her spirit with my love, as well as I knew how, day and night. When I felt her most strongly, I would let her know that no matter how awful her body looked, her spirit could heal it. I told her I knew her purpose had not changed; she was still whole, still beautiful, still wonderfully MJ.

MJ was gradually weaned off the respirator, and then taken out of intensive care. We made every effort to help her awaken, from talking to her to playing her favorite music, to insisting that the nurses and doctors not talk about her (only to her) in her presence. I knew she could hear and I could not stand her being treated as an "it." I could imagine how frustrating it must be to be trapped in a body you cannot use because the brain is not working properly.

MJ's coma gradually lightened, but as it did my mother became sicker. It was obvious she was dying. It seemed like she was carrying a burden only death could lessen: the burden of being too sick to be present for her child. Two hours after my mother died, MJ woke up, and the long, hard work of rehabilitation began.

These were perhaps the most difficult days of my life. I had to trust my deep sense that love can transcend and heal. I learned that this sense was not just a saying or a feeling, but the staff of life. This is what pulled me through the pain, kept me visiting my sister, helped me say goodbye to my mother, enabled me to be patient with my father.

And as I came through, my strength grew. I lost my fear of hospitals, doctors, "experts." I listened to them, asked lots of questions, and made my disagreements clear; I was, after all, my sister's advocate. But I was also changed inside. I was beginning to feel strong and to know what was real and important. The months that followed remained hard. There were many visits with my sister as she struggled in rehabilitation, and with my father as he recovered from my mother's death. MJ eventually learned again to talk, read, write, and walk.

In the middle of all this, Colin was born. I felt like it was the birth of the Christ child all over again. Life! I felt so blessed, and surrounded by those I love, that I finally began to mourn my mother's death. I realized that I loved her for her strength, for her honesty, and for the way she loved me without judgment. Her death did not diminish me; in some strange way, in dying she had once again given me life. I knew that to give my sons what she had given me, all I would need to do is be myself and do what is important to me.

Today MJ is living a fulfilling life, although I know it is different from what it would have been had the accident not occurred. She is active, happy, and has many friends. She volunteers at the local health care center, a home for people who need constant care due to stroke, illness, or age. She loves this work, and the people at the center love her. As a volunteer she can take the time to treat each person as a special individual. Her letters to me are full of stories, some sad, some funny, about the many friends she has made there. She is making a big difference in many peoples' lives.

The experience with my sister and mother was the turning point in my life. I became a much stronger person who dared to question "the powers that be." Most important, I learned I can trust my inner knowing. I understand what it feels like to "know" something even when logic tells me otherwise. I have a faith, which is often sorely tested, in the wholeness and meaning of the universe. When I listen to my inner knowing, and heed it, things usually work out. Doubt is my biggest personal enemy, and fear inevitably allows it in. In spite of my "knowing," I often struggle with this.

This period of empowerment was followed by continuing opportunities for personal change and learning. Following my divorce and becoming a single mother of three growing boys I was totally responsible, for the first time in my life, not only for myself, but for three other people. As so often happens to women after divorce, money became a major issue. There never seemed to be enough for all our needs, which triggered my fears about safety, trust, community, and, most basic of all, security. While I knew I had the inner strength to deal with whatever came, this didn't necessarily make the daily struggle any easier or help me to worry any less.

The most difficult part was being forced to collect welfare for two years (Aid to Needy Families With Children—ANFC—as it is called here in Vermont). For over a year only my closest friends even knew I was "on welfare." It felt shameful. I was still doing my work—publishing a newsletter (*Catalyst*), writing articles, speaking at conferences—just as I had always done, and I felt it was somehow wrong that I should need welfare. So many people told me the work I was doing was valuable. Yet here I was filling out countless forms, answering intimate questions about my finances and feeling like a second-class citizen. It seemed so ironic that I'd get calls for information about where to invest money, while I waited for my welfare check in the mail. If only people knew! I was often angry, though I tried to keep it hidden.

Release came when I became involved in the welfare/workfare debate here in Vermont. I realized by sharing my personal experiences I could help shatter the stereotypical image of a person on welfare. And lo and behold, stating publicly that I was "on welfare" didn't change people's opinions of me—or my work. Instead, it broadened their sense of who I am and what the goal of economic alternatives can be. I began to understand, deep inside (as opposed to intellectually), that creating an economy as if the Earth really matters must involve people, like myself, who are considered "marginal" in different ways, either due to class, race, ability, age, financial resources, sexual preference—whatever.

During this time, my work was challenged to support my family, not just itself. (The fact that it couldn't is what forced me to apply for ANFC in the first place.) Eventually I realized that *Catalyst*, the newsletter that provided the information and inspiration for the *Economics as If the Earth Really Mattered*, simply was not capable of providing my family with even a minimal income. It took me such a long time to come to this realization because I loved everything involved with *Catalyst*, especially the network of people and organizations connected with it. So I kept hoping things would change. Making the decision to cease publication (in March, 1993) was exceedingly painful and forced me to ask hard questions about my life and my life's work.

I couldn't just resign myself to living an ordinary life. The thought of a dreary 9 to 5 job would plunge me into depression and anger. I had spent over ten years creating my work, and I wasn't about to give it up. I agonized over this stubborn attitude of mine, wondering if it came from ego. After all, what made me so special that I should be able to do what I enjoy while so many others take menial jobs to make ends meet? Still, I knew that in order to be true to myself, the work I did for pay needed to embody the values of cooperation, respect, balance, integrity, and love of Earth. So I heeded my inner knowing to trust that my stubbornness wasn't ego; rather, it was my acknowledging who I am. I was asking a lot—but it was my personal "bottom line," and I stuck to it.

My commitment and trust were rewarded; I found a job working with a nonprofit organization committed to restoring and healing forests through the promotion of sustainable forestry. Regional economic self-reliance is one of the basic tenets of the emerging sustainable forestry movement, and this meshed perfectly with the work I'd been doing for the past ten years.

My welfare experience taught me a lot about the society we live in and about myself. It's difficult being a single mother in a society based on rugged individualism, and now I understand more about the hard choices people face and the reasons for the compromises they sometimes make. I have experienced the fear of homelessness and the resentment of not being acknowledged for who I am by the society in which I live. The flip side of this, though, is that I internalized society's definition of value—getting paid well—and applied it to me. This was so subtle I wasn't even aware of it at first. The longer I received welfare, the more entrenched this belief became. In ways I don't understand (but that I know to be true), this negative belief contributed to my poor financial situation. Things began to improve when I realized that my work is valuable, paid or not, and that I had choices. In retrospect, the decision to discontinue publishing *Catalyst* was the best decision I made because it created space—literally and figuratively—for something new to come into my life.

On another level, I learned that the real source of hope for creating positive change in our society lies in finding our power to work with other people. My experience taught me that traditionally disenfranchised people—people pushed to the margins of our social, political, and economic system—are where the real power to effect change lies. Many activists spend their time and scarce resources trying to "buy themselves a seat at the table," often compromising their integrity in the process. I don't believe this tactic will work in the long term. The issue for these folks is power (over), not justice. Working with people on the margins may be hard and it may cause the activist-organizer to face up to some difficult personal issues, even prejudices, but it is transforming work.

As you read through the many stories that follow, it is my hope that you will find those that speak most deeply to who you are, that they will inspire you to find within the power to work with others to create changes, and that together we will become invested in the common good.

Part II

HOME IMPROVEMENTS: ADJUSTING OUR CURRENT ECONOMY

Introduction

OUR ECONOMIC, POLITICAL, and social systems are responsible for much of the world's human suffering and ecological destruction. These systems must be totally transformed by a revolution of values, a transformation to ways of living that are decentralized, ecological, just, and joyful. However, we can't leap across the Grand Canyon in a single bound. Our acknowledgment of both current reality *and* the need for revolutionary change translates into working to integrate ecological, humane, spiritual values into our current system's existing institutions.

My own vision is that, over time (generations, most likely), some institutions will respond positively to value-based change and continue to thrive. Others will resist change, insisting on doing the old way and ultimately become extinct. Meanwhile, what we call alternatives today will increase in number and strength, providing hope and stability in our communities. This vision is idealistic, but it is also practical: Not changing our ways will surely lead to our own extinction, and much pain along the way.

Each of us has a gift to offer life. Some of us will actively create the alternatives, while others will work within existing businesses and institutions to change them. These two strategies are often seen as being at cross purposes — yet both are essential.

This section of the book looks at strategies to change the system from within, beginning with some cautions about the "green business" movement, and focusing on how we evaluate the current system (chapter 4). The "greenwashing" of major corporations, which is a different animal altogether, is addressed in Part III, "Breaking the Corporate Grip." Chapter 5, "Socially Conscious Investing," covers socially responsible investing, an

24

increasingly acceptable approach to integrate human and ecological values with Wall Street; "responsible banking"; and person-to-person financial relationships. Chapters 6–8 offer an overview of more practical, activist-oriented tactics to change "business as usual" with something for everyone to do.

For me, working within the system is a valid activity only as long as we keep in mind the goal—revolutionary change. The corporations whose stock comprises the vast majority of social investors' portfolios are in direct contrast (and often conflict) with these investors' stated values and goals. It is legitimate, and necessary, to ask questions about how support of such corporations at all (even "responsible" ones) can be a good thing when the system they depend upon to succeed (i.e., make profits) is responsible for so much destruction and pain. Is it possible to change the system while supporting the very institutions that are doing everything they can to keep it entrenched?

We will find the answers to these questions in the doing. As my mother would say, "Time will tell." Meanwhile, it is up to us to chart a path towards greater responsibility. It is up to us to keep on asking the questions. And it is up to us to know when we're making progress and when we're just getting sidetracked.

FOUR

Evaluating the Status Quo

HOW DO WE find out about the practices of businesses whose owners we don't know and live with? The activities of corporations can be uncovered and analysed through basic research. Researching corporations can be exciting. It is also time consuming and frustrating. In my opinion, the most important reason to initiate a detailed research project is to raise awareness beyond the immediate issue—to reveal patterns of destruction and exploitation and put the specifics about a particular company into a larger political and economic context. Following are some of the steps I've used to uncover irresponsible corporate behavior. Specific information is then provided to activist groups (especially students) launching boycotts and used as background for articles on rainforest destruction, the *maquiladoras*, and biotechnology, among others.

Research—Tools of the Trade

In order to make use of the actions recommended in this book, you will need accurate information on corporations and their products. How do you find out who's doing what? What sources of information can you trust? These are important questions because the quality of our information is more important that the quantity.

The first question to ask is, Why you are doing the research? Are you trying to make responsible decisions as a consumer, organizing a boycott, or working for change in an industry (e.g., waste management)? Are you fighting an incinerator, or are you working in local schools on an anti-styrofoam campaign? In each case, the kind and depth of information required is different. In some cases you will need company-specific data. In others you will need background information on an industry as a whole, or on production processes and environmental impacts. Be clear about what you need in order to avoid getting sidetracked—which is easy to do! Information for information's sake is not where it's at. Good research should lead to action.

Jeff Fedler, who works with the AFL-CIO and has conducted corporate research for years, offers the following advice for corporate researchers: Getting information is a frame of mind. You must be curious and have the ability to see connections between seemingly disparate and unrelated things. Passion and curiosity go a long way. Don't overestimate the intelligence of a company. Act stupid. Ask questions. Ask the same question in different ways—often the company will tell you what you want to know.

If you are fighting some fly-by-night operation in your community, you will have to dig deep. In such cases, you might not have a big name corporation to deal with (or maybe you do, but its identity is hidden from you). My advice is to contact an organization such as Citizen's Clearinghouse for Hazardous Waste, the Environmental Research Foundation, Greenpeace, or the Corporate Campaign for advice specific to your needs. It is not unheard of for grassroots organizers to hire private investigators in situations such as this.

The first thing I do when looking at a specific company is to call corporate headquarters and request all their printed information, which includes copies of their annual report, 10K and 10Q forms, company newsletters, informational brochures on products, and, in the case of chemicals and the like, safety or technical reports the company provides on these products. (Your library should have a book entitled, *National Directory of Corporate Public Affairs*, published annually by Columbia Books which lists addresses, phone numbers, and directors or managers at corporate headquarters and major offices e.g., community relations, investor relations, political action committee, or consumer affairs for most publicly held corporations in the United States.) I don't always ask for all these publications at once; usually I get the annual report and 10K first. When it arrives (usually in a couple of weeks), I read them through, compare them with information I already have, and then I call and request additonal documents, such as information on specific products or publications about overseas operations.

While I'm waiting for the company's materials to arrive, I look through books and other publications for articles relevant to that particular company or for information on areas in which the company is involved. I'll also contact organizations involved in issues related to the corporation's activities to see if they have anything useful to send me. For example, if I'm researching an agriculture or chemical company (sometimes it's hard to tell the difference), I read about pesticides in the Third World and use the information to frame questions for the company regarding its practices. This kind of information helps me to review the company materials more critically, too. Seeing connections comes in handy here. I often call the author of an article to see if s/he has additional information or insights that may prove helpful.

Once the company materials arrive, I go through them with a fine-toothed comb. Companies really blow their own horns. The annual report is designed to make the company look good to shareholders. All the bad stuff (what you're looking for) is left out. However, since corporate people see the world differently than you do, there are major clues as to the true face of a company in its report. The 10K also contains, by law, information regarding penalties, lawsuits, superfund sites, and other legalties. 10K's (and sometimes annual reports) can list overseas operations. The countries in which these operations are located can send off warning bells.

For example, oil companies with operations in tropical countries like Ecuador or Colombia almost certainly indicate connections to rainforest destruction. Why? These tropical countries have vast reserves of oil located in the rainforest, often where indigenous people live. Their leaders have committed to dramatically increasing oil production as a way of bringing in money. Chemical companies with operations in countries such as Mexico, Guatemala, Indonesia, for example, are probably involved in polluting air, water and land, and exploiting workers either because environmental and labor regulations are either nonexistent or lax, or the country doesn't have the money or political will to enforce them. Agricultural companies with operations in Latin America and the Philippines have been, and still can be, responsible for the displacement of indignous peoples and peasants from their lands, as well as for pollution and worker exploitation, especially among women and children.

How do I know these things? I rely on organizations located within the countries themselves, grassroots movements such as the Coalition for Justice in the Maquiladoras, and the U.S./Guatamala Labor Education Project, organizations that advocate for indigenous peoples, and excellent publications such as *The Ecologist* and *Third World Resurgence*, whose writers have field experience and a political-social perspective I respect. (See the Resources section for a complete list.)

If I have time, and my questions are lengthy or complex, I will write a letter addressed to the Chief Executive Officer. I try to start with something in their annual report that I would like more information about— pesticides, their involvement in biotechnology, forest management, or labor practices in the Third World, for example. If I have a particular piece of damning information from another source, I will quote it, express my concern, and ask the company to please respond. This is even more effective if I am doing the research on behalf of people in another country, I can quote from their letter. Make a copy of the letter you send.

If I don't hear in a month or so, I will call and refer to my letter. Usually, though, the company responds in some fashion sooner than this. In my experience it won't be the CEO who will respond. The letter will have been referred to someone else. If time is an issue, I will forgo the letter and start with a phone call to the main headquarters. Companies hardly ever admit to wrongdoing, and their responses usually inspire more questions. If I'm calling after receiving a letter, I ask to speak to the person who wrote to me.

Do not be put off by the runaround. Corporate research can be frustrating. When speaking to a company representative, act as though you know you have a right to the information, yet are aware that she is busy. (Generally you will be speaking to a woman unless you manage to get into the higher echelons of management.) If you are polite and friendly, chances are the person you are speaking with will be, too. But don't sacrifice your need for information to be nice, and don't let the opinion of the person at the other end of the line determine your behavior.

The tricky part comes when you are asking for more specific information on touchy issues, and they ask, "What are you going to do with this information?" You do not have to say, "I'm organizing a campaign to force you off the face of the Earth." Often I say I'm a researcher in the socially responsible investing community looking into the company's record on certain issues for a client. Sometimes I simply say I'm working on a report on agriculture or whatever, depending on what the company does.

I've had some very interesting conversations with various levels of company personnel as a result of my research, and mostly it's lots of fun. Make sure you note with whom you are talking and the date of your conversation. And keep a pen in hand to jot down pithy quotes—such as the time a manager at Georgia-Pacific told me in exasperation, "All the wood we use [in a plant in Brazil] comes from the rainforest," or when a senior vice president at UNOCAL told me their plans to deal with pollution off the coast of Tiwi (in the Philippines) from their geothermal plant there: "We're going to extend the discharge pipes farther into the ocean."

People working for a corporation generally believe in what the company is doing. They are not going to admit wrongdoing to you over the phone. While most people are cooperative, exceptions can be found in the oil and chemical industries, which have been on the receiving end of environmental accusations recently and can be rather defensive.

Of course, there is another level of information that you'll never get from the company. This is where a few good activist publications come in handy. You can also contact organizations specializing in corporate research. Sometimes these organizations will charge for reports or data-base searches, which can be expensive for a grassroots group or for an individual; ask yourself if you really need this level of information. If you do, maybe you can negotiate a compromise price, especially if the work you're doing is for a good cause.

Some useful sources of information include the Environmental Protection Agency's Toxic Release Inventory, which provides information, in pounds, of corporations' dumping of certain toxics into the air, water, and soil. The Environmental Research Foundation's database RACHEL contains information on a broad range of environmental subjects, such as chemicals, acid rain, water quality, biotech, and other hazardous materials. The Council on Economic Priorities' Environmental Data Clearinghouse offers detailed reports on numerous corporations for about $20 each. CEP is also involved in a Campaign for Cleaner Corporations, along with several other groups including the Sierra Club, Worldwatch Institute, and Greenpeace. The Data Center can be hired to search its files and send you copies of all the articles found on a particular company or issue.

By far the best sources of information are people living next door to a corporation's operations. These people can interpret public relations materials and verify if a company "walks its talk." For example, Scott Paper's neighbors know more about Scott than any of that company's personnel will tell you. A contact in the Philippines provided me with firsthand information regarding UNOCAL's operations that the company would never have admitted.

If you chose to go public or launch a boycott or other campaign, make sure your information is beyond reproach. Don't take a small mention in an obscure publication as the last word. Check it out. If you believe it to be true, use it to get verification from the company, if possible, or locate more details through other sources. It's better to keep quiet than come out with something and later have to take it back.

Good luck. And have fun!

Green Business

Green business has been getting a lot of press—and hype—lately. There are many shades of green, and discerning what's really green can be very confusing. On one end of the spectrum is the corporate trend towards greater awareness of the environmental impact of their activities. This can either translate into meaningful changes if the company is sincere, or into hype (and lots of expensive, flashy ads) if they aren't. It can be hard to tell the difference; one "green" program does not remake a company.

For example, Wal-Mart promotes their selling of ecologically friendly products, yet every Wal-Mart threatens to turn community centers into ghost towns. Proctor and Gamble participates in municipal composting, but such programs deal with tons of the company's own discarded, and some would say hazardous, product: disposable diapers. DuPont has reduced its U.S. toxic emissions, yet the company is still among the nation's top ten polluters. Chevron brags about its habitat restoration, but it's habitat they are responsible for destroying in the first place.

At the other end of the spectrum are the smaller-scale enterprises that have integrated humane values and environmental responsibility into their mission, and there are many variations in between. In the abstract ideal, a green business is one run with respect and care across the board—regarding workers, customers, suppliers, the community, and the environment. Sometimes this means going above and beyond the call of duty with regard to the environment or product quality or a donor program. In reality, though, "let the buyer beware"! One good product or action does not a green business make. At the same time, green doesn't necessarily mean perfect. It is possible to support a company because we like some aspect, while pressuring it to improve in other areas. Most people would agree that the trend towards responsible, or green business is a good thing, but we don't all necessarily see eye-to-eye about about specifics. Consider:

Small-scale energy projects (such as those employing hydro or wind) are generally seen as positive alternatives to large, more destructive projects, yet they still often meet with resistance from people concerned about the quality of local streams, habitat and what is called the "viewscape."

Plastic lumber from recycled plastic sounds good. But won't we have to continue using (and disposing of) plastic to ensure the financial success of these businesses? Wouldn't it be better to use less wood, to recycle the wood itself, and to learn how to live with the forest rather than exploit it for all it's worth?

Another trend in the marketplace these days that deserves some attention is products made from rainforest ingredients. The idea is that if people living in the rainforest can make a living sustainably from non–timber forest products, they will have an incentive not to destroy it. "They" generally means the people living in the forest, but to me it applies more to corporations and governments, who see value only in economic terms. "Value" takes on a deeper meaning to indigenous and land-based peoples who, when they have ownership and control of their resources, generally find ways not to destroy them. If this "use it or lose it" concept takes off, it will be applied to other endangered ecosystems and cultures. So we need to look at it carefully.

The most commonly used product to date is Brazil nuts, which are pressed for oil (used in cosmetics produced by The Body Shop), ground into flour or used chopped or whole. Rainforest Crunch is the best known product, a sweet nut brittle using Brazil nuts and cashews. The nuts are also used in granola, cookies, coffee, popcorn, and even dog biscuits. Most of the businesses involved in these "sell it to save it" ventures purchase their supplies from Cultural Survival Enterprises, which helped fund a Brazil-nut cooperative in Xapuri. (The Body Shop has its own arrangements with the Kayapo in Brazil).

The rainforest harvest is complex. If we look at this issue critically, we discover a history of severe exploitation when Third World and indigenous peoples become involved with—and then dependent on—outside, international market forces. People are treated as a means to an end, and their environment is exploited and destroyed as market demand increases. *The Ecologist* (July–August, 1992) described this process well:

> As production and exchange are enclosed by the market, economic activity is cordoned off from the other spheres of social life, bound by rules that actively undermine previous networks of mutual aid....As the market eats into the fabric of local self-reliance, commons regimes begin to atrophy. Their members can no longer rely on family, friends, neighbors, community, elders and children for support, but increasingly must go to the market.

Another issue to consider: Is it possible to save the rainforest (or any endangered habitat) by harvesting pieces of it to sell to consumers thousands of miles away? Successful harvest projects could encourage more colonists into the forest, further marginalizing indigenous people. Large businesses might start their own plantations of "economically valuable" resources. Cultural Survival even acknowledges this possibility: "It is inevitable that some of the most promising...commodities will...be produced on plantations and make it difficult...for forest residents to compete." (From a 1992 report by Jason Clay on "funding and investment opportunities for income generating . . . in the greater Amazon Basin.")

How can creating more "stuff" to buy save anything when consumption is a major cause of the problem to begin with? Are we only going to save those ecosystems and peoples that can pay their way on our terms? Are we going to let what works for business and the market determine our human rights and conservation objectives?

Finally, tribal peoples are are not in agreement on the benefits of the harvest. While some appear to welcome it, others most emphatically do not. The following exerpt is taken from *Indian Unity* (November, 1992), one of the oldest Indian-run newspapers in South America, produced by the Colombian National Indian Organization:

> In Europe and North America people believe that by buying certain products they are helping to protect tropical forests and indigenous peoples; this is called the "rainforest harvest." This is weakening the international campaigns in support of our struggles for our rights. People think that by consuming some product they are guaranteeing our protection. Our communities' independence is also weakened as our well-being is made dependent on western markets. There are many outsiders who are interested in profiting from our resources, manipulating environmental and indigenous issues for their own gain.

> Selling products is meaningless if we ourselves do not control the marketing projects and the natural resources, if we ourselves do not control our lands and have the right to say what we want.

I believe most businesses using rainforest ingredients really feel they are doing the right thing. However, I am skeptical as to whether their good intentions balance the potential for harm in the long term.

On the other hand, alternative trade organizations (ATOs), which market products made by indigenous artisans, refugees and peasants (e.g., weavings, jewelry, pottery, clothing, carvings) are an excellent example of "fair trade," and green business. ATOs work with artisans in countries in Latin America, Africa, and Southeast Asia whose goal, according to Catherine Renno, director of PLENTY's Fair Trade Program, "is economic self-sufficiency, which translates into self-determination so they can feed and educate their children, create health care, and provide clean water and sanitary conditions for their families."

ATOs value the skills and traditions of the people rather than the resources of the land. They work with cooperatives, whose members are often women with little economic opportunity. Often co-op members are displaced peasants or refugees. Sometimes they are indigenous people seeking to rebuild communities devastated by war, strife, and poverty. The Co-op America catalog carries products imported by ATOs such as Pueblo to People, Tradewind and Oxfam.

Another positive example is the story of Café Salvador. In 1990, Neighbor to Neighbor (N2N), a small grassroots organization, produced a television spot linking El Salvadoran death squads with Proctor & Gamble's (P&G) purchase of Salvadoran coffee, for its Folger's brand, the latest in N2N's campaign against Salvadoran coffee which included a boycott initiated in 1989. Finally, in 1991, P&G came around and asked what they could do to actively promote peace in El Salvador. A formal peace agreement was signed in El Salvador in 1992. At this point, N2N decided to work *for* something, rather than against. At the request of farmers collectively working the land they received as a result of land reform, N2N began to create markets in North America for the co-op's coffee. Today, thanks to a partnership among N2N, Equal Exchange, a Boston-based gourmet coffee company, and Oxfam America; the coffee co-op (La Magdalena) has a growing market for its coffee, Cafe Salvador, and the project serves as a model for economic democracy from the grassroots. Today, the farmers are getting paid a fair price for their coffee and the project has directly benefited its community; La Magdalena installed electricity in seventy homes with the increased income.

So what makes a business green? In general, we might begin by looking at businesses providing nontoxic alternatives to chemical-based products we use in our daily lives (e.g., nontoxic household and body care products, paints/stains and building products). Then there are products to help us stay healthy—vitamins, herbal alternatives to over-the-counter medicines, creams, oils and cosmetics (maybe you'll even discover some made near your home). Another consideration is the business's impact on the Earth. Soon, for example, we will be able to chose wood products made from wood grown and harvested sustainably. We can support organic growers. We can even find clothes made from organic cotton, and FoxFibre is a naturally colored cotton—it grows that way! (It is currently available in three shades of brown and two shades of green, which get darker with washing. Yellow, orange, blue-green, yellow-green and browns with more orange and red tones are being developed.) Clothing and shoe companies are making items from recycled plastic bottles and other waste. The bottom-line question for me is, What kind of relationships does the business have, and strive to have, with the Earth, with workers, consumers, and the community in which it is located?

The fact is all businesses, green or not, big or small, need to make a profit. This is a basic premise of business. How much of a profit varies from business to business. Stonyfield Farm, profiled in this section, cares more about the quality of its product and treating its employees well than it does about making a financial killing. Ben & Jerry's, on the other hand, is a publicly traded corporation and has to put profit first. This means juggling other values in such a way that honoring them doesn't detract from the bottom line, which can be difficult, as the company readily admits. Green businesses need to maintain a careful balance between social-environmental concerns (and actions) and the bottom line, which can make it difficult for them truly to be agents of transformation.

Green business is a transition strategy that can help us move towards a sustainable society. It is not the goal in and of itself. The current legal, economic, and social systems that shape business and the market do not provide the necessary framework to allow business to evolve toward what Paul Hawken calls an "economy of restoration." Today, the reality is it often costs more to do the right thing. This means more investment up front for energy efficiency; pollution prevention and the like (although many of these up-front costs save money in the long run); more costly ingredients (organic goods cost more than those grown otherwise); and a commitment to paying workers fairly. These all translate into a need to charge more for goods and services. If customers aren't willing to pay more, the business fails. So it is up to each and every one of us as customers to be willing to patronize such businesses when we discover them, so they can stay viable and provide a model for others.

Business is considered the most powerful force on the planet right now. Since it isn't going to disappear, it will need to be transformed, along with the systems that shape it. This will take businesses run by people with integrity, willing to go against the grain of standard business practice, who care—first and foremost—about relationships and who see the future in generations, not in quarterly reports.

Profile: Stonyfield Farm

Growing Up Green
by Paddy Garrett-McCarthy

Here in New England, almost everyone knows Ben & Jerry's—pioneers of great ice cream and socially responsible business. Perhaps not as many are familiar with New Hampshire's Stonyfield Farm Yogurt, though there are a number of parallels between the two companies: both sell dairy products, both are run by a pair of energetic entrepreneurs with a social conscience, both are dedicated to supporting local agriculture and communities, both started small and grew fast. In fact, the two corporations have a friendly relationship, often working together on issues of mutual concern, such as local dairy suppliers, container recycling, and community events. In any case, Stonyfield Farm is worthy of a closer look, both because of its yogurt and because of its unusual—and very successful—way of doing business.

Stonyfield Farm was founded ten years ago, before "green business" was a familiar concept, by two longtime agricultural and environmental activists who believed then, and still believe today, that it's possible for business to be socially responsible and still be profitable. Founders Samuel Kaymen and Gary Hirshberg's first goal was to "produce the purest, most natural and nutritious yogurt available." Although rapid growth and financial success have changed some things at Stonyfield Farm, their original values and commitment to quality appear as strong as ever.

The first Stonyfield Farm yogurt was made with milk from Samuel Kaymen's Jersey cows on his 200-year-old farm in Wilton, New Hampshire. Samuel, an engineer-turned-organic-farmer, and his wife, Louise, wanted to make wholesome, natural yogurt to feed their own family. They also sold quarts of plain yogurt to a few local health-food stores. At the time, the Kaymens were running a school they established in 1979 to teach agricultural and homesteading skills, The Rural Education Center (TREC). When financial support for the nonprofit school began to diminish several years later, Gary Hirshberg, then directing the environmental nonprofit New Alchemy Institute in Massachusetts, was recruited to formulate a business strategy for TREC. Intended initially as a way to generate revenue for the nonprofit center, the yogurt business grew quickly beyond that. The Rural Education Center went into dormancy while energies focused on developing a yogurt business. Samuel perfected the yogurt recipe while Gary got the business on its feet, and the first fifty-gallon batch of yogurt was produced in 1983.

After several years of making and selling yogurt from the hilltop farm, demand for Stonyfield yogurt began to exceed the farm kitchen's capacity. The kitchen-bathtub/wood stove used on the Wilton farm to mix and heat milk was replaced with modern stainless steel equipment at a sprawling processing plant opened in Londonderry, New Hampshire, in 1989.

Sales for Stonyfield Farm were over $14 million in 1992, and are expected to reach more than $25 million by 1996. There are some ninety employees in Londonderry, including Chairman Samuel Kaymen and CEO/President Gary

Hirshberg. Stonyfield yogurt is distributed nationally, and a recently established California facility will soon expand distribution into Mexico. In 1983, Stonyfield sold plain whole-milk yogurt in quart containers. Now it sells sixteen flavors of refrigerated cup yogurt, eleven flavors of hardpack frozen yogurt, and 14 flavors of soft-serve frozen yogurt. A new line of yogurt made with all-organic milk is being developed. Samuel says about Stonyfield's rapid growth, "I never, never thought it would get this big. I had no hope of it."

From the very beginning, the Stonyfield people were, in Gary's words, "dedicated to ensuring that the company makes a positive contribution to the marketplace, to the environment, and to northeast agriculture." They still insist that "doing business the way we want to do it is worth much more than money." So how do they want to do business? What's important? Let's look at Stonyfield's Five Mission Objectives, and how the company is trying to meet them.

1. To provide and sell the very highest quality natural agricultural products available.

Stonyfield yogurt is made with choice ingredients, starting with milk from Jersey cows, judged to be the sweetest and creamiest available. The yogurt is flavored with premium fruits and is sweetened only with fruit juice and honey—no preservatives, thickeners, or artificial ingredients of any type are used. The company insists that sugar will never be used in their yogurt, even though this would increase profit margins by about 5 percent. Stonyfield also refused to respond to demand for "diet yogurt" made with artificial sweeteners. The folks at Stonyfield are adamant that there be "No compromises!" in their yogurt.

Yogurt is made by inoculating warm milk with live bacteria. Unlike large-volume producers, Stonyfield uses an all-natural culturing process through which yogurt is actually incubated in individual cups; whole and low-fat varieties have a layer of cream that forms on the top of the cup during this process. Stonyfield yogurt is naturally thick from a bacteria culture that includes acidophilus and bifidus bacteria thought to be highly beneficial to health. While other producers rely on preservatives, Stonyfield's unique processing techniques—including heated incubation rooms and "chill cells"—give their yogurt a natural shelf life of fifty-three days—the highest in the yogurt industry. Stonyfield yogurt costs a little more than other brands. As Samuel remarks proudly, "It's a top product, all good for you, it has nothing bad, and people like to eat it."

2. To educate consumers and producers about the value of supporting family farmers.

Education has been an integral part of Stonyfield's vision from the start. Indeed the business grew out of Samuel and Louise Kaymen's rural-education endeavors. They sought not only to make wholesome, healthy food on their own farm, but to support and sustain local agriculture, while teaching consumers about it.

To address Stonyfield's commitment to consumer education, a visitor center was built at the Londonderry plant. Staffed by former teachers, the center hosts groups of school children and others interested in learning firsthand about nutrition, agriculture, and yogurt production. Revenues from modest admission fees are donated to farm organizations.

Stonyfield Farm yogurt cups provide information on yogurt, on farmers, and the company. Customers are urged to save endangered species, to promote responsible business, and to help prevent the use of growth hormones in cows. The biannual "Moos from the Farm" newsletter keeps more than 25,000 recipients abreast of Stonyfield employees, environmental updates, new products, public events, cow jokes, and yogurt recipes. Through Stonyfield's "Adopt-a-Cow" program, over 20,000 people have adopted a live dairy cow and learned about farm culture and values.

A significant example of Stonyfield Farm's commitment to promoting sustainable agriculture is its support of Oxfam America. Stonyfield provides a $5,000 cash prize to recognize the efforts of this both U.S. and international organization committed to sustainable agriculture. In addition, the company agreed to donate 4 percent of 1993 pretax profits to Oxfam specifically for support of domestic sustainable agriculture. Stonyfield cosponsors (along with Ben & Jerry's) National Public Radio's "Living on Earth" program, as well as the "Making a Difference" contest, where individuals describe environmental problems and propose solutions. (First prize is a tropical expedition for two to Costa Rica.) The company purchases guava and papaya for its yogurt from Cultural Survival, a charitable organization dedicated to helping native tribal peoples.

In a further effort to "walk their talk," Stonyfield has initiated a cash premium program that will reward farmers who implement sustainable agricultural techniques (e.g., soil conservation, improved animal care, and reduced herbicide and pesticide use.) Stonyfield has recently been negotiating this plan with Ben & Jerry's, which is supplied with milk by the same dairy co-ops.

3. To provide a healthful, productive, and enjoyable workplace for all employees, with opportunities to gain new skills and advance personal career goals.

Stonyfield management believes that the employees are what's most important at Stonyfield Farm. According to President Gary Hirshberg, "Our philosophy is basically simple: A happy employee makes a happy company." Gary credits Stonyfield's rapid growth and rising profits on "a good product and a workforce that literally won't quit."

Employees seem eager to talk about working at Stonyfield. They say that management cares about them, that they feel valued and listened to, that employees are really a part of things, and that it's fun to work at Stonyfield Farm. Based on interviews with company employees, *Inc.* magazine recently named Stonyfield Farm one of "The Best Small Companies to Work for in America."

Stonyfield Farm uses a team approach to management. The Operating Committee, comprised of senior managers of the four company departments— Operations, Sales, Accounting & Finance, and Research & Development—meets weekly to consider all operational, planning, and budgetary decisions. The Profit Management Committee, comprised of middle managers, meets monthly with the

Operating Committee. Informal employee committees, including Social Vision, Plant Design, Recycling, Employee Benefits, Safety, and Fun, receive the full support of management. Whole-staff meetings are held every three months. Employees are encouraged to participate in company operations and decisions.

Management believes that information empowers employees. "I'm always looking for ways to give information," says Gary. "I tell them about sales, about gross margins, about costs, about how much we're making and why." Some of that information is shared in staff meetings, and some is shared during employees' one-on-one lunches with Gary twice a year.

Input from employees has been valuable to Stonyfield Farm, and employees are rewarded for it. Employee suggestions for improvements have led to, among other things, a savings in labor costs of $0.15 per case of yogurt. Stonyfield believes in rewarding employees based on the company's profits. Employee rewards and incentives, given either as cash bonuses or as stock options, range from 18 to 23 percent of pretax profits. Last year every employee brought home at least $1200 in bonus. Stonyfield offers its employees the opportunity to purchase shares of private company stock after two years of employment.

Employees are encouraged to learn new job skills at Stonyfield. An employee-initiated Job Exposure program requires every employee to spend a day each year doing another employee's job. Candidates for all new jobs are first recruited from within the company. During recent growth, Stonyfield hired thirteen new supervisors, ten of whom were promoted from within the company; only three were hired from outside.

There are a number of moving-up-the-ladder stories at Stonyfield. One example is Lynne Turner, Company Promotions Manager, who works with the company's community, corporate, and nonprofit partners. Lynne left a career in advertising and took a large cut in pay to join Stonyfield three years ago, where she started in Accounting. "At Stonyfield, you will get as much responsibility as you want to take," she says. "The company is growing fast, and you really feel invested in that."

4. To recognize our obligations to stockholders and lenders by providing adequate return on their investment.

Stonyfield is still a privately held company. Despite numerous offers from potential investors (some as remote as Saudi Arabia) and the need for capital as the company expands, management is very cautious. They would like to "avoid Wall Street" and are considering possible partnership or co-owner agreements. "We do not want to be forced to make any compromises," says Samuel, "in our yogurt or in our company."

After several years without turning a profit, the company now has seen profits increase an average of 60 percent annually for the last three years. Sales, last year at $14 million, are expected to double over the next several years.

5. To serve as a model that environmentally and socially responsible businesses can also be profitable.

According to Stonyfield's philosophy, being "green" implies several levels of commitment. It means producing pure, healthy food. It means treating employees well. It means educating producers and customers. It means collaborating with other organizations to maximize positive social and environmental impacts. It means addressing environmental issues as part of doing business. The company has signed the CERES Principles, ten commitments to a healthy, sustainable environment (see following section), and advocates positive environmental and social changes through the network of businesses ACT NOW.

The most persistent environmental issue for Stonyfield Farm has been the use of plastic cups for their yogurt. According to Stonyfield's Environmental Coordinator, Nancy Hirshberg (Gary's sister), management reached the decision to use plastic after examining both paper and glass packaging options. "In relation to paper containers, plastic cups use fewer resources, result in reduced deforestation, and are more likely to be reusable and recyclable," she says. "In addition, paper food containers, because of the poly-coatings and the anaerobic conditions in most landfills, do not decompose. The processing of these paper products also produces dioxin, which can be highly toxic." Glass containers are not considered viable because of the wide geographic distribution area for Stonyfield yogurt and the tremendous weight and cost of transporting glass.

The current recycling market for plastics in the U.S. is dismal, at best. The high cost of collecting, transporting, and processing recycled plastic, along with remarkably low prices for virgin plastic, has made recycled plastic as much as twice as expensive as virgin plastic. Wide-mouth containers, such as those used for yogurt, are made through injection-molding, and cannot be recycled with containers (such as those for milk) made through blow-molding, due to different melting points. Stonyfield has made several switches in plastics to enhance recycling possibilities, with limited success. They currently use polypropylene (PP), a structurally strong but thinner-walled plastic, which has allowed a 20 percent reduction in the amount of plastic used. Stonyfield Farm is at work on a project to create a national polypropylene recycling infrastructure. The company is urging other yogurt manufacturers to switch to the same resin, thereby building the necessary volume of a single resin for recycling; they further hope to help build the consumer market for recycled plastic.

Stonyfield Farm intends to convert their Londonderry facility into a model of ecologically sound manufacturing, and has begun to implement plans for several major improvements: solid waste bailing to increase cardboard and plastic films recycling; conversion of a hydrochlorofluorocarbon (HCFC) refrigeration system to an innovative ammonia-based process; construction of a "grinding and recapture" facility to collect, recycle, and remanufacture Stonyfield containers into new products; building an on-site solar waste-water treatment facility, using technology pioneered by Hirshberg's New Alchemy Institute; and starting a pilot organic dairy adjacent to the plant.

This project is viewed by Stonyfield's founders as a "total education endeavor... an advanced level of what we [Kaymen and Hirshberg] were doing to promote sustainable agriculture and responsible environmental conduct before starting the company."

Nancy Hirshberg concludes, "It's only through innovative, collaborative projects like this that we believe we'll find solutions for sustaining life and preserving resources on our fragile plant. One thing is for sure, there are no simple solutions!"

Food for Thought: Will Stonyfield Farm continue to be driven by its values and accept "no compromises" as it grows into an international corporation? How can Stonyfield Farm best control its growth? What is the optimum size that will allow this business to achieve its goals of financial success and social responsibility?

Voluntary Reporting

Some companies are voluntarily incorporating an environmental ethic in their practices and providing an annual report on their efforts. The Coalition for Environmentally Responsible Economies (CERES) was created in 1989 to "to forge a new and forceful dialogue with corporations around the protection of the planet, an to establish a well-informed public that chooses where to invest its capital based on environmental, not just economic, performance." (Initially, the CERES Principles were known as the Valdez Principles "in honor" of the Exxon oil disaster.) Coalition members include social investors, environmental groups, religious organizations, public-pension trustees, and public-interest groups. Member organizations together represent more than ten million people and over $150 billion in invested assets (1993 figures).

The heart of the Coalition its the CERES Principles, a ten-point code (or environmental ethic) that member corporations endorse. The Principles "are seen as an ongoing process rather than a static statement. Endorser corporations commit themselves to the process of developing a standardized code of environmental conduct over the long term." This means signatories don't have to be environmental saints; rather, they need to commit themselves to gradually improving their environmental performance—and to document the process. A disclaimer attached to the Principles makes it clear signatory companies are *voluntarily* pledging to go beyond the requirements of the law. It also affirms that the Principles don't affect the companies' legal position, nor are they intended to be used against a signatory in legal proceedings. This disclaimer was added due to companies' fears that the disclosure required by CERES would create liability beyond that specified by state and federal laws. Liability concerns were holding some companies back from becoming signatories.

As of Summer, 1994, eighty-one companies had endorsed the CERES Principles. The Sun Company, the twelfth largest oil company in the U.S., became the first Fortune 500 company to sign on in 1993, and in 1994 General Motors signed on. Other endorsers include Atlantic Recycled Paper Company, Aveda Corporation, Ben & Jerry's, The Body Shop, Calvert Social Investment Fund, Clivus Multrum, Inc., Community Capital Bank, Domino's Pizza Distribution Corporation, Earth Care Paper Company, Esalen Institute, Ringer Corporation, Seventh Generation, Smith & Hawken, Stonyfield Farm Yogurt, The Timberland Company, Tom's of Maine, the H. B. Fuller Company, and Deja, Inc.

Signatory companies are required to complete the annual CERES Report regarding their environmental performance. The information provided will be made available to the public. Ensuring that the Reports are, in fact, the truth is an important consideration, especially as "bad-guy" companies sign on.

In order to "increase public trust," the CERES Internal Committee, comprised of signatory companies, was created in April, 1993, to address issues of policy including the validation of the accuracy of information contained in the reports. However, some activists justifiably question the ability of companies to police themselves and have suggested that an oversight team, consisting of credible organizations with expertise in areas of corporate accountability, waste, and toxics, review the Reports.

It is difficult to determine the impact CERES will have on overall corporate accountability in environmental areas. Most of the companies currently endorsing the Principles (with the exception of Sun Company and General Motors) face relatively few environmental challenges. Sun's chairman, Robert H. Campbell, said reaching CERES's goals would not be easy for an oil company, stating the company would do its best to follow the principles "within the economic reality of our business.... We have more emissions than Ben & Jerry's."

The CERES Principles
(Formerly the Valdez Principles)

Introduction: By adopting these Principles, we publicly affirm our belief that corporations have a responsibility for the environment and must conduct all aspects of their business as responsible stewards of the environment by operating in a manner that protects the Earth. We believe that corporations must not compromise the ability of future generations to sustain themselves.

We will update our practices constantly in light of advances in technology and new understandings in health and environmental science. In collaboration with CERES, we will promote a dynamic process to ensure that the Principles are interpreted in a way that accommodates changing technologies and environmental realities. We intend to make consistent, measurable progress in implementing these Principles and to apply them to all aspects of our operations throughout the world.

Protection of the Biosphere: We will reduce and make continual progress toward eliminating the release of any substance that may cause environmental damage to the air, water, or the Earth or its inhabitants. We will safeguard all habitats affected by our operations and will protect open spaces and wilderness, while preserving biodiversity.

Sustainable Use of Natural Resources: We will make sustainable use of natural resources, such as water, soils and forests. We will conserve non-renewable natural resources through efficient use and careful planning.

Reduction and Disposal of Waste: We will reduce and where possible eliminate waste through source reduction and recycling. All waste will be handled and disposed of through safe and responsible methods.

Energy Conservation: We will conserve energy and improve the energy efficiency of our internal operations and of the goods and services we sell. We will make every effort to use environmentally safe and sustainable energy sources.

Risk Reduction: We will strive to minimize environmental, health and safety risks to our employees and the communities in which we operate through safe technologies, facilities and operating procedures, and by being prepared for emergencies.

Safe Products and Services: We will reduce and where possible eliminate the use, manufacture or sale of products and services that cause environmental damage or health or safety hazards. We will inform our customers of the environmental impacts of our products or services and try to correct unsafe use.

Environmental Restoration: We will promptly and responsibly correct conditions we have caused that endanger health, safety or the environment. To the extent feasible, we will redress injuries we have caused to persons or damage we have caused to the environment and will restore the environment.

Informing the Public: We will inform in a timely manner everyone who may be affected by conditions caused by our company that might endanger health, safety or the environment. We will regularly seek advice and counsel through dialogue with persons in communities near our facilities. We will not take any action against employees for reporting dangerous incidents or conditions to management or to appropriate authorities.

Management Commitment: We will implement these Principles and sustain a process that ensures that the Board of Directors and Chief Executive Officer are fully informed about pertinent environmental issues and are fully reponsible for environmental policy. In selecting our Board of Directors, we will consider demonstrated environmental commitment as a factor.

Audits and Reports: We will conduct an annual self-evaluation of our progress in implementing these Principles. We will support the timely creation of generally accepted environmental audit procedures. We will annually complete the CERES Report, which will be made available to the public.

These Principles establish an ethic with criteria by which investors and others can assess the environmental performance of companies. Companies that endorse these Principles pledge to go voluntarily beyond the amendments of the law. The terms *may* and *might* in Principles One and Eight are not meant to encompass every imaginable consequence, no matter how remote. Rather, these Principles obligate endorsers to behave as prudent entities who are not governed by conflicting interests and who possess a strong commitment to environmental excellence and to human health and safety. These Principles are not intended to create new legal liabilities, expand existing rights or obligations, waive legal defenses, or otherwise affect the legal position of any endorsing company, and are not intended to be used against an endorser in any legal proceeding for any purpose.

FIVE

Socially Conscious Investing

SOCIALLY CONSCIOUS INVESTING involves bringing an acute awareness of social, environmental, and ethical concerns to one's investment decisions. There are many ways to invest ethically, and many considerations to balance, but the best decisions are those that integrate your life values and goals. This requires work. It means clarifying your personal needs and social values, and it means learning investment skills. Only then will you have the ability to make investment decisions that you are happy with—and that contribute to a world in which our children can live well.

Developing your Investment Criteria

Everyone has investment criteria, although they may be unaware of them. Developing conscious investment criteria will help you make better decisions, even if your final choices are gut-level.

The starting place for investment criteria are your core values, goals, and needs. Instead of thinking about money as a thing that helps us obtain other things, try thinking of it in the same way you might consider your work, your talents, and your skills: as another tool and resource for expressing your values and achieving your goals.

Some of the first questions to explore when making investment plans are:

1. What are my life goals? What values or beliefs do I hold most dear?

2. What impact do I want to have in the world?

3. What do I want to accomplish in my personal life?

4. What do I need to feel secure?

List general and specific answers to these questions; put aside some time to do this systematically. If it seems overwhelming and hard to begin, you can start simply by recording your thoughts. Alone or with a friend, sit in a comfortable place and let yourself imagine your desired future, then write down the thoughts as they come.

Talking with someone—a friend or a counselor—often helps; choose someone who can listen nonjudgmentally and facilitate *your* getting clear instead of arguing or offering advice before you want it.

Once you have an idea of your goals, ask yourself, How can I use money to support these goals? For example, if your number-one personal goal is to live in a clean, beautiful area, and your most important goals for the world are environmental conservation and improvement, how can you best use your money? Depending on other goals you have listed, the creative answers you come up with could be anything from buying a suburban home and donating to the Sierra Club, to starting an environmentally sound farming cooperative, to founding or supporting a fund that gives grants to activist environmental groups.

An Example: Values About Profit

Here are some of the different ways socially conscious investors might think about profit, fit it in with their other values and goals, and apply the mix to their investment choices:

Arla: "My grandparents worked very hard for the money I inherited. They intended it to be passed down in the family. If I invest it in a way that does not make a profit—at least enough to stay even with inflation—I would be letting the fruit of their efforts slip away and betraying the love they showed by providing this money."

John: "My grandparents and parents also worked hard at the factory my family owns, which is the source of my wealth. But the two hundred workers they employed also worked very hard. I think it's unfair that our system gives the profits from all that work only to those who have the money or luck to own the factory—especially when some of the owners, like me, don't even work there! So I choose not to invest for interest or profit. In fact, I'm considering giving away most of the money I have coming to me from my part-ownership of the family business."

Tom: "If I don't go for as much profit as possible on my money, while everyone else in the economic system does, I will eventually fall behind and my life-style will slip. I will be able to afford fewer and fewer of the things that make me comfortable, while my friends all move into nice homes and travel more."

Carol: "I've been torn about this at times. I agree with John that it is unfair that some people have the opportunity to make profits and others don't. But it's very important to me that I be able to provide my children with a college education. Saving and investing some money for profit seems like the only practical way to do that. My way of balancing my political views and my children's security is to invest in financially sound businesses that have excellent labor practices, democratic management, employee-ownership opportunities, and good on-the-job safety records."

Beth: "I feel the profit-making system is full of injustices, but I don't want the power of my money lost, either. My compromise is making loans that earn interest, but donating the interest to social-change organizations. That way the reward society gives for lending or investing money isn't lost—it actually goes to work to help change a system that's unfair."

Sarah: "The profit-making system is full of injustices, not the least of which is the lack of security for those of us who grew up without enough money. I've earned the little money I have to invest, and what scares me is how quickly it would go if my mom stops being able to work, which will be soon. I feel like I have to at least keep up with inflation. To balance my desires for a more equitable system and my need for security, I invest some of my savings in a socially responsible money-market fund and the rest at one point above inflation in a well-established community revolving-loan fund."

John: "I make zero-interest loans to a housing cooperative that helps low-income people to buy homes. If these folks had to pay interest, they couldn't do it, so my money is a very powerful tool to give a fairer footing to people who've been disenfranchised. I feel the money is doing more than if it were earning 20 percent interest."

Weighing Rate of Return, Risk, and Liquidity

Another step in developing investment criteria is to decide how fluid, secure, and profitable you want your money to be by asking yourself

1. How much money do I need to keep, risk-free?

2. How much do I want to invest? Lend? Give away?

3. What is the right balance of these uses of money for now?

4. How do I want that to change over the next five, ten, and twenty-five years?

5. How much can I afford to write off, if necessary?

Then there are the balancing questions that put different values together:

1. How much financial *return* will I give up in order to support an enterprise that excites me, that reflects particular goals or values I hold dear?

2. How much *risk* will I take with how much of my money to support an enterprise or project that expresses my social values and goals?

3. Given my personal *and* social goals, *how long* can a borrower use my money?

Naturally, some of these questions will become clearer as you consider specific investment opportunities. But examining them ahead of time establishes a base that can be helpful in deciding whether or not to make a particular investment or loan.

Two Examples of Investment Criteria

Abigail earns a modest salary as a community organizer and manages to save about $1,500 a year. She is the first of her family to have any savings at all and worries about having a buffer for herself and a little extra to help her family through hard times. But Abigail is also very committed to the work she does encouraging fundamental social change.

Abigail worked out a fairly explicit set of criteria. She wants her money to keep pace with inflation, be secure, be available at short notice, and if possible, support local community economic development initiatives. An unstated criterion was that her investment need little monitoring.

Abigail met her criteria by investing roughly half her money in a socially responsible money-market fund and the rest as a series of one-year loans to a well-established community revolving-loan fund. The money-market fund gave her liquidity, low risk, fair return, and acceptable social screens. The revolving-loan fund allowed her to support initiatives she really believed in with moderate risk, fair return, and acceptable liquidity.

Ron, who lives modestly but comfortably on a combination of inherited wealth and income, persuaded his grandfather to put the $400,000 he was leaving to Ron into a foundation Ron would manage. When his grandfather died, the foundation was born, and Ron had to decide where to invest its assets. He established the following investment criteria: 1) High return: The fund gives away only the income on its assets, and Ron wants to maximize the money available to give away; 2) Medium to low risk: "I can't let the foundation's assets disappear in a flash of the stock market"; 3) Liquidity available in four years: Ron, who has already given away principal to fund social change, may want to give more principal at that time; and 4) Local investment managers with whom Ron can build a relationship.

These criteria are not listed in any absolute order of importance; their relative importance to Ron shifted in light of specific investments he considered. Ultimately, he chose a fifty-fifty balance of investments returning a fixed rate of income and those returning a variable income at a slightly higher risk. Half the foundation's money went to a well-established alternative publishing house as a three-year mortgage loan, secured with the building the company was buying. The interest is tied to the prime rate, an important deciding factor, given Ron's criterion of a high return.

Ron put the other half of the foundation's assets into a stock-and-bond account managed by a local socially responsible investment manager. This manager offers a choice of social screens through which unacceptable corporations are eliminated, and Ron is using all of them: corporate citizenship, employee relations, energy, environment, product, and large-scale weapons production. Within that framework, the manager will pursue the highest possible income for the foundation at low-to-moderate risk.

Socially Responsible Investing (SRI)

The term "socially responsible investing" most commonly refers to fairly conventional investments—such as mutual funds or money-market funds—with social screens. The practice of what has become socially responsible investing has grown and spread considerably since its beginnings in the 1970s. In light of the Vietnam War, a group of concerned Methodists organized the Pax World Fund, a mutual fund that began operations in 1971. Its purpose was to avoid investments in all weapons, and to support instead companies producing life-supporting goods and services. In 1972, the Dreyfus Third Century Fund began investing in companies with "best-of-industry" records. Both funds are going strong today, and the Pax World Fund has expanded its screen to avoid nuclear power, South Africa, or the "sin" industries of alcohol, tobacco, and gambling. Companies are also screened for fair employment and sound environmental policies.

In the years since, the number of socially screened funds has increased to about a dozen. Most have fairly clear, if not all-encompassing, social and environmental guidelines for investment. In addition, the number of publications and books providing information for concerned investors has grown enormously, as have the number of financial consultants and brokers who work with socially oriented clients.

Today, SRI is no longer considered strange nor is it dismissed as a fringe movement. According to the Social Investment Forum, a national organization that promotes SRI, over $700 billion in investments are (as of 1993) under professional, socially responsive management. While this figure sounds impressive, it is important to keep in mind that the majority of the portfolios are screened for a single issue.

Social Screens

People involved in social investment are quick to point out that social investing means different things to different people. We are each unique and have our own priorities—there is no perfect screen that suits everyone. There are also no perfect companies. Investors must make choices based on their individual value systems, and they must rank their values.

What does this mean in practice? If you are an individual investor concerned about nuclear weapons, the environment, exploitative regimes, workplace issues, women's issues, and animal rights, it will be practically impossible to find publicly traded companies that are "clean" in all those areas. Obviously, then, if you wish to invest in the stock market, you must set priorities and make hard choices. You must decide what you absolutely cannot live with and what you do want to support—say, a clean environment or women-managed companies or worker-ownership. Based on your choices, you could then apply negative and positive screens to the companies you are considering.

Identifying and ranking the practices you want to avoid or promote is the first step toward creating a screen. The next step is to define economic needs and goals so that investments can satisfy both your financial requirements and social concerns. You must decide whether you want income now, in the future, or both, as well as how much risk you are willing to take. Then decide where to look for investments.

Investment Options

Besides the large corporations listed on the New York and American Stock Exchanges, you can invest in

- the stock of small to medium-sized companies that are publicly traded and sold over the counter (OTC) and on local exchanges (issued for sale in only one or a few states);
- mutual funds;
- money-market funds;
- municipal bonds;

- government instruments;
- banks and credit unions;
- small businesses; or
- other alternative investments.

Many investors, especially those with limited funds or first-time investors, chose mutual or money-market funds. Mutual funds pool the stock of many companies to form a diversified pool of investments. This diversification protects investors from large losses due to the failure of segments of the market. Money-market funds require and provide more liquidity than mutual funds, and consist of some corporate investments, short-term debt, and government issues supporting such things as small businesses, construction of moderate-income housing, and student loans. Mutual funds usually outperform money-market funds, which are sometimes only slightly more profitable than passbook savings accounts. There are several screened mutual and money market funds available for social investors (see Resources).

Municipal bonds are one method state and local governments use to raise money for specific projects. Interest varies according to the bond's rating and taxability and is paid every six months; the principal is returned when the bond matures (in a few months to several years). Changing tax laws can alter the bond market, so it is important to assess one's tax situation before investing in them. There are now three types of bonds. Fully tax-exempt bonds are issued to raise money for such governmental purposes as the building of roads and schools. Fully taxable bonds are issued to finance "private activity" (e.g., shopping malls, stadiums, convention centers, and the like). Fully taxable bonds pay a slightly higher interest rate than the tax-exempt bonds do. Finally, there are partially tax-exempt bonds to finance projects that are considered partly public and partly private. Bonds carry ratings, from AAA insured down to C, or are nonrated. The higher the bond is rated, the lower its yield—and the lower its risk.

Bonds allow investors to support particular local or regional projects. In addition, there are bond funds that, like mutual funds, reduce the capital risk. Calvert now offers a socially screened bond portfolio, and the Muir California Tax Free Bond Fund invests in California bonds concentrated in the areas of environmental protection, education, and housing.

At the federal level, various agencies issue government bonds to finance student loans (Sallie Maes), farm loans (Federal Farm Credit System), small-business loans (Small Business Administration), and home mortgages and housing construction (Federal National Mortgage Association, or Fannie Maes; Federal Home Loan Banks; and the Federal Home Loan Mortgage Corporation, or Freddie Macs).

Banks and credit unions are the places we usually put our money. They can be fine investments, or a concerned investor's nightmare. See "Socially Responsible Banking" later in this chapter for more on banks.

As you can see, there are many ways of investing your money in more traditional vehicles while still taking your personal values (at least some of them) into consideration. Which of these you choose, if any, depends on your personal financial situation and your values and preferences. If you need help in deciding where to invest, consult a financial planner who works with ethically concerned clients. Choosing a financial consultant is like picking a family doctor. Ask your friends for suggestions, visit, and ask all your questions. (It helps to have a few written down in advance.) Take as much time as you need to feel comfortable, and do not feel forced into anything because you feel ignorant or uninformed. You may interview several planners, brokers, or advisors before you find the person or organization that is right for you.

Social Investing's Hard Choices

I can't overemphasize how difficult it is to maintain total integrity when investing in major corporations. A company that has a wonderful employee policy may expose its workers to highly toxic chemicals. A women-owned company may promote an image of women less than desirable to feminists. Or a company with great parental leave and child-care programs may be polluting the environment.

You must also beware of corporate "greenwashing." Naturally, a company will promote its most positive aspects and avoid publicizing its problem areas. One good project does not translate into an excellent company. Today, it is possible to obtain fairly decent information on corporate practices in the United States—at least for larger, publicly traded multinationals. SRI funds and professionals connected with SRI have access to computer databases, publications, and reports that detail some of the worst abuses. It is possible to do your own sleuthing as well, with the help of grassroots organizations and computer databases. On my own computer, I have data on about forty major U.S.-based corporations involved in the chemical, paper, timber, oil, mining, waste, manufacturing and large-scale agriculture industries. If you are interested in doing some of your own research, see "Education and Research" in part 3, chapter 5.

In spite of best efforts, screens can sometimes have relatively large holes. For example, the November-December, 1992, issue of *Netback*, published by Good Money Publications, reported that some socially screened mutual funds had investments in nineteen companies that placed in the top 100 toxic polluters for 1990 (the latest year for which figures were available). At the time of Good Money's report, the only funds holding none of the polluters were Working Assets, the Muir California Tax Free Bond Fund, the three Parnassus Income Fund portfolios and the money-market portfolios of Calvert and Green Century Fund. All other screened funds held one or more of the top 100 polluters. Changes have most likely occurred since 1992, but it makes sense to see the current list of a fund's holdings before investing, in order to be aware of similar inconsistencies.

There is another caveat. It is increasingly common for companies to site production facilities in countries with lax or nonexistent environmental regulations and vast pools of cheap labor. While information about how a company operates in the United States is becoming more available, it is difficult—and sometimes impossible—to know for certain how they operate overseas, since many countries lack even minimal standards of corporate disclosure, and repressive governments go to extreme lengths to keep the rest of the world from knowing about their human-rights abuses.

Today's corporations are chameleons, having developed the ability to look like citizens of any country in which they are doing business regardless of their home base. In fact, some U.S. companies strive to *lose* their American identity to win broader acceptance and avoid political hassles. In the first chapter of *Abuse of Power* authors Dembo, Morehouse and Wykle write,

> If the symbiosis of corporate and societal interest ever did exist, it certainly does not now. Large multinational corporations have become more and more "disconnected" from the national economies of the countries where they are headquartered. As the scale and complexity of their operations have grown, so has the concentration of enormous economic and political power within them. Increasingly, those who exercise this power—i.e., senior corporate officials—are accountable primarily to themselves.

Social investors are becoming aware of the discrepancies between how companies operate in the United States and how they operate overseas. Researchers and social-investment firms are starting to tackle this situation by linking with international human-rights organizations such as Amnesty International, Asia Watch, the Lawyers' Committee for Human Rights, Coalition for Justice in the Maquiladoras, and individuals living in the countries who can see what is going on. Simon Billenness, a researcher with the social investment firm Franklin Research & Development, believes the social issue of the 1990s is human rights, and that social investors "are in a unique position to insist that multinational corporations support human rights."

Early efforts of the movement include Franklin's dialogs with PepsiCo and Amoco regarding their operations in Burma (both companies have agreed to provide a report on their Burmese operations and address concerns about their impact on human rights in that country). Franklin has also started looking at a company's domestic operations separately from their non-U.S. ventures, which are evaluated against internationally accepted human-rights standards. The U.S. Trust Company of Boston, the

Calvert Social Investment Fund's advisor, has added an international dimension to its existing social guidelines and plans to review corporate practices in countries such as China and Mexico. Working Assetts uses the International Bill of Human Rights as a guide.

This is a start. There is a long way to go, though, because hundreds of U.S. corporations have operations overseas, many in nations with repressive governments, including Indonesia, Hungary, China and countries in Latin America.

Along with human rights, concern for the environment is paramount, hence the development of environmental funds by investment firms not normally associated with SRI. For example, Merrill-Lynch and Fidelity Investments have both initiated environmental funds. Others include the SFT Environmental Awareness Fund and the Freedom Environmental Fund, funds invested, for the most part, in firms specializing in toxic and hazardous waste clean-up, air and water pollution control and clean-up as well as incineration plants. A small percentage of these funds' investments may be in more innovative ways of handling waste, but these constitute a tiny fraction of the portfolios' holdings.

There is no question that these funds' primary purpose is to capitalize on the public's concern about the environment. SFT Family of Funds' President Wes Groshans states, "This is a solid industry, regardless of what the social values might be. The industry is a tremendous economic opportunity at this time." Rosemary Mills-Russel, vice president of Merrill-Lynch, also notes, "It's difficult to say whether the interest is more altruistic or opportunistic."

They are referring to the waste-management industry, and the largest holdings in these funds are Waste Management and Browning Ferris, along with several of their wholly or partly owned subsidiaries. These companies are responsible for enormous amounts of pollution in almost every state, and their dumps and incinerators are being fought by community groups across the country. Both companies are notorious for gobbling up smaller businesses and monopolizing the industry. Citizens' Clearinghouse for Hazardous Waste has produced comprehensive reports on these companies.

SRI obviously has limitations. Still, it is a tactic taken by more people with money than ever before, which must be seen in a positive light. Wayne Silby, cofounder and chairman of the Calvert Social Investment Fund, believes "social screening [can be used] as a platform from which we create the emerging models for social change" if "we are resolute in directing the investment industry to viable approaches that speak to true social change."

Socially Responsible Banking

Most of us will have a savings account in a local bank or credit union long before we invest in a mutual fund or visit a financial planner to structure a portfolio of stocks and bonds. Our bank account is our investment, and the bank is the manager. How does the bank invest our money?

Banks can be fine investments (although interest rates on savings are very low right now), or they can be a concerned person's nightmare. Large interstate banks are more likely to have foreign investments, including exploitative loans to Third World countries. They are also more likely to be invested in the very institutions and corporations socially concerned people would rather avoid. Local savings and loans are much more likely to invest a larger percentage of their funds locally in the form of mortgage loans, business loans, and personal loans. The 1977 Community Reinvestment Act (CRA) requires that banks attempt to meet the credit needs of the community in which they are located. Banks must issue a public statement outlining the types of loans available to the community and also must disclose the percentage of loans made in the community. A bank with a high percentage of local loans might be a good place to open a savings account. The CRA has been a useful tool for community organizers trying to reduce the drain of capital, particularly because it allows community groups to participate in the review process a bank must go through before relocating or opening a new branch office.

Funds within conventional banks

Banks are beginning to respond in a variety of ways to depositors' concerns about how their money is invested. Several banks in my area, for example, stress their local or statewide focus in their ads ("Bank with us, invest in Vermont," one bank's ad states).

A leader in the banking sector is the Vermont National Bank, which instituted its Socially Responsible Banking Fund (SRB Fund) in 1989 to support affordable housing, agriculture, the environment, education, and small-business development. Today the SRB Fund has grown to more than $60 million and has the lowest delinquency rate of any department of the bank, even in today's difficult economic times. Vermont National Bank's experience demonstrates the viability of such funds. Hopefully, as news of its success spreads among depositors and members of the banking community, more conventional banks will follow its lead.

Profiles

Community Development Banks

South Shore Bank

The South Shore Bank in Chicago, the nation's first community development (CD) bank, has been revitalizing Chicago's South Side neighborhood since the early 1970s. South Shore was a middle-class neighborhood until beset with "white flight."

By 1973 the South Shore Bank was the only game in town—and it was threatening to leave as well, until a group of progressive bankers bought it. Since then the Bank has financed over 8,000 multi-family units, placed 3,500 persons from its job training programs, and assisted over 156 new firms—all while making a profit. The Bank is a federally regulated and insured, for-profit bank that operates as a subsidiary of Shorebank Corporation. Shorebank's other subsidiaries and affiliates include a real estate development company, a venture capital company, a development banking consulting company, and a community economic development organization that provides services such as job training and placement. South Shore is so good at what it does that it was awarded the 1992 Princeton Peace Prize for economic justice. And, during his campaign, President Clinton said he wanted to create one hundred South Shore Banks as a way to revitalize the nation's beleaguered communities.

Community Capital Bank

We have a long way to go to reach Clinton's goal. It is extremely difficult to start a bank from scratch, since a minimum of $1 million must be raised first (the actual amount depends on the location and population), yet that is exactly what a handful of enterprising bankers and supporters are trying to do. Community Capital Bank (CCB) in Brooklyn, New York, has actually succeeded.

In the fall of 1987, CCB's organizing group, headed by Lyndon B. Comstock (who left his job as a commercial lending officer at the First National Bank of Chicago to work on the Bank for Socially Responsible Lending, as CCB was called then) made a $5 million initial public offering for common stock. Comstock told me at the time, "We'll be going far out of our way to seek a group of shareholders who understand what we are doing. Our policy is not profit maximization but a profit adequacy strategy combined with a social strategy."

The bank opened for business in January, 1991, after five years of organizing, raising $6 million in stock subscriptions from individuals, corporations, religious organizations, community groups, and foundations in twenty-two states. During the process, organizers sent regular newsletters and updates to all interested people, investors or not, and offered numerous workshops and seminars on community development and community-based banking.

After one year in business, CCB had more than $10 million in total deposits, and more than five hundred institutional and individual depositors from New York City and across the United States opened accounts, including checking, savings, CDs, money market, and IRAs. The Bank had made fifteen community development–related loans from $25,0000 to $450,000. In 1993, CCB's boasted more than $20 million in total assets. Loans were made to St. Mary's Center, a nursing home for AIDS victims in West Harlem; a knitwear company in the Williamsburg section of Brooklyn; a minority-owned construction contracting company in Brooklyn; multi-unit housing in West Harlem, the Lower East Side and the Central Bronx; and a Ben & Jerry's franchise, store co-owned by Joseph Hollard and HarkHomes (a nonprofit homeless shelter), most of whose employees are homeless men.

CCB also now offers space to LEAP, a nonprofit organization whose mission is to provide technical assistance to new or expanding community development–related small businesses in New York City.

Endnote to Community-Development Banks

There are at least two other community development banks in formation—one in Washington, D.C., and another in Grand Rapids, Michigan. Another, the Elk Horn Bank and Trust Company in Arkansas (a subsidiary of Southern Development Bancorporation), had its beginnings after then-Governor Bill Clinton invited South Shore's parent company (Shorebank Corporation) to set up a development bank similar to South Shore in his state. Southern Development Bancorporation began operating in 1988 and has extended $19.5 million in investments in rural Arkansas.

Profiles

Minority-Owned Banks

Dwelling House Savings and Loan

Dwelling House Savings and Loan has the unusual motto "The institution that serves your need, not your greed." It loans money to poor, mostly black, people who would not qualify for loans at other banks.

The Dwelling House Savings and Loan Association was once a very different operation, open only part-time and disorganized. In 1957, Robert Lavelle, then a real-estate developer in the area, went into Dwelling House to obtain a mortgage for a client. Despite the client's excellent qualifications, the bank was unable to make the loan because all of its money was committed to paying back investors who had left. Angry, Lavelle gave them advice on how the bank could be run better. At that moment, literally, Lavelle was made a director and the bank's secretary. Lavelle recognized that the bank needed federal insurance to grow, but to do this it had to prove that it was self-supporting. It needed a separate, ground-floor location, and it had to be open full-time. So Lavelle partitioned his real-estate office, moved the bank into the new space, and opened it full-time.

Dwelling House then had three black directors, six white directors, and assets of only $67,000. By 1968, the directorship had changed to its present seven black to two white ratio, assets had climbed to $130,000, and the campaign to become federally insured had begun. The drive revolved around a subscription campaign to recruit people who pledged to save once the bank was insured. By 1970, they had succeeded in collecting enough pledges to obtain insurance. Dwelling House Savings and Loan was off the ground.

Dwelling House's lending policy is based on person-to-person contact and trust. Lavelle says,

> The banking rule is you lend at the highest rate you can to get to people at the lowest risk. Under that rule, how can a black person, a poor person, or a deprived person get a loan? When they first come in, we go through the same procedure as any bank. Only after that we have another dimension of trying to help a person. At that point, we say, "You don't meet the criteria. What can you say to make me lend you this money?" You really get them to face themselves and to know why we're going to do it.

Lavelle believes that marginal loans must be made because the needs of the black community must be met. He asserts that home ownership helps bring about quality schools, more and better services, and better police protection. This, in turn, generates a need for small businesses, which provide young people with positive examples and jobs.

Since 1957, the bank has authorized over nine hundred mortgages, as well as some home-improvement loans and loans to churches. Anyone can deposit in Dwelling House by paying postage both ways. "Everyone's mail box is our branch office," says Lavelle. Like all interest rates banks pay to depositors these days, Dwelling House's rates have dropped. Currently, the bank pays about 3 percent interest ("plus human") and deposits are insured to $100,000.

Blackfeet National Bank

The Blackfeet National Bank (BNB) is located in Browning, Montana, in the heart of the Blackfeet Indian Reservation, home to approximately 8,500 people, the vast majority of whom are members of the Blackfeet tribe. BNB opened for business in July, 1987, as the first and only tribally controlled (the tribe owns 94 percent of the outstanding common stock), reservation-based, full-service commercial bank in the United States. Initially capitalized at $1.05 million, today the Bank has $5 million in assets and has made loans totaling in excess of $4.5 million.

In addition to providing high-quality financial services to the reservation community, BNB aims to play a major role in plugging the leaks that allow tribal dollars to flow into off-reservation communities, reducing the economic viability of the reservation's own commercial sector. Historically, the reservation economy has been dependent on government transfer payments, federal and tribal employment, oil and gas production, manufacturing, and agriculature. Currently, there has been a decline in energy resource development and reduced federal and tribal spending, elevating the importance of agriculture, manufacturing, and tourism. BNB hopes to be able to provide the capital necessary to develop and expand Indian-owned and operated agricultural and commercial enterprises.

Credit Unions

Credit Unions are federally regulated financial cooperatives, owned and controlled by their members. They provide banking services and consumer loans. Credit unions can serve a specific group of people, such as state employees or employees of a large company, or the membership can be geographically defined, which is the case with community development credit unions (CDCUs). While most low-income communities are not well served by conventional banks, there are over three hundred CDCUs across the country providing basic banking services. In addition to accepting the deposits of members, CDCUs are allowed to accept nonmember deposits, which helps bring additional resources into undercapitalized areas. According to the National Federation of Community Development Credit Unions (NFCDCU), CDCUs currently manage more than $500 million in deposits. The NFCDCU can provide you with information on a CDCU near you. The Federation also manages a central fund, which can accept larger investments that are then channeled to smaller CDCUs.

Profiles

Self-Help Credit Union

The Self-Help Credit Union (SHCU) is perhaps the most well-known CDCU, and also one of the most effective and diverse. SHCU was founded in 1983 as a project of the Center for Community Self-Help. (The Center started three years earlier to help displaced workers start businesses.) There are two financing affiliates associated with the Center for Community Self-Help, the Credit Union and the Self-Help Ventures Fund (also started in 1983). The Credit Union is a federally insured depository institution, while the Ventures Fund is a nonprofit revolving-loan fund. The Center serves as the umbrella organization, provides technical assistance, and develops new programs and policies; together with the Credit Union and the Ventures Fund, they form the Self-Help Development Bank.

The Credit Union has come a long way from humble beginnings (the Credit Union was started with only $77 raised at a bake sale!). Since making its first loan in 1984, SHCU has lent over $40 million to North Carolina's small businesses, nonprofits and low-income home buyers. By the end of 1992, Self-Help made 469 housing loans totaling over $20 million. Eighty-eight percent of these loans were to minority households, and 62 percent were to single, female heads of households; the average income of families served was $22,000 per year. Also by the end of 1992, Self-Help made over $20 million in commercial loans to over six hundred small enterprises, creating or saving over three thousand jobs.

SHCU makes it its business to lend to nontraditional borrowers in depressed areas; to forge partnerships between public-sector development programs, private-sector capital, and local community-based groups; and to provide technical and managerial assistance where needed. Self-Help makes it possible for people to own homes and businesses who might never have the opportunity otherwise. According to Associate Director Kate McKee, "We value ownership as a development goal much more so than job creation or physical revitalization."

Investing in the Small Scale Investing Locally

Our investments are generally a hedge against an uncertain future. We try to save enough to help our loved ones and to cover our expenses when we can no longer work, or no longer wish to work. The hidden assumption—and tragedy—in all this is that few of us can depend on a supportive community to help our children get started, our relatives and friends during hard times, or ourselves as we get older. And so, if we can, we try to buy a measure of security by putting money by in places where it might grow.

The conventional wisdom about investments is that investing in bigger, more established companies and funds is the safest way to go. From a purely financial perspective, this may be partially true, especially if one spreads the risk by pooling both money and investments in a mutual fund, or if one invests in government-backed bonds. But many investors do lose money on the stock market, not to mention wilder markets like futures markets, and even the most solid-seeming bond is only as solid as the government it depends on.

On top of this, most large-scale markets are not set up to promote honesty, clarity, or investor (much less worker or community) control. For example, most of the investing in the markets is no longer tied to actual production; the chains of information between the individual investor and the people making the actual corporate decisions are long and tenuous; the flow of information is not usually good; the scale of operations are huge; and the intermediary salespeople do not necessarily share the investors' interests.

In short, few corporations or governments are truly accountable to the people who invest their time, energy, or money into them. Nor are they truly accountable to the communities or ecosystems in which they reside. Therefore, however socially responsible a large corporation or government may appear, especially relative to others, its very size and organization usually mean that it undercuts local, sustainable communities—and the security, comfort, and sense of control those communities can provide.

On the other hand, investing locally, in the small scale, offers the possibility of building community. It allows the investor and the organization to create relationships in which values other than purely financial ones may more easily hold sway, and in which each may more easily inform and influence the other. Besides invigorating such social relations, local investments can help invigorate local economies by keeping local money in local circulation. More personally, investing locally opens up for the investor another sort of return: a "use" return. By supporting organizations that are important in your life, (e.g., a food co-op, a theater, a local craftsperson or farmer), you can improve the quality of your life in the local community. Perhaps most important, investing locally—especially if you invest more than just money—can help you build more strands of security and satisfaction in the form of relationships, friendships, and local knowledge.

Types of Small-Scale Investments

Typically, if you invest in an organization, you own part of what you invest in. That is, you share the financial risks with the other owners (and workers), and typically, receive no financial return until you sell your share, or the organization is sold. You may, though, be able to share in the control of the organization, as well as the risks (if this fits your skills and interests). Sometimes, you can negotiate a regular return on your investment (a dividend of sorts). And, especially if you invest locally, you may also be able to negotiate some sort of use return.

It is also possible to loan money to an organization. Technically, a loan is a way of renting out your excess money. Generally, with loans, you take fewer risks and obtain a clear repayment plan, including interest. But it is possible to structure loans (e.g., without collateral, with little or no interest, that "roll over" rather than being repaid) so that they approximate investments. As with an investment, you may be able to negotiate something other than a financial return.

The following suggestions focus on loans, but much of the material, especially on screening, applies to investments as well. No matter how you decide to invest your money, you would do well to discuss your criteria, selections, and agreements with other experienced people including, perhaps, accountants and lawyers. You might also consider forming or joining a group of like-minded investors to share information, ideas, risks, and support.

Making Loans

On the face of it, making loans should be a safe and easy way of investing your money in small-scale opportunities. After all, you retain ownership of the money, grant the use of it for a time to others, and take rent for it in the form of interest during that time. But people who have lent money can tell you of bad experiences—things have gotten difficult, they have been given the runaround, been burned, or lost a friend.

Why does this happen? For one thing, our society has developed powerful impediments to our making such loans with ease and assurance. *First*, banks and other financial institutions have appropriated the functions and cornered the skills of lending. We find ourselves, as individuals, feeling mystified, powerless, and naive. *Second*, we have been convinced that the system is the *only* safe place to lend, that all else is risky. *Third*, we find money (though not property) abstract and hard to own up to. *Fourth*, while banks make their loans coldly and with regard to safety, risk, and rate of return, not social responsibility, we are immersed in a tradition that tells us *as individuals*; If something has social value, support it through gifts, donations, philanthropy—in short, through *subsidy*. To make loans yourself, you have to unload these debilitating assumptions.

Are you reacting to the coldness of banks by going to the opposite extremes, either avoiding loans or plunging in and acting as if you were making a gift? The main cause of feeling burned is making loans to people and businesses that they accept as subsidies.

Do you feel that money is too abstract to be real? Then realize that money is a medium and a storehouse of wealth.

Do you feel that the system is the only safe place? Consider the many people who have been burned in the system.

Are you afraid to go outside the system? Banks make loans so coldly because they rarely have good personal contacts with borrowers. You already have an advantage: You know—or can find out—how skillful, careful, persistent, enterprising, and committed your borrowers are.

In the small scale, it is *people* that you will be mainly investing in. Successful lenders put lots of time into finding and getting to know such people. And while some will not make loans to family and close friends, others do this very well because they have observed and assessed them so closely and carefully that they can really trust their own judgment.

With this in mind, let us look at the market for loans to small-scale enterprises. There is in fact no ready market, like the stock market, and no salespeople who will make it easy for you to buy. You are going to find your borrowers by direct contact. The hardest way to make direct contact is *on your own*. Instead, you will best reduce fear and hesitancy and turn the whole process into exploration and fun by getting continuing support and encouragement. Your personal network is the best place to start, and the resources in this book can help, too. Between these, you can find role models—people who have made loans already and will give you the know-how—and you can create support groups that will meet to share personal and technical concerns. Thus will you learn the ropes.

To test the waters, put out the word that you have loan money available. Make a list of people already in business and known to you or your friends who are doing things you support and approach them. Your first loans will usually be to people close at hand that you never considered until you decided that you really were ready to make loans.

The majority of small businesses you will know are probably pretty small and quite stable. They will include professionals as well as the obvious retail stores and restaurants; service businesses as well as small manufacturers and distributors; and mail-order people as well as artists and craftspeople. They may need help with expansion, special capital purchases, inventory maintenance, accounts receivable, refinancing previous debt, or moving their operations. If, for example, one needs a computer, it is possible for you to buy the computer, lease it and get a good tax credit, and take depreciation. Most lenders, however, prefer straight loans.

Screening Potential Candidates for Loans

The key to making a successful loan is *screening*. Before you even think about negotiating terms, get to know your potential borrowers and the business or organization they are operating:

1. Learn their plans in some detail.

2. Assess management's ability to carry out the plans.

3. Consider the stage of the enterprise: starting, stable, expanding, in a special situation, or in crisis. Screening of both start-up and in-crisis enterprises must be done carefully. Lending to strength is often the safer route, but your investment criteria might include accepting risks in the attempt to help worthy organizations in crisis.

4. Think about what the most effective loan might be: money, some tools, time, expertise, technical assistance, a referral, and so on.

When researching an enterprise, the business plan is a good place to start. If a particular organization does not have a business plan, you might want to ask that they develop one—or structure your discussions to gather the information you expect to find in the business plan.

A business plan is the investor's blueprint of a business. It is, most important, a written document that includes an analysis, detailed summary, and implementation plan of the proposed project. It should help a firm anticipate and deal with problems and help you judge the enterprise's future.

The initial, *intuitive* impressions of appearance, documentation, and form are very useful. The look of the plan should be appropriate to the project. A video production company that uses extensive graphics and charts in their business plan indicates they know what is appropriate for such a business. On the other hand, one might wonder about the fiscal responsibility of a start-up business that spends a lot of money on embossed folders.

Be sure to discuss the plan with the managers. How closely is the plan tied to what is actually happening? What questions does the plan raise for you? How helpful and insightful are the managers' answers?

The first section of the business plan itself is the summary and review. It emphasizes the strengths, background, and opportunities in the enterprise. The summary should include the history of the business (if any), its goals, its market approach, and its competitive advantage. Management skills and experience, financial and earning projections, and investment money required should also be included. As you read the plan and talk to the managers, try to determine whether the enterprise matches your investment criteria and whether the plan seems workable.

What are the goals of the business? Do the financial and nonfinancial goals of the enterprise match yours? At times, the personal financial goals of the management might get in the way of operating a successful business. Is the owner or manager committed to an integrated, socially responsible enterprise with both clear social goals and sound financial objectives?

Who is minding the business? Business experience and technical expertise are critical for success. If the venture is new, you should find out whether the managers have prior related experience and some previous business success. Small businesses usually fail because of poor management, so assessing management skills is essential.

It is also important to discover if the managers know what they do *not* know. Even after a business project is researched in depth, there are still going to be many unknown factors. A successful management is likely to admit and confront such unknowns honestly.

Finally, is the structure democratic, worker-oriented, and/or grassroots based? Is it consistent with the statement of purpose and objectives? Are professional advisers (accountants, attorneys, bankers, technical consultants, and others) available if needed?

How accurate are the financial assumptions? Since the advent of computer-generated financial projections, business plans have doubled in length. Therefore, you must pay attention to the quality of financial documentation, not just the quantity. It is the thinking process behind the financial projections that is critical. You need to know how sales assumptions were made, what the accuracy of expense allocations is, and how good any historical financial data are.

You should also be sure that the business has an effective accounting system that consistently and accurately monitors financial operations. Finally, make certain that the people managing the business have enough financial expertise to handle its level of complexity.

Is there a focus on marketing? For each venture, the marketing alternatives need to be clearly identified and matched to a marketing strategy that will successfully address the business opportunity. The firm must clearly define its marketing approach (determining a market need and satisfying it) and estimate the effect marketing will have in satisfying the potential customers. Hard data, careful analyses, and a precisely targeted market are the keys to a serious, successful marketing plan.

Once you understand the enterprise and the plan, you might want to evaluate the whole in light of the following:

Critical business risks. Every business has inherent risks; be sure you identify, discuss, and weigh them. A new herbal-tea manufacturer is trying to determine if the market is already saturated. A computerized psychological testing service is being managed by psychologists who have no business experience. A computer support business is too dependent on one experienced technician. Only one partner in a women-owned massage center has any marketing experience. None of these risks are necessarily fatal, but before you invest you should be convinced that the managers have a well-thought-out plan to deal with them.

Community and human benefits. Does the enterprise encourage useful employment of both people and resources? Does it provide products or services that serve the immediate community? Does it enhance local self-reliance, breaking the dependency on outside resources for development?

Action Plan. The action plan is a schedule for starting and maintaining a new business opportunity. It should be complete and realistic. A refugee-women's housecleaning cooperative scheduled language-training classes, work-skills workshops, and marketing-techniques development into a business plan and then did them.

Investment opportunity. Once you are convinced that there is an acceptable business goal, capable and experienced management, clear market opportunity, and realistic financial estimates, you should find out precisely how much money is required for the project and how it will be used. The published financial statements should help you determine if the investment is excessive (extensive capital improvements or high salaries) or appropriate (efficient technology or affordable equipment). Before investing, ask, Will the project succeed? Will it pay a fair return? Have the risks been identified?

You must take the time to read the business plan and talk with the managers. And you need to balance your own criteria against what the organization can provide. Sometimes you will need professional advice about things like taxes. And you must be sure the investment alternative you choose—stock, loan, limited partnership—is also in accord with your criteria.

Even a well-written, -researched, and -presented business plan will not guarantee success. The project is always at risk. However, management's experience and skills will increase a project's chance for success. Knowing this, you can shape intuition, first impressions, and a detailed analysis of the entire business plan into a dependable guide to social investing.

Negotiating the Terms
and Making the Loan

Once you have decided to offer a loan to an organization that meets your criteria, it is time to focus on the details of the possible loan. There are some very practical things you can do that make a loan more likely to work out well for both parties:

Negotiate. Do not be afraid to actively negotiate with someone who asks you for a loan. While many of us feel a sense of obligation to lend to friends and especially to family, with no questions asked, it is respectful to both you and to the other person to make a responsible, informed decision. Hence, you need to review your investment and loan criteria and ask for any information you need about the other person's situation.

Do not hesitate to ask for what you want. Explain your needs and your thinking, and ask if it seems fair to the other person. Choose a tone that seems appropriate, but still make sure you get all the content you need to make a comprehensive, workable agreement.

Make a written contract. If you decide you *do* want to make the loan or investment, negotiate an agreement that takes both of your interests into account. Put your agreement in writing—the more explicit and specific you can be, the better. Even if the loan or investment really matters to only one party, carefully writing up an agreement helps each party clarify her or his expectations and avoid misunderstandings, while providing a record either party can refer to should there be disagreements later. The agreement should include such information as

who will pay *how much* to *whom*;

when and in what form the payments will be received;

whether there is *flexibility* in the payback period;

if there is flexibility, how much;

whether *interest* will be paid;

if interest will be paid, *how much* and *when*;

how the agreement can be changed; and

how the parties will resolve unanticipated conflicts.

Written agreements should probably be as simple as is appropriate for a given situation. If the situation is complex, if there is a significant power imbalance between the two parties, or if one party is worried, it might be worth obtaining legal or other experienced advice.

Below are three loan agreements that vary in formality and complexity. They give some idea of the range of possible agreements. Note that they are not comprehensive; they are simply frameworks you can play with. You and the other party to the agreement have to design your own agreement that reflects the tone and content of your situation.

Promissory Note
$1,000
One Thousand Dollars

Berkeley, California
April 1, 1994

Elissa Brown (Payor) promises to pay Roger Pritchard (Payee), or order at place designated by Payee, the principal sum of one thousand only dollars, lawful money of the United States, with interest thereon from April 1, 1994, at the rate of fifteen percent (15%) per annum, compounded quarterly. Should principal sum plus accrued interest not be paid by due date, there shall be a late fee of $50.00. Payor may pay off this note in full without penalty on giving one month's written notice to Payee.

Payee and Payor shall have a meeting on or about February 1, 1995, to examine Payor's ability to pay off the note when due. There will be no charge for this meeting. Should Payor be unable to pay off this note when due, or should some other trouble develop, both parties shall first try to work things out. Should this not be possible, they agree to go to arbitration with Sterling Johnson or Paul Terry, or some other person chosen by Sterling or Paul who agrees to serve. Payor shall pay for the arbitration if there are any fees.

Payor agrees to exert all moral and work efforts to paying this note off on time. Should Payor die with the note unpaid, her estate shall be responsible for its repayment.

By_____
Elissa Brown
407 Hudson St.
Oakland, CA 94618
(415) 654-3795

By_____
Roger Pritchard
Financial Alternatives
1514 McGee Avenue
Berkeley, CA 94703
(415) 527-5604

Witnessed by_____

This is the form of a promissory note. First, the amount is stated. It is best to state figures both in words and numbers, as on checks. Second, the city and state are included. These establish jurisdiction. If you have an arbitrator, as in this case, the courts will back up the award, and the lender should make the jurisdiction as convenient as possible for her/himself. Third, the date of the agreement, which may or may not be the initial date of the loan, is added.

The first section of the note gives details of the promise to repay the loan. The names of lender and borrower (payor and payee) are given in full and the signatures match. The starting date is set out. The method of repayment is indicated. Then the interest rate, stated in terms of annual percentage rate (APR), plus time period for compounding, are added. Be sure the interest rate you agree on is not above the usury limits in your state, the courts will not back the lender up in case of trouble about that rate. The time period for compounding can range between a day and a year.

(Contact your state's department of banking and insurance for information.)

The most likely challenge to this agreement is Elissa's needing more time to repay. Both the meeting in February, 1995, and the late fee (which essentially helps pay for the extra time necessary to work out a new agreement) are included with that in mind. Further, two good friends whom both parties respect and trust are already named in case of irreconcilable dispute; if they cannot serve, they can name someone else.

The security for this loan is Elissa's moral commitment and her ability to work skillfully. This is stated *explicitly*. Had the lender wanted *material* security, that would have been included in another clause, or there would have been a separate security agreement filed or recorded with the county or state agency in order to establish the obligation on the particular property. Had the lender wanted a *cosigner*, s/he would have been named in the body of the note and would have signed, thereby becoming "jointly and severally liable" with Elissa. The lender could, alternatively, have asked for a *guarantor*. A guarantor has better protection than a cosigner, because s/he is cleared of the obligation if the terms of the note are changed without her/his agreement—something a cosigner cannot get.

Finally, the borrower(s) sign the note. The names, addresses, and telephone numbers of all parties can be included for easy contact.

In most cases, a simple agreement will suffice. You may wish to use an attorney as a consultant to check your already written agreement for errors and omissions, or you can entrust troubleshooting to your arbitrator, if you have one. Here I will use simple loan agreements as examples of the main points to be covered. Remember that space limitations preclude more than a very brief discussion and that not every consideration is examined. For more detailed information, consult a lawyer or paraprofessional.

Loan Agreement
$2,000   May 11, 1994

Marsha Samuels has loaned Bob Samuels two thousand dollars toward producing his second record album. Bob agrees to repay the loan in four installments: on September 1, 1994; December 1, 1994; March 1, 1995; and June 1, 1995. Bob will pay 6% simple interest to Marsha.

If necessary, Bob can make the first payment on December 1, 1994, and push back the whole repayment schedule three months; if he needs to do this he will tell Marsha by August 1, 1994.

Bob and Marsha may agree to change this agreement, and if they do so they will write up and sign a new agreement.

Marsha Samuels_____   Bob Samuels_____
Witnessed by:_____

Loan Agreement
$10,000   April 5, 1994

For value received, I, Robin Baker, for the Haverill Community Center, hereafter HCC, agree to pay to Betsy Hurley, or order, ten thousand dollars according to the following terms:

1. HCC agrees to pay $10,000 to Betsy Hurley, in cash, Massachusetts check, and/or U.S. bank check, in a total of ten monthly payments of $1,000 to be received by Betsy Hurley on or before the first of every month starting June 1, 1994, through the final payment on March 1, 1995;

2. HCC agrees to pay 10% per annum simple interest. Robin Baker and an advisor of her choice may elect a charitable organization as the recipient of this interest. If this option is chosen, Robin Baker will issue a check for the interest, payable to the charitable organization, and will send this check to Betsy Hurley with information about the group and its address so that Betsy Hurley can learn about the recipient organization. Betsy Hurley will forward the check to the recipient organization;

3. HCC agrees to secure this loan with the equity in HCC's building at 433 Sunshine Avenue, Chicago, Illinois;

4. The terms of this agreement may be changed only by mutual written agreement of both parties involved; and

5. HCC agrees to pay all reasonable costs incurred in the collection of this note.

Robin Baker_____   Betsy Hurley_____
for Haverill Community Center
Witnessed by:_____

The loan may be paid off in equal monthly payments; this is called an *amortized* loan. Or it may be paid off in one or more lump-sum payments; you will state the date(s) for payment or the circumstances (for example, attaining a turnover of $3,000 per month). State whether interest is accrued (added to principle) or paid to the lender on the date of compounding.

If you are concerned about the borrower's solidity or commitment, you may want to include an *acceleration clause*. This states that if a payment of interest, principle, or both (as specified) is late, then the *whole* loan is payable immediately if the lender so desires. If a borrower is drifting into difficulty, this allows the lender to try to get the principle back at an earlier stage.

The borrower may want a *prepayment clause* to permit a no-penalty prepayment if things go better than expected. In this case, the lender required reasonable notice so that she could find a new borrower by the time the loan came due.

After the loan goes into operation, it is best if the lender keeps track of principle and interest owed and records payments received. Banks will provide payment books on request.

Interest on loans is taxed in the year it is due. So if you have a note where compounding without actual payment of interest takes place, you still have to pay tax on the interest *payable*.

The true strength of the written note lies both in the process that led up to it (the businesslike relationship that has been established) and in the commitment on both sides.

When appropriate, say no. Sometimes the negotiations just will not work out, and you will have to end them. This is particularly hard to do in close relationships. Sometimes, money gets linked with love and respect even though they are unrelated. Being able to say no appropriately is necessary for you to be able to say yes at other times and really mean it. If you find saying no difficult, practice it, and get someone to back you up.

Payback Problems

A common problem is the borrower being unable to pay on time. If late payment will make you uncomfortable or will not meet your needs as a lender, then you should work out a contingency plan with the borrower as part of the loan agreement. As with other parts of the agreement, find a plan you will *both* feel comfortable with.

Some popular provisions in case of delayed payments include

partial payments;

an agreed-upon maximum grace period, with clear communication from the borrower throughout this period about when the lender can expect payments to begin;

a fallback emergency lender (who pays the original lender back, then assumes the loan permanently or for as long as the borrower is behind);

collateral that will be liquidated to pay back the lender by the end of a certain period of time; and

a clear communication/negotiation process for changing the payback schedule.

One innovative solution is practiced by Tracy Gary, who has made a great many loans. She and the borrower each put a little money (say, $10 a month) into a special account. If the borrower runs into problems in paying back the loan on time, this money will be used to hire a financial consultant to help the borrower figure out what to do. If the borrower never runs into trouble paying back the loan, the accumulated money goes back to borrower and lender. Tracy feels this protects her from the possibility of a lot of extra work and aggravation.

If you as a lender *definitely need* the money back, you will want to write into the loan agreement a secure, specific measure, such as collateral, that can be liquidated or a fallback lender who is willing to assume the loan.

Think carefully before specifying collateral. Often, traditional collateral—such as building or inventory—is an item the enterprise you are supporting cannot afford to lose. Do you really want to take possession of twenty thousand bicycle repair manuals, especially if you really believe in the organization?

An alternative you might want to explore is whether the borrower has anything to barter with you in case the repayment is not forthcoming. Since the best security borrowers can offer is often their skills, consider the skills as collateral! Here are three possibilities. First, the borrowers agree that if the venture fails, they will take a regular job in their particular skill area and pay the loan back over time at a fixed rate. Second, the borrower offers a list of six skills that the lender may use if needed as partial repayment at an agreed value in case of default. Finally, they seek out a three-way trade with another business or individual that owes the borrower services or money.

Conflict Resolution

It is important that the lender and borrower agree on a method for resolving possible, if unanticipated, conflicts. When loans are made warmly and without implied threats, a relationship of affirmation and support is established. If the loan gets into difficulty, the relationship is damaged. The feelings, attitudes, and intentions have to be respected if the relationship is going to survive the difficulty.

Initially, the borrower should agree to report to the lender if trouble is developing. By doing so and being open to ideas and help, the borrower steps out of the usual avoidance reaction, the relationship is affirmed, and an amicable solution is much more likely. Next, both parties agree to enter mediation or arbitration if things become more serious. Mediation will occur when both parties disagree but are trying to work things out; arbitration, when both parties know they cannot agree.

Together with the borrower, you might try selecting people you both know and respect who could serve as mediators or arbitrators. They should have common sense, some understanding of business, and high regard from both of you, especially the borrowers. As many as three should be named in the agreement—and, upon commitment, should be offered compensation, usually by the borrower.

When trouble develops, the primary problem is not usually the content, but the absence of a method for making *some* decision. Closely connected arbitrators can act quickly and compassionately. However, if you do not trust this idea, seek out mediation or arbitration attorneys and community services where you live, and learn about them—or help start a service in your community. They will be more expensive, but certainly cheaper and less energy draining, than continuing the conflict process in the courts.

It is important to note that having discussed and agreed, in advance, on a method for resolving difficulty will, *in and of itself*, make your loan agreement more secure. Support has replaced an implied threat, and you will find the clause rarely needs to be invoked.

Investing in People You Know

A common fear is that investing in a venture of someone you know or loaning money to someone you know will damage the relationship: "What if the borrower is not able to pay the loan or the investment equity back? I will feel resentful; my friend will probably feel guilty; and we will end up avoiding each other or in a nasty argument that will ruin our friendship!"

Using the guidelines above to work out clear arguments will prevent most problems and allay most of these fears. Here are some more ways to protect your relationship with family and friends when making financial transactions with them. The closer the relationship, the more attention you may have to pay to each of these areas.

Throughout the process of considering and negotiating a loan or investment, all parties should acknowledge feelings they are having about it. Listen to the other person's feelings (fear, hurt, envy, or something else) and honestly communicate your own feelings. Accepting feelings can disperse tensions. Repressing feelings may seem to work for the short term but will usually disrupt relationships over time. Explicitly communicate love and respect for the other person, unrelated to the financial transaction.

When saying no, communicate the reasons for your decision openly and thoroughly. Express love and respect, and be willing to listen to hurt feelings. Elaine Booker's experience illustrates the importance of communicating well and the fears one may face in doing it. Elaine, living in Cambridge, Massachusetts, was asked to lend $10,000 to a typesetting and graphics collective owned and operated by two of her friends in Santa Cruz, California. The business, Artstop, had been barely breaking even for three years. Knowing they needed capital for better equipment if they were ever to be financially viable, Artstop's owners attempted to raise $50,000. Elaine considered the loan for a month, did some research, and said no.

"Although I thought the work they were doing was worthwhile and I respected the individuals involved, the business did not appear financially viable to me," she explains. "They were asking for more money than I'd normally lend in one shot, and they were in a field in which technology changes rapidly, so there are frequent big expenditures for new equipment—otherwise, you go out of business because you can't compete. I'd had little experience with that type of business, so I had a firm that makes loans to alternative businesses, analyze their financial plan. The consultant said it looked like too high a risk; their firm would not make such a loan."

Elaine felt good about doing this research. In one brief long-distance phone call, she told her friends no. Later, she learned they had hurt feelings; they saw Elaine's refusal as a cold financial decision based on the consultant's recommendation. They felt that Elaine had not treated them with the respect they deserved as her friends and political allies. Says Elaine,

> I should have talked with them more openly about my reasons. Actually, I felt very torn, because I do respect their work; I believe in supporting collectives; and as an owning-class person, I have a strong belief in returning some of my wealth to working-class people by supporting their efforts. At the same time, I was scared that this business would go bankrupt, and I would lose all of this money that could be accomplishing good things elsewhere.
>
> If I had told my friends all that, they would have heard the part of me that wanted to say yes as well as the part that said no, and they would have understood the values behind my decision.
>
> At the time, I was afraid to voice these feelings, because I was afraid I'd then be pressured into making the loan. Now I know I made a mistake by not communicating more. I've refused other loans requested by friends without hurt feelings resulting, largely by telling them my reasons and feelings openly, and listening carefully to their feelings as well.

Be sensitive to the power differences that often exist between the lender/investor and the recipient. A borrower often perceives a lender as having more power, even though this may not be accurate. The borrower has a need, and the lender has the power to satisfy it. The greater the borrower's need and the more limited her or his options to borrow, the more acutely the borrower is likely to experience a power difference.

Once money has been loaned, the lender may worry that it will not be paid back, or that repayment will be late. The lender may now feel that the borrower has more power: the power to say yes or no to repayment. Ironically, the borrower probably continues to see most of the power in the hands of the lender to whom s/he is in debt.

Although power differences will exist as long as individuals continue to have unequal resources, we can make personal lending/investment experiences more empowering. Whether or not you agree to a loan, explain your reasoning and the values and criteria on which it is based, so the borrower can understand your decision and not simply experience it as an arbitrary exercise in control of financial resources. If you say no or can lend only part of what the borrower needs, let the borrower know of other resources s/he might contact. When you negotiate terms of a loan, make sure that you are carefully considering how both parties' needs can best be met.

In some cases, you may want to consider making a gift instead of a loan or an investment. If you very much support what the other person wants to do with the money and you believe s/he is unlikely to be able to pay it back, you may want to offer a gift. You can also work out creative options in between a loan and a gift (for example, a loan that becomes a gift if the borrower is in the red at payback time). For information in this section, I am indebted to: Paul Terry, Roger Pritchard, Chris Mogil, and Anne Slepian.

Part III

BREAKING THE CORPORATE GRIP

Introduction: It's Time to Get Tough! It's Time to Organize!

W HILE IN ALASKA a few years ago I saw television commercials depicting beautiful scenery, seemingly untouched by humans. Then a gentle, mesmerizing voice began talking about—you guessed it—the oil industry! The camera shifted a bit to show an oil well in the midst of all this pristine beauty. These were the first attempts by the oil industry to wriggle their way back into the hearts of the Alaskan people still reeling from the devastation wrecked by the Exxon *Valdez* oil disaster. Despite corporate public-relations efforts, polls show that a large number of people in the United States are growing increasingly distrustful of anything corporations say. Hoping to change this, corporations are spending more money than ever to tell us how much they care about our well-being and the environment.

Virtually all major oil, chemical, and paper companies—including DuPont, Dow, General Electric, Chevron, Monsanto, Westinghouse, Arco, ICI, General Motors and Weyerhaeuser are involved in what are often referred to as "greenwashing" campaigns. Corporations are forming coalitions designed to promote themselves and win public approval for

76

their products. Examples include the American Plastics Council ("Take another look—at plastic") and the Chemical Manufacturers Association's "Responsible Care—A Public Commitment" initiative.

Many people are aware that under the green mask lurks a polluting monster, while others decide to give a company the benefit of the doubt. And some people who don't totally believe the ads do think that, since people can change, so can corporations, and we need to give them the chance. "At least they are trying," they say. But have any positive changes come about as a result of corporate greening?

Corporations point to commitments to toxic-waste reduction and the use of more environmentally benign production processes. Many, however, simply relocate the most polluting production processes to countries with lax environmental regulations. Furthermore, Citizen Action surveyed the fifty facilities with the biggest drops in toxic emissions for 1990 and found that most of the reported decreases were due to reporting changes and loopholes in the law, not process changes. For example, the EPA's delisting of ammonium sulfate alone accounted for 450 million pounds less toxic emissions reported for 1990 versus 1989. Even the most "progressive" companies still dump millions of tons of toxins into our air, water, and soil each year.

Another tactic companies take is to claim they are improving wildlife habitat when the reality is they are simply trying to restore land their own operations destroyed. For example, Chevron's oil drilling in southeastern California destroyed habitat essential to the San Joaquin kit fox, listed as an endangered species since 1967. So the company had to construct artificial dens. Chevron's "People Do" campaign promoted their den construction as a way of protecting the fox from coyotes—without mentioning that the company (not the coyotes) was responsible for destroying the natural dens in the first place. Overall, Chevron's campaign consisted of about ten television and print ads touting their concern for wildlife and the environment. In addition to the kit fox, ads focused on the grizzly bear and the endangered El Segundo Blue butterfly. All the environmental efforts of the company were in response to destruction caused by their own operations. And the amount of money spent on the actual restorations was a fraction of the public relations budget to publicize them.

So, while companies talk a "green streak," our environment is getting dirtier. While some cities have somewhat cleaner air and some rivers are healthier than they were twenty years ago, other places that had clean air and drinkable rivers twenty years ago find they no longer do. Forest destruction and many forms of pollution are at an all-time high. The ozone layer is being destroyed, and more of us are dying of cancer and immune-deficiency diseases than ever before. Our bodies contain toxic chemicals and even breast milk is contaminated. In fact, there is hardly a corner of the planet that hasn't been affected in some way by industrial development.

The moderate reforms advocated by governments and supported by industry are an insult! It is time to wrest ourselves from the corporate grip on our lives and on the planet. We must articulate an ecological and humane vision of the future, devise strategies to get from here to there, and then *do it*.

Our strategies must include tactics to weaken the corporate beast. This section discusses some of these tactics as part of a comprehensive, national/international movement. Actions such as letterwriting and boycotts need to be coordinated with education and practical alternatives to the status quo. Remember, the world cannot change unless people change. Fear and isolation make us weak. Strategies that start in our communities and neighborhoods and build, with love, from the grassroots increase our trust and commitment to each other and to the Earth and make us strong.

It's Time to Organize
by Richard L. Grossman

> The laws of the land are supported by the use of violence; that is, the use of physical force to make people obey the law....If you're trying to change things, first you have to know that violence can be used against you, and second, you have to know what strategies to use in order to change the system, given that situation.
> —Myles Horton, *The Long Haul*

If you take action as a result of reading this book, you will become part of a large, historical, citizens' movement for social justice. This can be exciting and empowering, but it can also be dangerous.

Myles Horton advises that we be clear about our situation before we decide how to change. I believe we need to understand—really understand—that exercising our citizenship today is very much subject to government—and corporate—violence. We can see this from the FBI's two-million-dollar infiltration into Earth First!, from the bombing of Redwood Summer organizers Judi Bari and Daryl Cherney, and the way government and industry officials declined to look for the culprit. We can see this from our government officials' readiness to mobilize vast resources for death and war when they believe their basic control over resources and events is at stake.

So we will have to talk to one another, and to people with different perspectives, about the destroyers' desire for power, which preserves their control. We will need to talk about our situation, and what changes we actually need, instead of what those in charge of the violence and their camouflagers tell us is "realistic" and "acceptable." We'll have to talk candidly and frankly.

We need to understand how laws and other "solutions" have been used to create false senses of success, to decrease citizen vigilance, and to scatter citizen attention and energy. Over the past fifty years Congress has enacted scores of anti-poverty, labor, civil rights, and environmental protection laws. Many were considered "landmark" achievements, and were achieved only after persistent struggle by significant citizens' movements.

But today, we can see for ourselves what citizens were demanding in each instance and what was actually enacted. Maybe the discrepancies will help explain why, despite all these laws, wages and working conditions have been worsening, poverty has been increasing, destruction of ecological systems and public health have been intensifying, individual rights have been eroding—all while ownership has been concentrating, corporate profits have been skyrocketing, and our federal government has become the greatest poisoner and destroyer in the cosmos.

If we looked, we would see that the debate and demands by many workers in the 1930s sought greater protection of workers' rights than the Wagner Act and the creation of a National Labor Relations Board provided. That some people believed the National Environment Policy act should have been much stronger, should have provided authority for citizens and communities to stop and transform the polluters. That the Surface Mining Reclamation Act was originally intended to ban strip mining totally, not just "regulate" it. That early versions of the Humphrey Hawkins Full Employment Act were intended to guarantee each citizen the right to a job, just as the intention of early organizers for what became the Occupational Safety and Health Act was to stop the destruction of people at their places of employment, not legalize it.

We need to learn our history. We need, as Daniel T. Rogers writes in *Contested Truths*, to revive "the radical language of the [American] Revolution." Then we will see that even the Declaration of Independence and the Constitution and the Bill of Rights were the final products of many compromises; that there were people in those days who believed, for example, that one of our inalienable rights was the right to "property," that is, control over our own labor. If these people had been better organized, or stronger, if they had kept tighter rein over their leaders, perhaps they would have had to compromise less. They could have left us better tools to use against corporations and our governments today.

Many of those who came before us struggled hard to help others understand the situation by provoking revealing debate, by demanding what they wanted. Today, exploiters, polluters, and politicians and the press and academia are doing a terrific job at limiting public debate and citizen demands, especially with regard to our labor and the Earth's resources. Few labor or environmental groups—much less elected officials—even talk timidly about stopping destruction or unemployment at their sources. They behave instead as if the next politely listened to Congressional testimony, or euphemistically titled legislation, or pious presidential promise, will turn the tide. They join with the exploiters and the polluters and the media to honor legal charades of the past. They declare a mealy-mouthed "Clean Air Act" or an EPA decision that permits lead poisoning of most drinking water for decades or the latest Forest Service or Nuclear Regulatory Commission decision to permit a little less harm this time, to be celebrated as "victories" for the environment and public health, and "models" for the future.

We need to recognize that we cannot turn to the entrenched organizations of our movements or to our elected officials for ideas and strategies. We can't even turn to them for encouragement. Indeed, we will have to figure out ways to neutralize or transform these organizations, as well as our relationships with our elected officials.

We must also talk about how corporations and their colleagues in government, with the help of many labor and environmental organizations, have weakened, diverted and contained citizens' movements; how they have undermined the democratic process; obscured and rewritten American history; divided people against one another; intimidated and killed. We must show how they have learned to cloak themselves skillfully in the flag; to invoke Divine Right under the cover of empty phrases like the "invisible hand" of the "free market"; to legitimize violence at home and abroad behind jubilant economic theories; to isolate citizen protesters as un-American, and to terrorize decent people with job and economic blackmail.

We must demand what the Earth really needs, what our communities actually require, to start restoring themselves. We must talk about stopping the destroyers at the country's places of business, and how this will require taking political and economic power—and legitimacy—away from the destroyers.

We'll have to break through taboos that industrialists have created about their "managerial prerogative." We'll need to challenge their boring refrain that only "they" can decide what products to make; only "they" can determine investment, technology, and production processes; only "they" can design the societal arrangements for citizens to fulfill our needs; only "their" economists can define "productivity" and "efficiency;" only "their" rhetoricians can define "progress"; only "the government" can determine the role of the United States of America in the world.

We'll need to tell ourselves that it is not un-American for us to see the destruction which is going on in our communities, in biological systems, and all across the planet. It is not un-American for us to trace this destruction back to its source and then to organize to dismantle these sources.

We can help other people realize it is not un-American to think and talk about what is in this book. It is not un-American to help one another penetrate the camouflage, distortions, and lies of the polluters, the politicians, and the press. It is not un-American for us to demand a real say in how we use the resources of this land, how we produce, what we produce, how we own our labor, what our president does with our armed forces, what our courts do with our Bill of Rights.

We have as many rights as we take. American history has been a constant struggle between the people and the institutions over these rights, and over the wealth and power that possession of these rights confers. Since before the Revolution, citizens have been struggling to maintain and increase our rights and there have always been bleak periods like our own. But people have persevered—we shall probably have to keep persevering forever.

Today, there is something more: We have learned that it is not enough for people to win our rights. Rivers, mountains, oceans, soils, plants and animals must also have their rights recognized and preserved. We are their advocates. We have an obligation to demand and take action in their names.

So we'll be thinking and talking and struggling for what the Earth and we actually need. We'll have to think strategically, for the short haul and the longer hauls, how best to withdraw our support from institutions and leaders who are antidemocratic, concealing, unaccountable, and false. We'll need to figure out how to disrupt—in most Gandhian manners, of course—business as usual in our city councils, our legislatures, our factories, our banks, our forests, our waters, our streets, our courts, our Pentagon, our Federal Reserve Board, our National Labor Relations Board, our Environmental Protection Agency, our unions, our conservation groups, and around our kitchen tables.

We know that we cannot stop the destruction and repair the harm overnight. We know we cannot easily dismantle the destroyers who have lawyers and laws, publicists and propaganda machines, politicians, universities and the press, money and the army. But we also know that despite their violence, and the arts of violence, over time we can make the changes we need. We know we can free our minds and our communities and our planet from irrationality and fear. We know we can take action in solidarity with other citizens of the Earth, and in solidarity with its flora and fauna. And we know that we can redefine for ourselves what it means to be conscientious citizens of this country and conscientious citizens of this Earth.

SIX

Making an Impact as an Individual

Letterwriting Campaigns

THE MOST COMMON action suggested in the "What You Can Do" boxes at the end of articles in environmental and social-justice publications (aside from sending tax-deductible donations) is "Write to..." While writing letters rarely effects change directly, letter-writing campaigns, especially when in conjunction with boycotts and other forms of action and protest, can raise awareness. It is easy to sit down and write a letter, it entails no risk, and it usually elicits a response of some kind. This can be rewarding and may lead to other actions over time.

In 1989, I wrote an article on rainforest destruction for *Organica*, a quarterly publication of Aubrey Organics. Accompanying my article was a sidebar the editor titled "Corporations Destroying the Rainforest." (When I sent this article to *Organica*, the sidebar was called: "Corporations Involved in Tropical Countries.") Coca Cola was included because they import orange-juice concentrate from Brazil for their Minute Maid orange-juice products. Readers, angry that Coke was "destroying tropical rainforests," wrote stating they would no longer buy the company's products.

Coke's reaction to the letters was amazing. Upon arriving at my office one morning there was an anxious message on the machine from the editor of *Organica*. She just received a rather threatening registered letter from Michelle Beale, Coke's Senior Vice President of Public Relations. I called Ms. Beale, who requested that I retract my statements regarding Coke's involvement in rainforest destruction. I agreed to explain to *Organica*'s readers that Coke wasn't in there with chainsaws, but I would not exonerate them from responsibility. Instead, I offered to write a follow-up article explaining the complicated process of rainforest destruction so readers would have a more complete understanding. She was happy with this, even though it would still implicate Coke.*

I asked Ms. Beale how many letters Coke had received as a result of my article. She told me, "Anytime we get more than twenty letters on the same subject, a red flag goes up." At the time of our call, which was only three months after my article appeared, they had received over fifty letters, and they were "very concerned."

Tips for letterwriting

Letters must be short and to the point.

They should by typed or legibly hand-written.

Stick to what you know is true. Any misinformation discredits your entire letter.

Identify yourself as a customer up front. Corporations really care that you like their products and continue purchasing them. When you say you like their soup or bread or crackers, but will no longer be buying them because of a particular problem, they will take notice.

Tell the company what you want them to do. If you want more information from them regarding their operations, ask for it. If you expect them to stop using pesticides in their forest lands, say so. Be specific.

---

*For the record, Coke does not have orange plantations in the rainforest. They have contracts with large landowners in the southern part of Brazil for their imported concentrate—"far from the nearest rainforest" as Coke's many responses state. Rainforest destruction has a complex history that parallels the history of colonialism. The issue of who owns and controls the land is directly relevant to rainforest destruction in Brazil, and elsewhere. When large landowners control the most arable land in a country and grow crops (oranges, for example) for export, the people who live there can't grow food to feed their families or sell in the market and are gradually forced onto more and more marginal land, often into the rainforest, to eke out a living. This process is well documented. Therefore, Coke and other large-scale agricultural corporations with plantations or contracts in tropical countries do contribute directly to rainforest destruction.

Be courteous and thank the official for his/her time. Say you are looking forward to a reply.

Keep a copy of your letter as well as any responses you receive.

A letter you compose yourself is much better than a form letter or preprinted postcard. If you are a teacher, and you're getting your class involved, encourage kids to draw pictures and tell how they feel in their own words. (This applies to all letter-writing campaigns, whether they are directed at corporations, legislators, government organizations, or individuals.)

Letters are always more effective when they are numerous and directly targeted towards specific corporations or individuals, and when the message is basically the same in each letter (i.e., about the same issue).

Corporate Responses: What to Expect

Corporations and public officials will respond to your letters. The letter sent to you will be exactly the same as the letter sent to every person who wrote about that issue. Corporations do not like to admit that they are doing anything wrong. Expect their reply to deny or avoid the issue your letter addressed. Letters will include statements such as: "[Company XYZ] takes pride in being an environmentally responsive company. There is genuine concern at all levels in the corporation about manufacturing useful, high quality products while simultaneously maintaining a healthy, aesthetically pleasing environment for all."

When a company feels it can't get away with denial, the reply might include reports, maps, or other information for the purpose of assuring you they share your concern for the environment or oppressed peoples or whatever, but their product or activity is justified given society's needs. Corporations will also attempt to discredit the source of your information.

For some examples of what you might expect, see chapter 4, "Evaluating the Status Quo." Corporate research, as it involves correspondence with corporations, will provoke many of the same responses.

Profile

Global Response

Global Response (GR) is a network of dedicated letter-writers who care about the Earth and want to do something about it. They state,

> To respond effectively to [the threats to our environment] requires a worldwide network of dedicated activists who will be "on call" to communicate public concern on matters of global environmental urgency. While we can effectively lobby and achieve real change in our own backyards, we must now take action on the far greater challenge of global awareness and global action.

GR's main areas of concern are rainforest destruction, atmospheric contamination and ocean dumping, protection of marine mammals and fisheries, wildlife and endangered species and nuclear proliferation. There is no fee to join GR, although contributions to cover printing and postage are greatly appreciated, of course. When you join, you receive their monthly *Global Response Action* sheet. These are simple, brief, and informative. They state what the problem is, what needs to be done, who to write, and where to get more information. Letters are targeted to corporations, national officials, universities, international bank officials (such as the World Bank), among others. In exchange for their free monthly mailings, members agree to write letters on at least one *Global Response Action* each month.

GR publishes a brief for young people, "Young Environmentalist's Action," which is also available in Spanish, an excellent (and free) tool for teachers.

For more information, contact Global Response at P.O. Box 7490, Boulder, CO 80306, (303) 444-0306.

Being a Responsible Consumer

In the United States, about one percent of the population owns about one third of the resources—and controls much more. Todd Putnam, former editor of the *National Boycott News*, now with the *Boycott Quarterly*, believes every time we buy a major brand, we contribute to the widening gap between the haves and the have-nots, the powerful and the powerless. He states, "Our present political system is...the logical result of our consumer choices....It is our bottom line that determines the bottom line of the business community. The absence of values in business merely reflects the absence of values in our own purchasing decisions." Therefore, in addition to paying attention to the specifics of the products themselves, we also must examine the values of the corporations that make them. While we cannot shop and save the world, as some would have us believe, our purchasing dollars can support innovative, life-respecting businesses and local economies.

One of the easiest ways to be a responsible consumer is to "buy local" as much as possible. In Vermont, we have a state-sponsored initiative that encourages Vermonters to buy Vermont products. Our "Vermont Seal of Quality" also means Vermont's products are recognized outside of the state as "the best." (Oregon has a similar program.) At the supermarket I can purchase local milk, cheese, eggs, and other dairy products as well as snack foods, condiments, and canned goods. At the co-op and other local stores, I can also purchase locally made herbal preparations, body-care products and cosmetics as well as organic produce and meat. Excellent local bakeries distribute to supermarkets and to food co-ops alike. In addition, we have a Vermont-based producer of processed meats such as bacon, sausage, and hot dogs, and soon there will be a cannery that will aid the development of more small food-processing companies. Of course, many are already familiar with Ben & Jerry's Homemade ice cream. There are local craftspeople, organic farmers, and farmers' markets statewide during the season.

The point is that once we open our eyes and look at the addresses on the packages, we may be surprised at how often we can support our neighbors when we buy our everyday needs. Sometimes these products are a little more expensive than their mass-produced counterparts, but the difference in price is in some ways an investment in the community and, in the case of local, organic produce, in your own health.

Patronizing locally owned small businesses rather than large chains is also important. With the advent of shopping malls and warehouse stores such as Wal-Mart, our downtown areas have been drained and often rendered lifeless. Supporting local independent merchants is very important in maintaining strong local economies, with all their potential independence and diversity.

Still, even in locally owned mom and pop stores, most of the products are manufactured by corporations. To make ethical purchasing decisions easier, each year the Council on Economic Priorities (CEP) publishes a pocket-sized guide, "Shopping for a Better World." In 1993, this guide was geared towards teens ("Students Shopping for a Better World") and rates 166 producers of the goods teens buy: clothes, snacks, CDs and tapes, cosmetics, fast food, for instance. CEP's 1994 guide, "The Comprehensive Shopping for a Better World" includes food, household products, personal care, clothes, computers, cars, appliances and more. Companies are rated on the environment, minority advancement, women's issues and public disclosure of information, as well as animal rights and nuclear weapons.

We've been hearing a lot lately about "green products," a rather generic term (along with "green business") that can mean many things—or nothing. How can you tell if the "green" on the label is more than an advertising ploy? To give you a sense of what you're looking for, here are a few questions to ask:

Is there unnecessary packaging?

Is the product made from recycled materials?

Is it biodegradable under conditions that make sense for the product? (It doesn't matter if plastic degrades in the presence of light or air if it is buried in a landfill where it comes in contact with neither.)

Can it be recycled, or better yet, reused?

Do you know anything about the company's policies and political activities?

Is the product produced by a large company with factories in the Third World?

Does it take a lot of energy and resources to make the product? If so, how long will it last?

If it's a wood product, where does the wood come from? (Do not purchase products made from tropical hardwoods such as teak or mahogany.)

Is it organic?

Is it tested on animals?

Read food product labels carefully: Does it contain chemical additives or toxic ingredients?

Seek out sources for nontoxic household chemicals and cleaning supplies.

Do you really need it?

Even with good information, becoming a responsible consumer is not easy. Changing habits such as buying patterns is remarkably difficult. And once we change one set of habits, we often begin to notice other layers. For instance, one might begin to wonder about ways to reduce the effects of our consumption on people in the Third World. Still, what we buy and from whom are decisions we control; let us use even that little bit of power.

Environmental Labeling

The following organizations are in the process of developing systems to evaluate consumer products for their ecological friendliness. Each system has its own criteria, which is limited in scope, but at least it's a beginning. These programs are consumer driven, based on the assumption that educated, concerned consumers can send a strong message to producers, a process that will ultimately force changes in industry.

Scientific Certification Systems, Inc. This product-testing company based in California announced its first round of certified products in late 1990—mostly recycled paper products. Since then, SCS has evaluated various plastic products for recycled content and biodegradability. They have also added a Forest Conservation Program, which certifies whether wood is grown and harvested sustainably. (This program is criticized by others in the sustainable forestry/certification movement as being too broad. The fact that SCS is evaluating some smaller holdings of large paper companies [e.g., Boise Cascade] for certification is also a matter of concern.)

Green Seal was launched in June, 1990, as an independent, nonprofit, national labeling program. New standards were recently announced for general-purpose household-cleaners and for clothes washers, dryers and dishwashers. The household cleaners standard includes provisions for toxicity to humans and aquatic life, biodegradability, phosphate and VOC (volatile organic compounds) content and content of toxic metals. The standard also requires reduced packaging and includes a test to see how well the product works. Standards for clothes washers, dryers and dishwashers specify energy and water use and reduced, nontoxic packaging with recycled content.

Good Housekeeping Institute has established "Green Watch" awards for significant contributions to the environment.

Smart Wood Program is a certification program for sustainable wood products sponsored by the Rainforest Alliance. The program initially focused on tropical wood but has recently expanded to include temperate and boreal regions in the United States and Canada. Guidelines include maintenance of the "environmental functions" of the forest, sustained yield, and positive impact on local communities. Smart Wood does not support the conversion of natural forests to plantations, and each country is examined on the basis of guidelines that allow for local needs.

The Environmental Choice Program (ECP) was established in 1988. Today over seven hundred products and services carry the EcoLogo, the program's seal of approval. This Canadian program is sponsored by the government with standards developed by a sixteen-member board of independent expert volunteers appointed by the Minister of the Environment. Standards have been developed for products such as detergents of types, household appliances, recycled paper and plastic products, energy-efficient lamps, diapers, some automotive products, and various building products.

In the United States, responsibility for policing environmental claims rests with the Bureau of Consumer Protection of the Federal Trade Commission. Barry Cutler, director of the Bureau, commenting on labeling programs, said his office is "looking at two basic questions: Are the manufacturers' environmental claims deceptive? and Is there competent and reliable information to substantiate both the expressed and implied claims being made in environmental advertising?" Cutler went on to say, "We do not view certification programs…as the simple answer to complex issues.…Such programs themselves have the potential to be deceptive. Each such program will have to be evaluated individually for compliance with applicable federal law."

So far, the U.S. government hasn't become actively involved with certification. It's up to individual consumers to make intelligent choices based on available information and common sense.

SEVEN

Making an Impact as a Community

Community Organizing

LETTER-WRITING AND BOYCOTTS—pretty tame on their own—can become powerful tools for change when part of a comprehensive, national/international campaign that involves education, practical alternatives to the status quo, and a wide constituency such as parents, students, teachers, businesspeople, and clergy: in other words, community organizing.

Organizers today are challenged with having to learn new skills—especially those involving complex interpersonal relationships; all the "isms," blatant and unconscious; and empowerment, first of ourselves and then others, so we can accomplish our goals.

Linda Stout, founder of the Piedmont Peace Project (an organization in rural North Carolina committed to mobilizing low-income people to vote and to influence public policy on peace and justice issues), has made some important observations based on personal experience. Linda grew up in the rural Piedmont of North Carolina, is a thirteenth-generation Quaker and the daughter of a tenant farmer. Her first job was picking tobacco at the age of ten. She was forced to drop out of college and take work at the local hosiery mill after a year because her parents were turned down for a

89

college loan for lack of collateral. Early experiences with the women's movement made her feel "excluded" and "inferior." Similarly, as a volunteer in the peace movement, Linda explains,

> I constantly experienced attitudes and comments that made me question my own worth. I became painfully aware of my lack of a college degree, my "different" way of speaking, and my lack of knowledge about important events and people. For the first time in my life I felt really stupid.

> In order to overcome the inferiority and shame I had been taught, I had to understand that poverty was not the fault of myself or of my parents. I had to learn to be proud of who I was. Going to Nicaragua in 1986 I met people who were proud of being peasants. They didn't like the conditions they lived under and fought a revolution to overcome them. But they were proud and did not blame themselves for the conditions that affected their lives. They understood classism and saw it as the most difficult problem facing folks from the United States who were going back to organize. I returned from that trip with a new knowledge about myself and the work we needed to do in helping other poor people see how classism and racism have affected us personally.

Linda came home and started the Piedmont Peace Project. She discovered there were no models for multi-racial, low income groups working on peace issues. There were no peace education materials written for people with low reading levels. They were on their own.

> Our motto became, "We cannot make a mistake, except to give up." We learned to ask folks how they wanted to participate and what could motivate them to take action. We began to identify and address the barriers, both personal and institutional, that keep us from participating in peace and justice work....We had to create new ways of holding meetings, doing outreach, and developing educational materials. We had to take into consideration people's fears and insecurities about taking on leadership and power when it was not a part of their experience. We had to "translate" models.

PPP discovered that the models they developed worked well with many mainstream, middle-class folks, too, enabling them to reach a broader group of people than the more technical and difficult materials produced by most peace groups. And women felt much more comfortable participating, because PPP threw out the rules and developed new processes that felt comfortable to them. Linda stresses that "PPP is not an organization that works to help poor people, or advocate for them, but rather a group of people that works for changes in our own communities and wants to have a voice in public policy at the national level."

Organizers in these times must learn to deal effectively with personal issues and prejudices and know how to channel the anger in the right direction. Another major challenge is understanding the barriers to participation. Linda explains,

> I often describe the barriers as an invisible wall. Many people, especially middle-class white folks, especially middle-class men, walk right through the wall and never see it. But low-income and persons of color keep hitting the wall and being turned back. Others make excuses and say, "Well, they're poor folks who are too busy trying to survive and don't have the time or energy to come." The wall includes everything from language, to how one defines a leader, to how meetings are held and facilitated, to how organizational priorities and budgets are decided.

Linda offers some basic principles to building a successful organization (from *Peace Work*, Sept. 1993, "Why Aren't We Winning?" by Linda Stout, see Resources):

Address social change: It's fine to do social service, but it's not a step to addressing the root cause.

Work across race and class lines: Value each group's skills and knowledge and include indigenous organizers and leaders.

Educate on the large picture: Make connections, care about both the global and the local.

Be persistent!

Another successful community organizer from my own backyard is Theresa Freeman, who founded Vermonters Organized for Cleanup (VOC) in 1983. Theresa's work in Vermont stands out among organizers for her unique ability to bring so-called ordinary working-class people into activism:

> My current organizing/leader work began because my town, Williamstown, Vermont, became a Love Canal. One of my children was showing symptoms of exposure to a toxic soup of dry-cleaning chemicals that were dumped behind the plant flanking our two schools. The plant had dug "pits" or holding ponds behind their plant and dumped liquid chemical waste into the ponds, which ran down the hills into our town and onto the school yards. These ponds also off-gassed into the air, and stacks from the plant emitted regular doses of these chemical gases.
>
> Headaches, fatigue, nausea, cold symptoms, leaking urine, muscle aches and pains were some of the symptoms people in Williamstown experienced. Eleven women teachers out of nineteen were being seen by a gynecologist for menstration problems.

We fought for testing of the air, water and soil, and were shocked to find chemicals all throughout our community: in the school, in the public drinking-water supply, on our dirt road system, in our landfill, and in private homes around the plant.

Because the local small-town officials followed the government line of the Reagan administration—"no real problem"— and did next to nothing, my friends and I built two different organizations to deal with citizen action, forcing cleanup, evacuations, and response from the government. A third community group exists now to follow clean up and the hooking up of a clean public water supply eight years after the fact. My family finally moved off the site four years ago. Our organization involved more than half of our town's eight hundred people, held meetings, rallies, pickets, law suits, and legislative changes, and set the tone for citizen involvement for all of the environmental work going on in Vermont. I know this because we were the first toxic-waste site, and became known as the Vermont Love Canal. Government policies formed because of our actions, and citizen activity was highlighted by personal growth and struggle.

Community Organizing

by Theresa Freeman

A community organization is different from an advocacy organization. Advocacy work tends to hire people to go out and pass laws, to get more services for their clientele, and so on. Advocacy groups are the direct antithesis of community groups, where people do their own work. Advocacy organizations empower their staffs; community organizations empower the membership. Community organizing in a people's organization requires action using a mixed bag of skills and techniques that are learned by members of a community group. For me, whatever happens in a community setting, the participants' development comes first and foremost, and however long that takes is okay.

What Do Organizers Do?

Organizers use skills common to a variety of professions, from teaching to community development, to farming, and most other activities. In every case, organizing reflects individual life experience.

Organizers are dreamers. I love to hear what other people think, dream, and want! Dreamers, their voices clear with hope and self-confidence, are more secure in their seats of love and nonviolence. Basic qualities like these can bear fruit of a new, more just society. Discovering the voice, the power within, is the basis of all struggle and the foundation of stopping all oppression. Seeing ourselves as free makes it easier to act free. Being able to act free and conceive of a new way makes it more likely to happen—and at least we are aware of when it is *not* happening.

Organizers help people grow. People need space and support to develop their own opinions and to realize they have a right to their own voice. The greatest job of a person working in community is to unlock the dignity of the group, to encourage the voices. A person with a voice is more likely to feel secure dreaming about what the new society should look like. Finding one's voice means tapping an inner power that allows the brilliance in each of us to spark.

Organizers break down broad concepts and put them into ordinary street language. Goals such as stopping pollution or eliminating ozone depletion or changing the system have limited meaning in the streets. An organizer helps define these broad, unrealistic dreams and helps make them attainable goals using words that ordinary people understand. It is necessary to demystify information, take it out of the hands of the so-called experts, and make it work for us.

Organizers practice listening very hard. Many times we are corrected and argued down before we get to say what our thoughts really are! This is destructive. Many of us have been denied the luxury of having someone listen to us. Often we are not allowed to speak, and therefore feel rushed to put forth our ideas. Listening, for me, takes the form of reflective questioning to help a person say exactly what they mean. Reflective questioning uncovers and helps a person sharpen their point of view. Reflective questioning can preserve dignity, assure good listening, and help uncover the brilliance of yet another stifled genius.

Organizers also try to listen to a group's position. They write summary statements and goals, and get corrected, uncovering the real motives and goals of the group. This requires clarity, patience, and downright stubbornness when things become muddled. Eventually, as the organizer reflects the groups views more accurately, the whole group will come to a better understanding of its position.

Organizers let democracy happen. Free to speak one's mind, a person can be creative, take leaps of faith, and often will say something everyone goes wild over. The soul unfolds when trust and faith are present in the group. When trust evolves and real discussion happens, democracy is operating in a group. Organizers must both work hard for this, and let it happen when it occurs.

Organizers are dedicated to working within a group (as opposed to being dedicated to the advancement of individuals). Building a group is very tough work. Moving beyond personalities is a task of the group. Personality conflicts and disagreements can get passed over for the sake of the agenda. In good groups, however, personal conflicts *are* group business, and need to be aired. If there is significant disagreement among members that cannot be resolved publicly, then people can work one-on-one, but groups should try to resolve difficulties in a way that everyone can be aware and help people get along. It's hard, but worth it.

Organizers record the truth. More organizers need to write about the process of development of people, and to help people doing the work tell their own stories. Most organizers think of the outcome rather than the road to get there. While there are excellent manuals on how to organize, nowhere there is a compilation of titles by those heroes and heroines who have helped us to get where we're going. Our history needs to be written and preserved.

Organizers press on.

Skills, Tactics, Tools

It is a mistake to think that anyone can apply these community-organizing skills who is *not* deeply involved with the community. No one can enter a community from outside and "organize" it. Each and every community is highly organized already. Tools for organizing are only aspects of organizing. When tools are used as part of a whole package, we can see a group unfold and come into its own, and take control of the issues or problems that affect them.

Meetings. Meetings are about actions. An organizer helps people run their own meetings. A planning or core group develops a simple agenda prior to the meeting. Additional agenda items are added by members at the meeting. Facilitation is a skill that can be learned by all group members. Facilitators need to know how to keep the discussion on track without cutting anyone off, how to control a meeting if outsiders try to take over, and how to help the group reach a decision. People need to understand the difference between discussion and decision, and every member should be able to support the decision.

Flyers. Flyers get the word out about meetings and other events. A flyer answers the following questions: who, what, when, where and why. They should be written in people's own language and should always have a phone number, name, and address, making it possible to trace the material to real people in the community.

The community newsletter. Periodic reports on progress and programs are essential to keep a group together. Also, it is important to educate and communicate with others. In my group, the newsletter is written by members with some articles contributed by the staff. A people's newsletter can count on being called unprofessional by some, but members relish seeing their own words in print, especially in their own publication. We have resisted creating a slick and costly newsletter, preferring to spend the money in other ways.

Fund-raising. All aspects of community organizing cost money. How this money is raised and spent determines how long people can afford to fight. It is necessary to set up concrete fund-raising plans; these can include canvassing, dues and memberships, events such as dances, suppers, raffles, auctions—the list is endless when community people decide how they are going to pay their bills. Grants from foundations, businesses and individuals are also ways of bringing in funds. Fund-raising can be difficult if you need to raise a large amount of money for a project. Some organizations, such as the Peace Development Fund, offer trainings in fundraising, and there are numerous books and grantmaking guides that can help. Talking with someone who has a successful track record is a good first step.

Research papers. Producing useful information for a community is essential. Thomas Jefferson said, "When the people are well informed, they can be trusted with their own government." Striving to understand any issue is a chore, and those with research skills can be valuable if they share them with others. Information should be given to a community group when they request it, or when they are open to receiving it. A struggling community can suffer from information overload, and members may leave meetings because the technically minded folks have the floor most of the time and other skills are underused. Research committees are useful for making reports, but they should adjust their language and style to suit the audience.

Speaking to the press. Dealing with the media is one of the most important tools available to a community organization. An organizer can help people write press releases, practice speaking, and decide which press people to focus on, but she should not be the person out in front. Organizers can arrange rides, go over details, help with presentations at press conferences, and research history, but no more. I tell community people that they couldn't possibly say anything worse than what has already happened in their community—all the great crimes have already been committed.

The press does not necessarily see itself as a communication network. In fact, your goal to educate your community can be in direct conflict with the newspapers' goal to sell papers. It may be hard to interest a reporter in your topic. Many reporters do not have a sense of what you consider justice, and you must do your best to get your points across. Remember radio talk shows, general flyers at supermarkets, and weekly shopper papers. You can tape a public-service announcement (PSA) for free or for a small fee at many radio stations. As a last resort, you can take out a paid ad.

Holding a conference. Putting on a conference can build a sense of community in a group when participants reach clear goals. Having fun and being engaged is part of a conference, but the outcome should include plans that can be building blocks for ongoing work. Good results require a planning team that sets criteria to evaluate the event (i.e., How do we know if we've had a good conference?)

Protest rally. A rally is indicated when local people decide that a particular target or issue must be exposed and brought home in a way local people will understand. They also provide experience for members in press work, public speaking, organization building and the like. Producing a good turnout for a rally, marching, shouting slogans, and getting arrested can be great fun. However, all activities, especially getting arrested, should be agreed upon and planned in advance. Before the rally, the group decides upon the rally's theme, whether or not forming coalitions could bring greater success, and how to present the issue so that just about anyone feels comfortable participating in some way. People will need to keep abreast of other events or organizations that could "crash" the rally or affect it in some other way. If large numbers of people are expected to attend, you will need to do advance press work to prevent the local group from getting lost in the excitement.

Testifying at legislative hearings. Legislative hearings are important, and many community members can take part. Organizers do research and compile necessary reports, but someone in the community should take the speaking role. If the group needs an expert, it can retain one—but it's far better to help a community person become a "citizen expert," and it aggravates the "powers that be" no end.

In general, the public believes legislative hearings are dog-and-pony shows. They believe "no one is listening"—in fact, staffers and legislators often get up and leave when ordinary citizens start to speak. In spite of this attitude, it is important to make legislative hearings work for grassroots people, and for grassroots people to work with lobbying groups to try and take control of the compromises made in the name of the people. An organizer must consistently balance the desire for justice with reality, and one way to teach the truth about this balance is to put people in situations they can evaluate on their own.

Filing lawsuits. Lawsuits can be a realistic option for a community organized in a particular struggle, but this is not a way to save a community. Only lawyers who can accept direction from their clients should be hired, and then *only* to fight the legal aspects of the case. Lawyers are *not* community organizers; they are paid to know the law and fight in the courtroom. They should be kept abreast of the group's plans, but they need not attend meetings.

Hiring experts. Like lawyers, experts should do and say what the people want and should be paid under these agreements. It can be hard for an expert to understand that while they may have all the technical data at their fingertips, they do not understand its social and political implications for the group. They may feel they have answers for everything—even outside their field. Good experts help people understand information, they have respect for the people's ability to learn, and are not interested in jargon.

Challenges in Organizing

Denying our own background. Each organizer must understand her limits of experience within her culture, class, and race. Too often organizers try to deny their own individual experience and struggle to be on the right side of every issue. Trying to be everything to everyone can hold back serious organizers.

Organizers should choose groups with whom they feel they can work well, and recognize what groups make them especially uncomfortable. We can strive to expand our skills at working with different kinds of people, but we need to accept our class, racial and ethnic backgrounds, as they are part of us.

Power. Organizers are most effective when they are part of a group, not when they are leading one. We need to examine who is doing the work and why. The goals of an organizer can conflict with the goals of the organization. How often have we seen the work of a group derailed by the best-intentioned organizers, who come up with their own version of the group's goals? How often do we allow other groups to distract us from our goals?

Women as organizers. Women who organize face special problems. We experience sexism in our work, the culture oppresses us, our own minds oppress us, and a community group will and does oppress a woman organizer.

Sexism, like racism, limits each one of us forever. Every woman and every man benefits when a person stands his or her ground in a group and refuses to be caught in a sexist web of interaction. We are still learning this.

Women organizers are often riddled with guilt over leaving their own families. This is a double message in our society: Be a good mother and at the same time get out there and work! I am not willing to leave my own family night after night, or to agree that good organizers must be single, divorced, or beset with other problems.

Community organizing is the key to bringing about any kind of change. There are some excellent resources available, including Theresa Freeman's *Organizing: One Woman's Experience, A Field Guide for Community Workers*, available only from VOC, P.O. Box 120, East Calais, Vermont, 05650, for $10.50; *In the Tiger's Mouth: An Empowerment Guide for Social Action* by Katrina Shields, from New Society Publishers; and *Organizing for Social Change*, by the Midwest Center for Organizing, Seven Locks Press.

Consumer Boycotts

Boycotts can be a powerful tactic that enable us to vote with our dollars in the marketplace. According to the Institute for Consumer Responsibility (ICR), which published the *National Boycott News*, the number of boycotts doubled in the first years of this decade. The *Wall Street Journal* dubbed 1990 "The Year of the Boycott" and asked whether the 90s would be the "Decade of the Boycott." There are hundreds of ongoing boycotts in the United States, organized, for the most part, by nonprofit groups operating on small budgets. 1993 was one of the most successful years ever with victories declared in boycotts of General Electric (producers of nuclear weapons), General Motors (who uses animals in crash tests), South Africa (aparteid), American Airlines (homophobic policies), L'Oreal (animal testing) and Colorado (gay rights).

Here's a little known fact: The boycott is named after a British captain, Charles Boycott. The Irish had a particular dislike for this soldier and decided to treat his family like lepers when he tried to enforce a harsh landlord's rules. The Boycott family survived under seige for almost a year with provisions sent from England before the captain was finally forced to return there for early retirement. This first so-named boycott illustrates the point: Boycotts are effective.

Each year, several boycotts capture the media's attention, making headlines and turning into sophisticated battles that can smear a company's reputation, hurt sales, and make it more difficult to continue business as usual. Some examples include boycotts against the state of Colorado in response to Amendment 2, which prevents the passage of any law that would allow gays and lesbians minority status; against Adidas, Browning, Florsheim, and Puma for using the skins of threatened Australian kangaroos for shoe leather; against McDonald's for conducting unfair practices towards urban employees; and against Scott Paper for their poor forest management in Nova Scotia.

How companies deal with boycotts has changed. Ten years ago, companies rarely responded to a boycott, writing them off as the products of fringe radicals. Things are very different today. In some corporate circles, boycotts are considered a form of economic terrorism—and are taken very seriously. Even the mere threat of a boycott by an influential organization can have a major effect. It is important to consider this when launching or developing new strategies for a boycott. For example, Campbell Soup Company decided in January, 1993, not to use genetically engineered tomatoes in their products after a threatened boycott by the Foundation on Economic Trends. (The tomatoes were developed by the Calgene Company of California with major financial backing by Campbell.)

Some companies have developed sophisticated counterattacks to boycotts. Most attempt to divert attention away from the boycott issue by directing attention to something good the company is involved with. Or they may question the integrity of the group calling the boycott. To aid them in fighting a boycott, corporations commonly hire glitzy public relations firms to create strategies to counter the boycott. This can actually backfire, since the plans are often leaked to the boycotters or the press. For example, after the boycott against Nestlé was launched, the company hired the public-relations firm Olgivy and Mather to devise a strategy to destroy the boycott. The plan,"Proactive Neutralization," suggested infiltrating and redbaiting groups that supported the boycott. Action for Corporate Accountability was able to get a copy of the company's plan and release it to the press, causing Nestlé's plan to backfire. Not only was Nestlé seen as a bad guy by the public, employees began to question the ethics of their employer.

Therefore, it is important to have well-researched and documented information. *The simple truth is your greatest tool.* Boycotting groups have nothing to hide, while the companies have a great deal they would rather keep hidden. The public is generally mistrustful of corporations to begin with, so your message needs only to be truthful, simple, and repeated over and over.

Another tactic corporations employ is to switch the controversy to arenas over which they have more control, such as institutions or the government. For example, in the Nestle boycott, once the issue reached the level of the U.S. Senate and the United Nations, Nestle could bring its lobbying strength into play easier than it could against a massive grassroots adversary. Boycott organizers then had to divide resources to fight the company in several institutional settings, each requiring a different strategy.

Boycotts are often criticized for reacting to a problem, rather than addressing the root causes of problems. An article in *National Boycott News* (Winter, 1992/93) addressed this issue:

> What such criticism fails to understand is that lasting 'change' does not result simply from changed circumstances, but from a changed perspective of existing circumstances. Boycotting puts into motion the chain of understanding that leads to individual empowerment. Changes in society are the reflection of changes in individual consciousness. Change happens one person at a time. When we change ourselves, we change our world.

Tips for Organizing a Boycott

While there are no "how to's" written in stone, a history of boycotts has provided nonprofit groups with useful blueprints for organizing, fundraising, and strategic development. Remember, *a boycott is a tactic in an overall strategy to achieve a goal.* A consumer boycott remains the single most powerful way to bring pressure against a company. It is the only tactic against which corporate megabucks and political maneuvering will have little effect and which takes place in an arena the corporation cannot control.

Identify the problem and your adversary. Look closely at potential targets. If there are several possibilities, will you boycott them all or pick one or two? For example, you can target a company that is the worst offender, the industry leader, or the one with the highest visibility. Do you want to go after a company that is already somewhat sympathetic to your demands and therefore most open to dialogue and change, or perhaps the company that is most vulnerable in some way? Companies with a high number of easily recognized consumer products make the best targets, and are also most vulnerable to a consumer boycott.

Contacting the company. After choosing your target, write the company about your concerns. After the company replies, respond with a letter stating that they give your concerns more serious consideration. Ask to be referred to a person directly involved in the disputed issues. (Unless, of course, they agree with you and provide a timeline for change that you can support—a highly unlikely response). If the company's response continues to be unsatisfactory, outline your concerns again, requesting that the company respond with a plan to deal with them. If they don't, submit your own plan with a timeline. Let the company know you are prepared to initiate a boycott, but stress that the lines of communication are open. If the company still doesn't respond with a plan that meets your concerns and timeframe, tell them you will announce a boycott at a press conference on a specific date. Again, let them know the lines of communication remain open. Then do it.

Pre-Boycott Planning. Before publicly announcing the boycott, it is important to be very clear about your long- and short-term goals and how you will measure the boycott's overall effectiveness. You must also decide which products to target: all of them, or a few high-profile products? What about the products of subsidiaries? Connect with other groups (local, national, international) who might be willing to cosponsor or endorse the boycott. These can be groups working on similar issues or groups opposing your target for other reasons who can get the word out to their constituencies. Ask them to send letters to the company expressing their support for the future boycott action. Keep the company informed of all cosponsors and endorsers as the boycott progresses.

You must also define the process to be used to reach any settlement of the boycott. What is your bottom-line? How can the company satisfy your concerns? Make sure your expectations are achievable. For example, wanting the company to disappear off the face of the Earth isn't a reasonable boycott demand. Becoming clear about your terms at the outset is important to avoid confusion and misunderstanding later.

The Boycott. Hold a rally and press conference to kick off the boycott. Request that cosponsors hold similar events in their communities. Ideally, the primary event should be held in the city where the company's main office is located. The rally should be colorful, innovative, and empowering. You can have speakers, make use of drama, masks, costumes, street theater, and music. The event should be exciting enough to draw television, radio, and print media.

A boycott logo that will be used over and over is an excellent idea. Press releases should be sent to as many media outlets as possible, including international media for multinational corporations. (Get cosponsors to help). Make sure the press releases arrive two weeks in advance of the rally. You may want to follow-up some press releases with phone calls just to make sure they were noticed. (In general, two weeks is a good lead time for press releases if you want decent coverage in a timely fashion.) Other nonprofits or social-change organizations are good sources for media addresses, and local Chambers of Commerce may maintain a media list. For national or international media, the library, as always, is a good resource for current information.

Fund-raising and Support. Who and where is your main power base—churches, the grassroots, schools, environmental groups, or others? Develop a realistic budget and figure out where the money will come from. It is important that your strategies match your resources. Fund-raising is the bane of all nonprofit groups and is increasingly competitive. Funders, particularly private foundations, are fickle, jumping from popular issue to popular issue, generally wanting quick-fix results for their bucks. Direct-mail campaigns are overflowing mailboxes of an ever-skeptical public, while churches and other sources of funds are overstretched to fill the gaps left by administrations that have ignored domestic needs. A well-thought-out fund-raising plan is essential to a successful boycott campaign.

Be prepared for the long haul. Boycotts are a lot of work and require a sustained effort over time. While the McDonald's boycott was successful in just six months and the tuna boycott took only two years, the Nestlé boycott (for pushing infant formula in the Third World, resulting in thousands of infant deaths) has been going on since

1988—and this is its second installment! And INFACT's successful boycott of General Electric was initiated back in 1986.

Publicity. Your long-term strategy should include ways to keep the boycott in the public's awareness. Some boycott groups decide to publish regular updates. Keep boycott publications (see Resources) informed of any progress or activities. Make use of existing print media, develop workshops for schools, and create a video that can be sent anywhere to spread the word. Work your network. Keep your materials simple and to the point. Have more detailed information (in the form of reports, and articles, for example) for those who request it: reseachers, journalists, educators, or activists.

These suggestions are just a beginning. Planning is essential to any boycott campaign, along with the ability to constantly reassess one's strategies and tactics given existing resources. One key to a successful campaign is the ability to be flexible enough to take advantage of your adversary's moves. While strategies will change over the course of the campaign, they must always reflect the overall goal. This is why it is important to be clear about this right from the beginning. It is all too easy to waste important resources when your goal is not clearly articulated and kept in view.

Current Boycotts

The tobacco industry is INFACT's latest target, their goal being to stop the marketing of tobacco to children and young people around the world, and to stop the tobacco industry's actions that undermine public health efforts, including its interference in public-policy making. The campaign was initiated in October, 1993, with an initial phase of putting the industry on notice that consumers are opposed to its abuses and are willing to take further action if they don't stop. The three main targets of the boycott are Philip Morris, RJR Nabisco, and British-American Tobacco (BAT). These companies all have nontobacco-related divisions, making them an excellent target for consumers.

Texaco is being boycotted because of that company's wanton disregard for the rainforest environment of the Ecuadoran Amazon. During its twenty-year involvement in Ecuador's rainforest, Texaco has built an infrastructure for the exploration of oil that includes a vast network of roads that opened the forest to a colonial invasion by poor, land-seeking farmers. The Trans-Ecuadorian Pipeline, built by Texaco, has spilled more than 16 million gallons of oil, most of it in the Oriente region. (To put this in perspective, the Exxon *Valdez* spilled about 10.8 million gallons in Alaska.) Spills from secondary pipelines are unmeasured, but, according to Judith Kimerling in her book *Amazon Crude*, "the smaller flowlines discharge approximately 10,000 gallons per week of petroleum into the

Amazon." Kimerling continues, "Hundreds of oil wells generate more than 4.3 million gallons of toxic wastes every day, virtually all of which are spilled or discharged into the environment without treatment." Texaco's development in this region has threatened the survival of the eight indigenous tribes of the Oriente that depend on the rainforest; the Quicha, Cofan and Huaorani peoples have been displaced and exposed to new diseases for which they have no resistance. The colonists have overhunted the animals indigenous peoples rely upon for survival, and fishing grounds have been polluted.

In 1992, Texaco's operations were handed over to Petroecuador. Carlos Esquitini, Ecuador's Deputy Secretary of Energy, states in Kimerling's book, "Texaco has been in this country for twenty years. Texaco was our professor. They taught us how to produce and pollute. They never taught us how to clean up the mess."

Other U.S.-based oil companies are currently (or will shortly) be exploring or drilling in concessions in the Amazon. Texaco boycott organizers say that in order to establish a useful precedent for dealing with these other companies, Texaco must be held responsible for cleaning up its mess.

Bovine Growth Hormone (BGH). The Food and Drug Administration (FDA) approved the synthetically derived growth hormone, which increases a cow's milk production by 10 to 25 percent, for use in February, 1994. Further, the FDA does not require that dairy products containing BGH be labeled, so consumers will have no way of knowing if it is present in milk, cheese, ice cream, or other milk products. Some companies, responding to consumer demand, are pledging not to purchase milk from farmers who use BGH, and they will state this on their products. However, there is no one actually checking on farmers' claims, so the producers and consumers will simply have to trust. This is a very serious issue, since our whole milk supply could ultimately be contaminated. Organizations fighting BGH are including boycotts in their strategy. One such organization, Food and Water in Marshfield, Vermont, is targeting Land O' Lakes.

(Many thanks to Janice Mantell, Todd Putnam and *Boycott Quarterly* for information used in this section.)

Taking Back the Charters, Taking Back the Law*
by Richard L. Grossman and Frank T. Adams

Corporations cause harm every day. Why do their harms go unchecked? How can they dictate what we produce, how we work, what we eat, drink and breathe?

How did a self-governing people let this come to pass? Corporations were not supposed to reign in the United States.

When we look at the history of our states, we learn that citizens intentionally defined corporations through charters—the certificates of incorporation. In exchange for the charter, a corporation was obligated to obey all laws, to serve the common good, and to cause no harm. Early state legislators wrote charter laws and actual charters to limit corporate authority, and to ensure that when a corporation caused harm, they could revoke its charter. During the late 19th century, corporations subverted state governments, taking our power to put charters of incorporation to the uses originally intended.

Corporations may have taken our political power but they have not taken our Constitutional sovereignty. Citizens are guaranteed sovereign authority over government office-holders. Every state still has legal authority to grant and to revoke corporate charters. Corporations, large or small, still must obey all laws, serve the common good, and cause no harm. To exercise our sovereign authority over corporations, we must take back our political authority over our state governments.

We are out of the habit of contesting the legitimacy of the corporation, or challenging concocted legal doctrines, or denying courts the final say over our economic lives.

For most of this century, citizens skirmished with corporations to stop doing harm, but failed to question the legitimacy of the harmdoers. We do not use the charter and the chartering process to stop corporate harm, or to define the corporation on our terms.

What passes for political debate today is not about control, sovereignty, or the economic democracy which many American revolutionaries thought they were fighting to secure.

Too many organizing campaigns accept the corporation's rules, and wrangle on corporate turf. We lobby Congress for limited laws. We have no faith in regulatory agencies, but turn to them for relief. We plead with corporations to be socially responsible, then show them how to increase profits by being a bit less harmful.

How much more strength, time, and hope will we invest in such dead ends?

Today, corporate charters can be gotten easily by filling out a few forms and by paying modest fees.

Legislatures delegate authority to public officeholders to rubberstamp the administration of charters and the chartering process. The secretary of state and the attorney general are the officials most often involved. Sometimes they are elected; sometimes they are appointed.

In all states, legislatures continue to have the historic and the legal obligation to grant, to amend, and to revoke corporate charters. They are responsible for overseeing corporate activities. But it has been a long time since many legislatures have done what they are supposed to do.

---

*Excerpt from *Taking Care of Business: Citizenship and the Charter of Incorporation,* by Richard L. Grossman and Frank T. Adams, 1993, Charter, Ink. Reprinted by permission.

In Illinois, the law reads: 12.50 Grounds for judicial dissolution. A Circuit Court may dissolve a corporation: (a) in an action by the Attorney General, if it is established that: 1: the corporation obtained its certificates of incorporation through fraud; or 2: the corporation has continued to exceed or abuse the authority conferred upon it by law, or has continued to violate the law…; or 3: in an action by a shareholder, if it is established that…the directors or those in control of the corporation have acted, or are acting, or will act in a manner that is illegal, oppressive or fraudulent;…or if it is established that dissolution is reasonably necessary because the business of the corporation can no longer be conducted to the general advantage of its shareholders.

After entering an order of dissolution, "the Court shall direct the winding up and liquidation of the corporation's business and affairs."

In Delaware, Section 284 of the corporation law says that chancery courts can revoke the charter of any corporation for "abuse or misuse of its powers, privileges or franchises."

New York requires dissolution when a corporation abuses its powers, or acts "contrary to the public policy" of the citizenry. The law calls for a jury trial in charter revocation cases.

The Model Business Corporation Act, first written in 1931 by the committee on corporate laws of the American Bar Association, and revised twice since, is the basis for chartering laws in more then half the states and the District of Columbia. Although strongly protecting corporate property, this model law gives courts full power to liquidate the assets of a corporation if they are "misapplied or wasted."

It requires the secretary of state "from time to time" to list the names of all corporations which have violated their charters along with the facts behind the violations. Decrees of involuntary dissolution can be issued by the secretary of state and by courts.

Corporations chartered in other states are called foreign corporations. Corporations chartered in other nations are called alien corporations. Legislatures allow foreign or alien corporations to go into business in their states through this same chartering process. Either may establish factories or do business after obtaining a state's certificate of authority.

In Illinois, foreign corporations are "subject to the same duties, restrictions, penalities and liabilities now or hereafter imposed upon a domestic corporation of like character."

When we limit our thinking only to existing labor law, or only to existing environmental law, or only to the courts, or only to elections—or when we abide by corporate agendas—we abandon our Constitutional claim on the corporate charter and the chartering process.

When we forsake our Constitutional claim, we ignore historic tools we can use to define and to control the corporation. We pass up strategies which can inspire citizens to act. We fail to demand what we know is right.

We must name and stop what harms us. John H. Hunt, a member of the Equal Rights Party, wrote this resolution in 1837:

"Whenever a people find themselves suffering under a weight of evils, destructive not only to their happiness, but to their dignity and their virtues; when these evils go on increasing year after year, with accelerating rapidity, and threaten soon to reach that point at which peaceable endurance ceases to be possible; it becomes their solemn duty coolly to search out the causes of their suffering—to state those causes with plainness—and to apply a sufficient and a speedy remedy."

His resolution was passed unanimously by cheering mechanics, farmers and working people during a mass rally in a New York City park.

Around the nation, citizens are no less willing—and are quite well prepared—to educate, to organize and to agitate.

Citizens who have been to folk schools or labor colleges understand that by learning together and teaching ourselves corporate history, we can hone the skills of citizen sovereignty and power.

We can read our state constitutions. Libraries containing our states' constitutional histories, corporate histories, and corporate case law can provide details about what earlier citizens demanded of corporations, what precedents they established, and which of their legal and organizing methods we can use to our advantage.

We can demand to see the charters of every corporation. We need to know what each charter prohibits, especially if it is an old charter. Armed with our states' rich legal precedents, and with our evidence of corporate misuse or abuse, we can amend or revoke charters and certificates of authority.

When corporations violate our Constitutional guarantees, we can take them to court ourselves. Corporate officers can be forced to give us depositions under oath, just as elected officials who spurned the Constituion were forced to do by the civil rights movement—often in courtrooms packed with angry citizens.

New Yorkers used to get sufficient and speedy remedy through injunctions against corporations. We can revive this tradition. Surrounded by citizens and their peers, judges can be encouraged to enjoin corporate officials from doing further harm, or from stripping the corporation's assets, or from moving the company away.

Stockholders have authority to seek injunctions and file dissolution suits if they fear managers are acting illegally, oppressively, fraudulently, or are misusing or wasting corporate assets.

As in the first half of the 19th century, would-be or on-going incorporators must be made to ask us for the privilege of a charter. We can set our own criteria: workers must own a significant or majority share of the company; the workforce must have democratic decision-making authority; charters must be renewed annually; corporate officers must prove all corporate harm has ceased. For starters.

Who defines the corporation controls the corporation. We cannot command the modern corporation with laws that require a few days' notice before the corporation leaves town, or with laws that allow the corporation to spew so many toxic parts per million. If we expect to define the corporation using the charters and putting legislators on our civic leash, we must also challenge prevailing judicial doctrines. We cannot let courts stand in the way of our stopping corporate harm.

Legal doctrines are not inevitable or divine. When the liberty and property rights of citizens are at stake, as former Supreme Court Justice Louis D. Brandeis said, "the right of property and the liberty of the individual must be remoulded...to meet the changing needs of society."

The corporation is an artificial creation, and must not enjoy the protections of the Bill of Rights.

Corporate owners and officers must be liable for harms they cause. No corporation should exist forever. Both business judgement and managerial prerogative must meet the same end as the colonial trading companies' delusion of divine authority.

Our sovereign right to decide what is produced, to own and to organize our work, and to respect the Earth, is as American as a self-governing peoples' right to vote.

In our democracy, we can shape the nation's economic life any way we want.

A Sample Citizens' Resolution

Chartering a corporation is the citizens' historic right, and a civic responsibility. Many corporations serve the common good but too many cause injury, corrode our democracy, and poison the Earth.

To halt corporate harm, we citizens must redefine the corporation, reclaim our sovereign authority over the corporation, and when necessary, revoke charters of incorporation.

We urge local and state elected officials to adopt this Resolution:

Whereas, only citizens have sovereign authority to grant charters of incorporation; now,

Therefore, be it resolved, that the legislature of this state:

Redefine the process and criteria for granting corporate charters to our specifications; and,

Restore civic authority over the governance of existing corporate charters to our specifications; and,

Finally, revoke the charters of harmful corporations, and revoke the certificates of authority of harmful foreign and alien corporations operating in our state.

Investor Activism

Investor activism is a strategy available to investors that can help force corporate change. While these tactics can only be utilized by investors, they can play an important role in a diversified corporate campaign. When combined with a consumer boycott, shareholder action can hit a company where it hurts most—in the bottom line.

Divestment

When it is part of a larger campaign, divestment can put a lot of pressure on companies. But as usual, vigilance is necessary. Some corporate breaks from South Africa, for example, were far from clean. Coca-Cola sold its

South African operations to black South African entrepreneurs and continued sales through a South African franchise. General Motors and IBM also continued sales in South Africa, despite their official withdrawal from that country. Successful divestment campaigns put pressure on the target companies, and particularly on institutions depending on the companies. Cosmetic restructuring, such as occurred during the years companies were divesting from South Africa, and the willingness of less scrupulous investors to buy the divested stocks, limit the economic pressure on the companies and the government, but they do not necessarily stop the bad press. Divestment means we personally are not supporting a bad situation or a repressive regime.

Shareholder Action

Shareholder resolutions can be used to promote a wide range of changes in corporate policy. They can be effective in bringing issues and concerns to the attention of management and of the other stockholders and are most often filed to raise awareness, rather than with the expectation that the resolution will actually pass. Media attention can make such resolutions even more effective. Large institutional investors (such as pension funds) and churches have been the most effective in bringing resolutions to a vote.

All owners of common stock in a corporation are entitled to vote on corporate policy and elect the directors who run the company. Each share is worth one vote. If a stockholder can't attend the annual meeting in person (and most do not), one votes by proxy. Before the annual meeting, the company sends out information about candidates for the board and about any resolutions being submitted for consideration. One votes and mails the proxy back before the meeting. Participating in the company's decision-making in this way is more than a right—it is a responsibility. More shareholders are becoming aware of this—and of the possibilities for change from within—than ever before.

Anyone who owns at least $1,000 worth of stock and has owned it for at least twelve months prior to the filing deadline may submit a shareholder resolution, a formal proposal requesting that the company take certain actions. The Securities and Exchange Commission (SEC) made the $1,000, twelve-month requirement to discourage people from buying a single share of stock just to hassle a company. Investors get around this requirement by pooling funds. All shareholder resolutions are included on the proxy statements to be voted on by all stock owners.

When submitting a resolution, one must pay careful attention to SEC regulations so as not to give the corporation an excuse to ignore the resolution. Corporations can, at their discretion, decide not to include a resolution, but to do so they must send notice, along with their reasons, to both the filer and the SEC. Regulations govern the content as well as the submission process itself. Resolutions must meet the SEC's defination of "legitimate shareholder concern": the subject must be significantly related to the business of the company, may not be of a personal nature, may not concern "ordinary business practices," and must be within the company's power to grant.

The past few years have seen a huge increase in the number of shareholder resolutions submitted for consideration and in the diversity of issues addressed. As a result corporations, together with the SEC, are attempting to broaden the definition of what are considered "ordinary business practices," thereby limiting the types of issues shareholders may bring to a vote. Activist shareholders aren't giving up without a fight, however. In June, 1993, the U.S. Trust Company of Boston, the New York City Employees Retirement System (NYCERS), and the Women's Division of the United Methodist Church filed a suit against the SEC seeking a reversal of its ruling that bars shareholder resolutions on social issues, such as employment, from proxy statements. The suit stems from an SEC decision that permitted Cracker Barrel Old Country Stores, Inc., "to exclude from its proxy statement a NYCERS-sponsored shareholder proposal prohibiting discrimination in the workplace." (Since February, 1991, Cracker Barrel has been the target of boycotts and demonstrations for firing gay or lesbian employees.) The SEC stated that employment policies are "ordinary business."

The situation is far from resolved however, since in April, 1993, a federal court issued an injunction barring Wal-Mart stores from mailing its 1993 proxy materials without including a shareholder resolution calling on the company to report on its equal employment opportunity and affirmative action programs and purchasing from women and minority vendors. The judge in this case felt that the resolution involved "a significant policy consideration" and does not fall into the catagory of "ordinary business operations."

The Interfaith Center on Corporate Responsibility (ICCR) is a coalition of approximately two hundred fifty Roman Catholic and Protestant orders, dioceses, denominations, and agencies with combined portfolios totaling over $35 billion and is extremely effective in organizing shareholders (individuals and institutions alike) into powerful alliances in order to have the most impact. ICCR coordinates shareholder actions, boycotts, divestment, letter-writing campaigns, and vigils challenging corporations' policies on a number of social-justice issues, including South Africa, equal employment, the arms race, infant formula and pharmaceutical sales in the Third World, environment and energy concerns, corporate governance, Third World debt and the responsibilities of U.S. banks and alternative investments. ICCR is also an excellent resource for general information pertaining to shareholder activism—for example, the latest developments in the SEC situation mentioned earlier.

In 1994, ICCR members sponsored 302 resolutions to 138 companies, frequently cosponsored with pension funds, other institutional investors, and individual investors. Included among the cosponsors were New York City, Minnesota, and New York State Pension Funds; several labor unions; mutual and money fund managers; Friends of the Earth; Jesse Smith Noyes Foundation; other nonprofit groups; and numerous individuals. 1994's resolutions were more diverse than ever (in the 1980s most resolutions involved South Africa or disclosure). More than thirty companies—including Alcoa, Allied Signal, AT&T, Arco, Boeing, GE, IBM, McDonald's, PepsiCo and Weyerhaeuser—were asked to endorse the CERES Principles (see chapter 4, "Evaluating the Status Quo"). American Express and Merrill-Lynch were asked to report on why they are underwriting Hydro-Quebec's James Bay Projects. Several companies were asked to adopt smoke-free facilities or to stop or limit cigarette advertising. International banks were requested to develop criteria to evaluate loans to Third World countries. AT&T and General Motors were asked not "to evaluate the environmental and human rights context" in which they operate the *maquiladoras*. Executive compensation was an issue for many shareholders, as were toxic wastes and emissions. Old issues such as infant formula sales in the Third World were also still on the agenda.

When integrated into a larger effort—including letter-writing campaigns, boycotts, divestment strategies, and media attention—working within the company can be an effective way of encouraging corporate responsibility. A success story: ICCR members had been questioning Monsanto about its weapons production since 1979. In 1983 they asked it for the first time not to renew its contract with the Department of Energy. When Monsanto's contract to operate its Miamisburg, Ohio, facility for the manufacture of nuclear-weapons components came up for renewal on September 30, 1988, it was not renewed. Wylie B. Hogeman, Monsanto's president, stated that the decision "would enable Monsanto to more fully concentrate on its major businesses."

More recently, in 1992 a resolution endorsing the CERES Principles was submitted at Sun Company's annual shareholder meeting. (Sun is the twelfth-largest oil company in the United States). Although the resolution was supported by only 6 percent of the votes, management agreed to meet with the Principle's backers and were able to reach an agreement after talks convinced them the Principles were in line with Sun's own efforts to reduce waste and pollution. The result: on February 3, 1993, Sun became the first Fortune 500 company to endorse the CERES Principles.

To the extent that shareholders become informed and aware of their responsibility as owners, corporations will be forced to become more responsive. For maximum power and visibility, it is essential to join together with other shareholder groups and organizations. Shareholders often own stock in several companies targeted for the same reason. Although specific companies are targeted, the *issue* is the focus. In conclusion, any action that could endanger a company's bottom line is bound to be taken seriously, especially if there is the threat of publicity.

Direct Action for the Earth

*by Brian Tokar**

Every social movement in U.S. history that has ever made meaningful change has employed methods of direct action and civil disobedience. From the earliest acts of defiance against British rule in colonial America, direct action has played an essential role in furthering democracy and social justice in this land. Today, direct action is playing an increasingly important role in our efforts to protect the Earth's ecosystems from the abuses of corporate domination.

History of Direct Action

The history of the United States is full of inspiring examples of people struggling for justice and equality. Despite our government's claims to represent the cause of democracy in the world, it has invariably sided with the interests of privilege and power, both at home and abroad. Time and again, people have had to go outside the system, mobilizing public outrage, creating alternative institutions, and often resorting to extralegal means to see justice done.

The abolitionists employed direct action in their struggle against slavery, beginning over one hundred fifty years ago. While supporting rebellions of enslaved blacks in the American South, abolitionists organized boycotts of goods produced with slave labor and built an Underground Railroad of safe houses and transportation routes to help fugitive slaves escape their plight. Escaped slaves and their supporters also staged sit-ins and eat-ins on railroad cars and steamboats, anticipating some of the methods of the 1960s civil rights movement. The first public campaigns for women's rights were pioneered by women who refused to remain silent at public meetings that officially welcomed only men. By the early 1900s, women were organizing hunger strikes, along with some of the first demonstrations at the gates of the White House. Early labor organizers endured the efforts of both employers and the government to silence their activities. Everything from work slowdowns to blockades and sabotage was employed by unionists in defense of their right to organize.

Throughout the late 1950s and early '60s, civil rights activists marched through segregated towns, sat-in at lunch counters and other public facilities, and stood firm against the violence of a system determined to keep African American people "in their place." The methods of nonviolent resistance advanced by Dr. Martin Luther King, Jr. and others helped reveal the injustices upon which the American social system depends, and offered a striking example of moral force standing firm against the system's innate violence.

---

*Brian Tokar is the author of *The Green Alternative: Creating an Ecological Future*, (revised edition, (New Society Publishers, 1992). He covers environmental issues for *Z Magazine* and other periodicals; lectures around the country on Green politics and other ecological movements; and teaches Social Ecology at Goddard College in Plainfield, Vermont. He was an organizer of the 1990 Earth Day Wall Street Action.

As the U.S. military escalated its involvement in Vietnam and thousands of American men were drafted to fight a war the government could not adequately explain, people's frustration and outrage began to grow. Protests against the war evolved toward open acts of resistance, as young men publicly burned their draft cards, and thousands of people demonstrated against both the Pentagon and local military bases.

When the top-secret Pentagon Papers were revealed in the early 1970s, it became clear that the antiwar movement had substantially slowed the escalation of the war and prevented the likely use of nuclear weapons against the Vietnamese. Domestic opposition forced the pullout of most U.S. troops and pushed all sides, however reluctantly, to the negotiating table.

Throughout the 1970s and '80s, direct-action campaigns for peace and disarmament have shaped public opinion and policy in the United States and many other countries. Sit-ins at congressional offices helped slow the flow of U.S. aid to Nicaraguan mercenaries and Salvadoran death squads, and women's peace camps in many Western European countries helped build pressure for renewed superpower arms negotiations. Students on many campuses built mock shanty towns to protest their universities' refusal to divest from South Africa.

Direct action in the environmental movement began as an outgrowth of the campaign for nuclear disarmament. Greenpeace began launching ships to stop nuclear-weapons tests near Alaska and in the South Pacific, and soon broadened its focus to include an international campaign against the hunting of whales and seals. Their actions continue to be dramatic and well-planned so as to attract the greatest-possible media attention. Through the efforts of Greenpeace, the idea of direct action in defense of the Earth has been firmly implanted in the public consciousness.

A Model for Direct Action

It was the antinuclear-power movement of the late 1970s that first combined ecological direct action with widespread public organizing and mass mobilizations. In the spring of 1976, eighteen New Hampshire residents were arrested for walking onto a nuclear construction site in the small coastal town of Seabrook. A few months later, 180 people repeated their action, and the following spring nearly 2000 demonstrators tried to occupy the site. Over 1400 were arrested, and most were imprisoned for two weeks in National Guard armories for refusing to pay bail or compromise with the authorities. There, in prison, they cast the mold for a brand new kind of antinuclear organization, one committed to nonviolent direct action, consensual, small group-based democracy; and, for many, a sweeping vision of social transformation.

While working to stop nuclear power, New England's Clamshell Alliance sought to create a new kind of activist community— community based upon feminist group process, participatory decision making, and personal and cultural as well as political change. Similar alliances of activists sprang up all across the country, staging blockades, occupations, and nonviolent backwoods raids on nuclear construction sites, utility headquarters, and nuclear-weapons facilities. The nuclear industry's growing economic difficulties contributed to a rapid shift in the political climate that virtually halted the expansion of nuclear power in the United States. The widely decentralized antinuclear alliances that emerged nationwide established a model for ecological direct action that thrives to this day.

This model owes its strength and success to several elements. First is the commitment to decentralized, grassroots organization. People seek to organize themselves in a way that fosters personal empowerment and creates living models for a society that can live in harmony with the Earth. There are countless difficulties and hurdles along the way, but the spirit of consensual democracy speaks to people's deepest hopes for a different kind of world. Empowerment begins with the individual, as each person knows that his/her personal feelings and ideals will be fully respected by the group. Forms of oppression such as sexism and racism can be addressed at the personal and community level. Small groups of like-minded people are free to engage in whatever actions are appropriate to advancing the cause within their own communities. Decentralized structures seek to break down the hierarchies and top-heavy power relations that have plagued more traditional political formations.

The primary vehicle for this is the *affinity group*. Since the 1970s, activists have formed small, close-knit affinity groups to participate in direct-action and community-building efforts. Whether in a large demonstration or in personal-change work, people can be more effective in tense situations if they can count upon the support and shared thinking of a small group of like-minded people. The idea goes back to the Spanish anarchist movement of the 1920s and '30s: before the civil war in Spain, small, autonomous groups of revolutionaries known as *grupos de afinidad* helped free large areas of the country from the control of oppressive institutions and landlords. Today, affinity groups come together for direct action and often continue to work in their community as autonomous collectives within larger movement organizations.

A second element is nonviolence. Approaches to nonviolence vary from the personal and spiritual to the politically pragmatic. It is clear that the violence of the system cannot be defeated on its own terms: The corporate state's ability to inflict pain and suffering upon its opponents is endemic. Public refusals to cooperate with violence, however, can expose the system's weakest links. Power and authority in society are sustained by the quiet compliance of most people; the withdrawal of compliance by those who clearly have morality and justice on their side can, in a sustained campaign, confuse and upset the balance of power. This has been a key to the success of nonviolent campaigns throughout history. Nonviolent methods vary from passive resistance and acts of personal witness to mass blockades and some forms of sabotage.

Finally, ecological direct-action movements are engaged in promoting viable alternatives that are in tune with a more ecological vision for the whole society. Most people passively accept the injustices and atrocities of modern industrial life because they simply cannot imagine any better way. Breaking through this culturally enforced passivity is a key to the growth of any movement, and this requires real-life examples. Direct-action movements have become engaged in planning for alternative energy sources and drafting sweeping proposals for the restoration of wilderness. They have helped form working cooperatives and alternative communities, while fighting for direct, face-to-face democracy within the larger society. The merging of oppositional and reconstructive currents makes it possible to tap the profound discontent that lies just below the surface of an Earth-denying society such as ours.

Ecological Direct Action Today

Many different approaches to direct action have emerged from today's ecological struggles. Features of the basic organizing model outlined here have been taken up by communities of people fighting toxic dumping, waste incinerators, and local weapons manufacturers. As corporations move many of their most polluting facilities away from urban centers, people in far corners of the United States increasingly face outlandish "development" schemes with the potential to severely disrupt the lives and health of people and ecosystems. Time and again, nonviolent direct action has played an important role in keeping the polluters at bay and helping communities of people empower themselves to create a healthier way of life.

The grassroots movement against toxic chemical pollution has emerged over the past decade as probably the most successful—and least publicized—people's movement of our time. In communities throughout the country, antitoxics activists have mounted successful community organizing and political pressure campaigns against corporate polluters. When dangerous projects have gone ahead despite overwhelming public outcry, people have increasingly turned to direct action. In some communities, direct-action campaigns have tapped experiences and organizing skills that go back to the early days of the civil rights movement.

In one poor, rural county in North Carolina, people discovered that their local landfill had been chosen as the final repository for thousands of truckloads of PCB-contaminated soil recovered from sites all over the state. In one of the largest public protests in the rural South since the early '60s, over five hundred people—black and white—were arrested trying to block the trucks. The dumping went ahead, taking over a month to complete, but the people of Warren County prevented their landfill from continuing to be used as a toxic repository for the entire state. Similar actions have occurred on a smaller scale—and have had a dramatic impact upon race relations—in many Southern communities where poor people of all backgrounds share the burden of some of the most toxic industrial facilities in the entire country. The Warren County actions helped spark a widespread movement for environmental justice that is transforming activism in the South and across the country.

Monkeywrenching

A considerably different approach to environmental direct action has been advanced by the Earth First! movement, which began as a loose-knit band of radical wilderness advocates in the Southwest. Earth First! gained considerable notoriety in the 1980s for its promotion of sabotage, or "monkeywrenching" as a way to protect ecosystems from the ravages of industrial-scale logging and other assaults. Edward Abbey's popular novel, *The Monkey Wrench Gang*, follows the adventures of a band of renegades committed to stopping the exploitation of their beloved desert lands by all means of disruption and sabotage, and Earth First! set out to replicate their successes—and their outrageousness—in real life.

Earth First! was formed as an alternative to the increasingly staid, buttoned-down ways of the large, Washington-based environmental groups. Earth First! devised detailed plans for the reclamation and expansion of wilderness areas that were often being compromised away by more mainstream groups, and backed up their demands with demonstrations, sit-ins, road blockades, and sabotage. Planting spikes in trees to prevent their cutting, taking out bulldozers and other heavy machinery, removing survey stakes, and barricading Forest Service offices are only a few of the late-night tactics employed by Earth First!ers in their pursuit of "No Compromise in Defense of Mother Earth."

These methods sparked considerable controversy in the media, in the environmental movement, among activists committed to more traditional forms of political action—and within the Earth First! movement as well. The media, along with some environmentalists, accused Earth First! of terrorism. Others asserted that monkeywrenching was inconsistent with the broader movement's commitment to nonviolence. Earth First! emphasized its commitment to not harming any living beings, and to preventing harm to workers by clearly marking areas where trees had been spiked; indeed, this was the only way that spiking could actually prevent trees from being cut.

Over a period of years, the exploits of Earth First!ers have helped raise the protection of native ecosystems to a major regional and national issue. Their uncompromising demands and methods have helped more mainstream groups heighten their own demands for the protection of ecologically sensitive areas and sometimes resist the pressure to strike damaging compromises with logging companies, developers, and complicit government agencies.

A major split occurred within Earth First! when some activists began to see the growth of public activism to defend the wilderness as potentially far more valuable than monkeywrenching. Activists in the redwood forests of northern California began reaching out to loggers and their families, who are often as much the victims of the exploitative practices of the big logging companies as the forests are. One company, Pacific Lumber, which owns much of the remaining old-growth redwood forest, had been the victim of a hostile takeover by the Houston-based Maxxam conglomerate. As with most such buy-outs, the costs of the takeover were to be paid off through the rapid liquidation of Pacific Lumber's assets: in this case, the redwoods themselves. Earth First!ers fought the cutting of the redwoods by petitioning state agencies, going to court, blockading logging equipment, and scaling giant redwood trees that were about to be cut.

Soon, alliances with the loggers and mill workers began to bear some fruit, with the help of the Industrial Workers of the World (IWW), an anarchist-leaning labor union which, in the early twentieth century, had gained a considerable following among the loggers of the northwest. Pro-logging interests countered by polarizing communities and threatening violence. In response, activists chose to renounce tree spiking, a tactic feared by the workers, and concentrate upon bringing thousands of people to redwood country in the summer of 1990 to take action against corporate logging.

It was known as Redwood Summer, in memory of the Mississippi Freedom Summer of 1964, when students and other activists converged upon Mississippi to support the struggle for desegregation. For the entire summer, activists from across the country camped in the redwoods, rallied at timber-company headquarters, and ventured into the woods in small groups to blockade logging roads. Some forest defenders learned to live for days at a time on platforms near the tops of trees threatened with destruction. Redwood Summer was seen as an overwhelming success, and inspired similar actions in other parts of the country as well as in Canada where, since 1993, thousands of people have participated in actions against the cutting of ancient forests near Clayoquot Sound on the rugged west coast of Vancouver Island. However, it also sharpened the divisions within Earth First!, pitting advocates of alliance-building and a widened political focus against those who shunned public activism and preferred to limit themselves to individual expressions of outrage, such as monkeywrenching.

The same year brought the twentieth anniversary of the first Earth Day, and activists from around the country turned to direct action to counter the growing cooptation of environmental consciousness by corporations promoting consumerism. With large infusions of corporate advertising, Earth Day became identified with the message that everyone was equally responsible for the destruction of the Earth. Individual solutions—recycling, planting trees, and buying different products—were offered as the only answer, and the role of corporations in systematically destroying ecosystems for profit was being lost in the shuffle. A broad coalition of Green activists, antitoxics organizers, students, antinuclear activists, ecofeminists, gay activists, urban squatters and others emerged to support a call for a demonstration at the New York Stock Exchange on Wall Street for the Monday following Earth Day.

Demonstrators were unable to physically close the Stock Exchange, but it was clearly not a day for "business as usual" on Wall Street. Arriving stock brokers and office workers were greeted by crowds of people highly aware of the role of the corporate economy in endangering our future. There was anger and there was singing. There were banners and costumes and barricades. Some demonstrators sought dialogue, others preferred to simply get in the way. A noontime rally highlighted the victims of toxic corporate practices, and the connections between environmental, social, and economic injustice. Even the mainstream media acknowledged that the Earth Day Wall Street Action successfully challenged the corporations' efforts to turn Earth Day into just another marketing gimmick, and helped refocus public attention on the institutions chiefly responsible for our environmental crisis. It was an important example of the power of direct action to bring people together across lines of political interest, and to bring ideas to the public which are normally ignored by the corporate-controlled media.

Forms of Direct Action

Direct actions can differ as widely as the people and groups that take up the call. They vary considerably in size, scope, and locale. They can involve huge mobilizations of people, one brave individual, or a small close-knit group. They can physically prevent harm to living beings and ecosystems, halt the normal functioning of complicit institutions, attract widespread public attention, and serve as acts of personal witness. Direct actions take place on land or sea, on city streets, inside corporate offices, and deep in the woods. They can be perfectly legal, or they can involve acts of civil disobedience and the risk of arrest.

The choice of actions usually reflects the personal inclinations and creativity of participants as much as the particular political situation they may face. Every new situation offers new possibilities and new ways of getting a message across, informed by the sense of urgency that comes when more conventional means have proven insufficient to overturn an injustice, make an institution accountable, or find a meaningful alternative to business as usual. Sometimes, actions emerge from a carefully thought-out strategy, but often a wider campaign will evolve from the simple urgency to halt a particular atrocity through direct action. Actions combine a deep-felt personal commitment with the desire to further a movement's longer-term goals, often creating an excitement and exhilaration all their own.

Most direct actions involve both public symbolism and direct interference with business-as-usual. Some actions are designed primarily to raise public awareness and outrage, or to draw attention to an issue of which most people are not yet aware. Some eschew public attention and media coverage and are designed mostly to get in the way. Most actions share a little of both. How "symbolic" or "direct" an action might be reflects the style of action, its role in an overall campaign, and the degree of public awareness or support for the action's goals. For example, a blockade of a toxic shipment might be judged by its success in mobilizing long-term public opposition, as well as by how long it actually delayed the shipment. Releases of laboratory animals by animal-rights activists can draw public attention to laboratory conditions, while saving the lives of individual animals.

The immediate and longer-term effects of an action are sometimes viewed as competing goals. Those seeking a clear political message may opt for a more orchestrated action, while those seeking to maximize the obstruction of business might insist upon elements of spontaneity and surprise. The interests of furthering a movement may be best served by one approach or the other, depending upon the timing and circumstances. An institution's most symbolic point of vulnerability may differ from where it is physically vulnerable. Ultimately, the effects of a particular action can never be predicted in advance. A well-planned action will take both its symbolic and direct elements into careful consideration.

The role of civil disobedience and arrest in an action campaign also requires serious thought. Often, the occurrence of arrests at a demonstration will bring greater media coverage; seeing people being arrested for a cause can certainly raise public awareness of the urgency of that cause. This has been evident at countless disarmament and antinuclear demonstrations in the past fifteen years. Arraignments and trials that follow mass arrests can help keep an issue in the news, and arguing one's own case in court can be a particularly empowering and effective undertaking. In a few cases, activists have been acquitted by juries on the grounds that their illegal actions were necessary to prevent a greater harm from being done (the so-called Necessity Defense).

However, a desire to provoke arrests can sometimes distort the focus of an action and limit its effectiveness. For example, activists will often meet with local police officials before an action to encourage communication and explain the movement's commitment to nonviolence. But when arrest is the primary focus, such meetings can turn into elaborate negotiations over the specifics of arrest scenarios. In Seabrook in 1978, such negotiations led to the cancellation of a massive occupation of the nuclear construction site after movement spokespeople were pressured into accepting a deal offered by the state attorney general. In other cases, activists have unwittingly helped the police set the stage for rapid arrests, minimizing their action's direct impact.

In the '90s, activists continue to be willing to risk arrest for their beliefs, but fewer people are choosing to take action *in order* to be arrested. In many actions, people prefer to keep moving rather than sit in one place, so as to heighten the degree of obstruction while postponing the risk of arrest. For example on Wall Street in 1990, less than a quarter of the people actually involved in blocking the Stock Exchange were arrested by police. In San Francisco, periodic "War Chest Tours" of the downtown financial district have succeeded in disrupting business without provoking arrests. For longer-term actions, supporters can help to maintain an occupation or blockade for many days even though only some people might choose to stay and be arrested when threatened with a police order to leave. For actions that may involve heavy legal penalties, such as monkeywrenching, people will go to elaborate lengths to avoid being detected. On the other hand, many peace activists have willingly done considerable jail time for damaging sensitive weapons facilities and then publicly turning themselves in.

The political purpose of an action can also vary, depending upon the movement's goals. *Some direct actions are designed to pressure institutions to make changes in policy, while others seek to take power away from those institutions.* For example, the Pledge of Resistance against the Reagan administration's war in Nicaragua was focused upon cutting off aid to the U.S.-financed *contra* rebels, and succeeded in pressuring several members of Congress to change their votes. On the other hand, the burning of draft cards and draft-board files during the Vietnam War was part of an overall movement to change policy, but protesters' primary purpose was to impede the draft boards' ability to function.

Some of the most empowering actions involve the reclaiming of people's right to satisfy their basic needs, as opposed to the interests of property and social control. Urban squatter movements are some of the best examples of this, and have become symbols of resistance in major cities across the United States and Europe. In Berkeley in the late 1980s, a group of homeless people and student activists occupied a long-abandoned building owned by the University of California. After the University evicted the occupiers and tore the building down, people returned a few weeks later to plant a garden on the site. The garden helped feed homeless people in Berkeley for the duration of the season and beyond. "Take Back the Night" marches have been organized by women in many cities to reclaim city streets from pervasive sexist violence. Food Not Bombs groups have been springing up all across the country to feed homeless people in public places in open defiance of official restrictions and neglect.

Successful actions rely only partly upon the mass media to communicate their message; a well-planned action conveys its own message to the surrounding community as directly as possible. Many sabotage actions have succeeded in slowing logging in particularly endangered areas without anyone notifying the media at all. Building a strong community of resistance around a particular facility, such as a weapons or chemical plant, may be more important in the early stages of a campaign than gaining media attention for every action. On the other hand, an event such as the Earth Day Wall Street Action will rely upon alternative media and personal contacts to make it happen, but can be very dependent upon the mainstream press to communicate its message to a wider public. Activists have created many new ways of communicating directly with the public, from underground newspapers and wall posters to human billboards positioned along major highways. In smaller communities, they may decide to canvass a town door-to-door to explain their purpose. In larger cities, activists have taken to altering the messages on large commercial billboards to create messages against war, pollution, and the sexist images that pervade advertising itself.

Whether through the media or more person-to-person means, a successful action conveys a clear message about its purpose and goals. The more creatively the message is communicated, the more support will be aroused, and the more likely it is that people will think beyond their reflexive support for law, order, and the status quo. *Actions that combine civil disobedience with a strong visual or theatrical element are often the most effective politically and the most fun for participants. The more outrageous the better!*

Organizing for Direct Action

There are several basic steps to organizing a direct-action campaign, and we can only briefly summarize them here. The sources listed in this book's Resources section offer a wealth of ideas, suggestions, and specific examples of direct-action strategies. Direct-action organizing has become a virtual art form unto itself. Studying successful examples from the past can offer valuable ideas and inspiration to help you get started, but the best ideas come from personal experience. See you on the streets!

Pick a focus. Choose a location that clearly symbolizes the problem you are addressing. Ideally, this will also be an important link in the continuing perpetration of a particular atrocity against the Earth. Highly significant direct actions have been carried out at corporate headquarters, construction sites, shipping and loading docks, government offices, officials' homes, military bases and recruiting stations, illegal dump sites, public roads and bridges, financial districts, research installations, tourist attractions, television studios, and just about anywhere the interests of profit and poison mingle. Pick a site that is accessible and relatively easy to reach if you wish to attract large numbers of people. If numbers are not a priority, almost any place will do. Sometimes there is an obviously weak link in the chain of destruction. Occasionally you can even catch someone in the act.

Choose a particular strategy or style of action. This will, of course, change and evolve over the course of a campaign. It may be best to start small. Some actions are announced months in advance; others rely upon an element of surprise. Notify the media whenever it is appropriate, the earlier the better if you wish widespread coverage. Be as visually engaging as you can. For public actions, be sure to include a wide community of supporters, and try to involve them in your planning. Involve others in your planning where possible; the benefit of other people's experience and perceptions can make a huge difference. As we have seen, every situation and every group of people will bring unique elements to your decisions about strategy.

Form affinity groups. Affinity groups have proven to be an essential element in direct actions, both large and small. They provide an important setting for sharing skills, planning tactics, and offering both personal and logistical support. In large demonstrations, they help counter feelings of isolation and make scenarios more flexible. They can also offer some protection against police infiltration. Encourage groups to form out of already existing circles of friends, neighbors, and co-workers. Some members may join a group for a particular action or series of actions, while others will continue to work together on other community projects between actions.

New affinity groups often form at a *nonviolence preparation session*. Preparation, often referred to as nonviolence training, originated with Gandhi, and is another important ingredient in direct-action organizing. Preparation sessions help develop a set of common skills for nonviolent action, including group-process skills, legal information, and nonviolent ways of responding to potentially volatile situations. Many local peace groups have a pool of experienced trainers, and the War Resisters League maintains a network of trainers all over the country. Preparation sessions explain the logistics of an upcoming action and help empower people to continue working together for change. Many affinity groups emerge from their first action together with a wealth of ideas for further actions that they can carry out, either on their own or with the support of other like-minded groups.

Organize a support system. Effective direct actions require support of several types. This is especially true if people will be risking arrest. Support functions include communications, legal assistance, and media work. If people are away from home or are detained for any reason, people back home may need to be notified, plants watered, appointments cancelled. Backwoods actions may require help with food and medical needs. These roles are generally filled by supporters who will not be participating in the riskier parts of the action. They allow everyone to play an essential role, whether or not they are willing to take all the risks. Every affinity group has one or more of its own support people to account for members' personal needs, and larger actions may require more elaborate coordination of the tasks that will benefit everyone. In most affinity groups, support roles are rotated among the members: At least one person needs to agree to "sit out" a particular action to carry out the often very-demanding support role. Supporters have been arrested in some instances, despite questionable legality, in an effort by the authorities to thwart the demonstrator's well-laid plans. Participation in direct action at any level is never truly without risk.

Provide for evaluation and follow-up. One action is rarely sufficient to permanently alter any situation. Activists should plan to gather after an action has been accomplished to evaluate what was done and to begin planning for the future. In the case of civil disobedience, legal proceedings might take some time, and it is important to maintain close communication among the defendants. This is a time for community-building, networking, and thinking ahead. Affinity groups might plan a retreat together, or organize some study groups. Sometimes, the situation might demand that people go right back to the site of action to prevent further environmental damage the very next day.

Systematic evaluation and follow-up can help sustain a community of activists through many difficult campaigns. Activists that are healthy and well supported for the long haul will be much better able to spring into action again when the iron strikes. Our own creativity and the strength of our solidarity are the only limits.

Part IV

CREATING THE ECONOMY WE WANT

Introduction

W HEN WE ARE dependent on the workings of corporate capitalism for things we need in our daily lives, not to mention our jobs, that's where the economic and political power will reside. Restructuring our economic, political, and social institutions and processes is necessary if we are to shift power back to the people. This requires that we work locally and regionally to create the kinds of institutions, systems, and relationships that can sustain us.

Let's take a moment to envision a different future. Take a deep breath, sit back for a moment, and relax. Close your eyes and imagine what it would *feel* like to live in a self-reliant, ecologically and economically diverse community where people and nature supported and enhanced each other—a Whole Earth Community. Let your imagination run free:

What does your town look like? What kind of work do you do? What kinds of businesses are there? Where do your children go to school? Where are the parks, rivers, forests, swamps, and other natural areas? How does it feel to be in them? What qualities do they add to people's lives? Where does the town's energy come from? What kinds of industry is there? How are monetary exchanges made? What is the town's relationship with neighboring towns? With the region? With the nation and other nations? How do people organize their daily lives? What do people do for fun? What kind of food do you eat; where does it come from? Where do your clothes and other necessities come from? How do you feel about the future, your children's future?

This is my vision: The overwhelming first impression is a feeling of peace and exhilaration. Doubt, worry, and fear related to the economy are gone because the work I do is valued by my community. Here, work is a true expression of who we are. Class, race, sex, and sexual preference are non issues. Diversity among people is honored. Elders and children are also honored.

People work hard producing most of the things we use in our daily lives (e.g., food, clothing, housing, infrastructure, and communications) and on developing and maintaining relationships with other communities and regions. We trade and otherwise engage in exchange with other communities, regions, and nations. We continue to restore the environment from the ravages of past exploitation and research ways of providing for our human needs that don't further stress the Earth.

Storytellers, historians, healers of all types, mystics and philosophers, artists, musicians, and teachers are respected by the community for their unique contributions—which translates into material support. Federal currency is used when necessary (especially for trade outside the region); barter networks, work exchange, local currencies and trust predominate.

Manufacturing does take place, trees are cut and natural resources are utilized. But since we no longer define ourselves by our possessions, we consume less. Most of us have come to see natural resources as gifts rather than commodities, which has dramatically changed our relationship with nature. One of the unexpected benefits of this change is a new partnership between human and nonhuman species, an evolution that occurred so gradually it was hardly noticeable at first. Now, whether we are working in the garden or walking in the woods, we are able to communicate in various ways with all of nature. This has opened our hearts in such an amazing fashion that our lives are permeated with joy and awe—the most wonderous gift of all.

Your vision may be different from mine. No matter. I've talked with enough people to trust that regardless of the details, the essence (or energy) of the vision usually is based on a foundation of common values, including cooperation, trust, compassion, healing, equity, balance, and respect—the values necessary to bring about an economy as if the Earth really mattered.

This section looks at some of the strategies, processes, and models that offer an alternative to "business—and living—as usual." I propose a community- and regionally based grassroots approach to economic development that requires integration, cooperation and synthesis. It necessitates bringing together all constitutiencies—right from the beginning—to discuss problems and approaches. It is site-specific: What works for one community may not work for another. But there are tools, models, and strategies that can be employed and changed as needed to suit specific needs.

Ideally, the time to begin developing community-based economies is before disaster strikes. If we wait until the major employer in town moves to greener pastures, or downsizes, we start in a place of panic and fear. When many fear for their economic security, it is harder to see the possibilities in smaller-scale, grassroots approaches to economic development.

Putting the difficulties aside for a moment, there are advantages to be had by engaging in a community-based development process (aside from working toward that long-term vision). On the practical side, we shorten the feedback loops. Feedback—information on how we're doing—needs to be incorporated at all levels of decision making, from the family to the national and global. Unfortunately, today's feedback loops are so large the negative impacts of decisions often aren't discovered (or heeded if they are discovered) until it is too late, or almost too late. This a major reason why today's trend toward "global management" of ecosystems, economies, and politics is so dangerous: It limits or prohibits the input of indigenous peoples, local communities, regions and even nations, thereby cutting off the greatest source of feedback on how their management is doing.

On the other hand, when decisions are made locally, any negative repercussions will be felt and noticed sooner, enabling people to make changes before collapse occurs, a process that applies to economic and social systems as well as to ecosystems. Since all systems are connected, negative environmental feedback effects economic and social decisions, and so on.

The time has come to do it ourselves. During the past several years, people in cities and rural areas alike have developed models for creating some aspects of a community-based, bioregional economy. We have learned a lot, and there are success stories. We still have much to discover, not the least of which is how the principles and models can be integrated into a community in such a way that the community as a whole is transformed. *The direction we take, beginning at this moment, is up to us.*

What would it take to make our visions real? John Seed believes it will take a miracle, albeit a simple one:

> All that it would need would be for human beings to wake up one day different than they were the day before and realizing that this is the end unless we make these changes, and then deciding to make the change. That doesn't seem like a very likely thing to happen, but on the other hand the whole road that we've traveled is so littered with miracles that it's only our strange kind of modern psyche that refuses to see it.

This sentiment might send some into despair. To me it offers a strong ray of hope, because miracles—or what we perceive as miracles—happen every day. During the hard times after my sister's accident, I learned that miracles are born of hard work. They don't just happen; and even if they appear to, when you think about it, and look back at events preceding the miracle, you will see a chain of events involving struggle, belief in possibilities against all odds, and commitment to doing whatever it takes to change things. These events incorporate action, reflection, prayer, hope, and gratitude for progress, however small and tentative, not to mention or disregard the inevitable moments of anger and despair.

So it's not a matter of sitting back and hoping humans wake up some morning different than we were the night before. It's understanding where we are and holding a strong vision of where we want to go, implementing strategies and creating transitional structures and processes that can help us get there. It's reaching out, working together, educating, supporting, making mistakes and starting over. It's building coalitions, strengthening relationships, opening to possibilities and partnerships of all kinds.

This part of the book offers examples of transitional structures and processes that can help us bring about a world not dominated by greed, consumption, competition, or exploitation. Some of these strategies work in partnership with existing institutions or take advantage of current legal structures, others do not. All have the potential to bring about positive change if we are willing to take one step at a time, take risks and enter uncharted territory with an open heart and mind. Making a miracle is hard work, but also fun and most certainly exciting. The choice is ours!

EIGHT

Economics of Community

Building Strong Economies from the Bottom Up

B ACK IN 1967, C. George Benello, a visionary and activist in the area of creating democratic workplaces, wrote

> To effect significant change nothing less than a different dynamic and motive system must be created, and so the requirement of building anew is an imperative one....In the end, it is a philosophy of the person and of human possibility that is in question. [We] must confront the organized power of dehumanization that has grown so tremendously in this century and created the wasteland culture we see around us....It is not enough to be...committed to the right philosophy. One must act.*

The workplace is even more dehumanizing today than that it was in 1967, and industry is becoming more mechanized, requiring fewer workers. Combined with Third World flight (corporations relocating production facilities in countries with few if any environmental regulations and a cheap labor force), these factors have resulted in sixteen million jobless people in the United States in 1991 and what has been called

---

*From "Wasteland Culture: Notes on Structures and Restructuring for Change," published in *Our Generation*, Vol. 5, No. 2. 1967.

the "pauperization of work." More of us are living in poverty than ever before, and young people feel disheartened and discouraged about their futures.

Communities around the world are seeking solutions to our economic, social, and environmental ills. Worker ownership and various other models of democratically managed businesses are growing in number and are providing their worker-owners with job security as well as creative and rewarding work.

We are challenged to create alternatives on a scale that feels hopeful and realistic to workers and that are, in Benello's words, "humanized and democratic in structure but not utopian in the sense of demanding heroic measures of their members, such as rejection of private property, total equalization of income or a zero-profit orientation." While many activists embrace these values, they are a hard-sell to most workers and business people.

In order to face these challenges, we must shatter some myths about the best way to do business and even redefine our definition of work. In the United States we tend to think each business must be complete in and of itself. It needs to include designers, producers, marketers, public-relations people—the whole bit. Large corporations take this concept even further by owning or controlling not only the processes of production and distribution but the sources for raw materials as well.

Economic-development professionals generally think in terms of large businesses, which employ two hundred or more people, when examining ways to improve a region's economy and provide more jobs. Reality disputes this conventional wisdom, since small businesses create more jobs than do large corporations. Smaller businesses may actually be better financial bets in today's economy than large companies. In Vermont, for example, large corporations such as GE and IBM have downsized or restructured hundreds of people out of jobs in the past few years. Since manufacturing jobs are higher paying than jobs in other sectors, laying off hundreds of workers in a rural state such as Vermont is a double blow to our economy with a dangerous ripple effect. It appears that smaller businesses are more stable in the long run. It makes sense, then, to turn to smaller, more stable manufacturing companies. The question is, How?

Community-Based Planning for Economic Development

Rocky Mountain Institute's Economic Renewal Project is an organization founded by Amory and Hunter Lovins in 1982. The institute has two overarching themes, resource efficiency and real security. The Rocky Mountain Institute (RMI) believes that security cannot be provided by the Pentagon from the top down, but must be created from the bottom up. They argue that people feel secure to the extent that their basic needs are met and to the extent that they live in a sustainable economy under a legitimate government.

The Economic Renewal Project is a practical program designed to address real community needs, build the economy from the bottom up, and thereby create real security. The staff of RMI facilitates this process in local communities, but their goal is to help each community take charge of its own economic destiny. The program's Four Principles of Economic Renewal are

Plugging the Leaks. A healthy economy is one in which money circulates within the community rather than being poured out. The Project helps community members examine how and why money leaves and then begin to explore to what extent they can provide more of their needs themselves. Although commerce from outside a community provides a variety of products and services that add substantially to the quality and vitality of our lives, there is no doubt that local communities can provide for more of their necessities. RMI states,

> In every town, many goods and services which are purchased out of town are, or could be, produced and/or marketed locally. Such greater self-reliance means more than saving money. Without a strong local economy, there is little basis for strong regional, and ultimately national, commerce. In this sense, a lasting recovery on Wall Street must begin on Main Street.

RMI's research indicates that the amount of money a typical town spends on energy purchased from outside is equivalent to the payroll of 10 percent of its population! For example, Osage, Iowa, (population 3,800) created the equivalent of sixty new jobs by implementing a variety of energy-efficiency programs. $1.2 million that leaked out of the community to pay energy bills each year now stays in people's pockets and generates more local wealth.

Support existing business. Invest in yourself! Most new jobs are created by small businesses, not large industries. Encouraging existing businesses to run more efficiently and to expand provides a stronger, more sustainable foundation for healthy economies. As RMI says, "A program of supporting a community's existing economic base flows logically from our first objective. Once you identify the items now purchased outside of town which could be produced locally, community businesses can move to fill those market opportunities." In Lane County, Oregon, a program called Oregon Marketplace helps local firms obtain contracts previously awarded to out-of-state firms. In its first year, nearly one hundred new jobs, over $2 million in local contracts, and more than $1.5 million in capital investments were created.

Encourage new enterprise. As some businesses die and others emerge, communities can encourage new firms that build on local strengths (e.g., the existing labor force, infrastructure, and resources). For example, apple growers can process their apples into juice and sauce locally, rather than shipping them elsewhere, and businesses can turn recycled materials into locally useful products. These sorts of choices provide jobs and much-needed capital and also make it unnecessary for people to import substitutes. For example, in Delta County, Colorado, a local community-development corporation (CDC) helped start a business that uses waste paper and local coal to make "heat bricks," a heating fuel half the price of firewood. The same CDC helped set up a mill that processes alfalfa and hay into pellets, thereby making it possible for local farmers to make money while putting fallow land back into production.

Recruit compatible business. Select particular industries that will build on underutilized resources and meet needs not being met by existing businesses. New enterprises can bring in more capital, technical expertise, the economies of scale, and participation in national and international networks. If these complement local resources, the new company will help revitalize the economy.

It is essential that community members ask themselves many questions before inviting new industries to locate in their town. They must sort out future goals for the community and be sure new arrivals advance these goals. Will the new company bring in its own employees? Will it utilize community resources only to export its profits? What of air and water pollution? What are the chances that the industry will pack up and leave after it has taken maximum advantage of community members and resources? RMI advocates a cautious approach to the recruitment of new business and industry, believing that by targeting the most promising and appropriate businesses, communities will be able to make best use of resources and time.

A community that has plugged its leaks won't be as desperate to settle for just any economic activity, regardless of whether it fits local conditions. With a vibrant economy, a community can be an attractive place for businesses to locate, without the need for expensive inducements. Responsible industry also feels more confident moving to a community where values and goals are clearly stated, and where the public and private sectors act together to achieve those goals.

Economic renewal is most effective when all sectors of the community participate. The point of the project is for community residents themselves to determine how they want their community to grow and develop. The Economic Renewal Project helps community residents, who may have no knowledge of how to proceed, analyze their economy and develop their own solutions to its problems. This process is less expensive than traditional consulting, and it gives community members real ownership of the results. RMI's process is both educational and action oriented; it leaves people with a much better idea of the workings of their economy.

What follows is a description of one form the process can take. RMI offers training seminars for local leaders, citizens, and planning professionals preparing to conduct the Economic Renewal Process in their communities. RMI also offers several publications that can help.

Mobilize the Community. Local stakeholders are recruited to participate in an orientation session that informs them and inspires their active participation in the community's strategic-planning process. These people then recruit friends and allies to participate in the second step.

If the community is so deeply divided that constructive dialog is impossible, RMI recommends bringing in a mediator—a respected person who is not on either side of the controversy—before moving on. This could even be someone from outside the community. The purpose is to rebuild respect and communication.

Envision the community's future. The visioning session follows plenty of fanfare—posters, newspaper stories, talk around town—that brings out as many people as possible. Because most people want to get on with it, the Economic Renewal Project develops, in one meeting, a rough picture of what residents perceive as their preferred future.

Identify what you have to work with. Before deciding what to do to work toward your preferred future, you need a clear picture of what you have to work with. The local economy is divided into several areas, such as access to capital, business environment, infrastructure, human resources, natural resources, and quality of life. Subgroups are formed, and citizens pick a group to work with. Economic Renewal offers workbooks with a descriptive summary of each area and questions each subgroup asks, along with worksheets that help them to identify problems, needs, assets, and windows of opportunity. Local experts should be encouraged to join subgroups in areas of their expertise. If technical professionals are brought in, RMI cautions that they remain advisers only. Local people must remain in the driver's seat.

Discover community economic opportunities. In their subgroups, participants explore local opportunities by identifying how local problems and needs might be served by assets and opportunities that were listed in the previous step. Segments of prior meetings include subgroup reports to the whole, so that everyone can see the bigger picture. Again, RMI offers workbooks to help with this step.

Generate project ideas, using what you have learned. Participants brainstorm project ideas that their community might pursue.

Evaluate and select project ideas. Ideas are evaluated for their practicality, sustainability, consistency with the community's vision, and potential for opposition.

Develop projects. This is the hard part. The publication *Financing Economic Renewal Projects* (from RMI) can help the community think through how to secure funding for its projects. Think, too, about models presented in this book: revolving-loan funds, socially concerned investors and their networks, alternative ways of structuring business and land ownership that can lower costs and spread risk, and developing a form of community currency. Contact people involved in related work elsewhere; find out how they raise their funds. Check out national and state community-development programs and grants, and look into innovative forms of public/private partnerships.

The Economic Renewal Project has a revolving-door policy, meaning that participants may leave or enter the process at any point. People are able to commit to what feels comfortable, knowing it is acceptable to leave as well as to become involved later in the process.

Much of the important work is conducted in the subgroups. By working in these small groups, participants develop a real understanding of how the local economy is affected by their chosen resource areas. They read case studies with an eye toward finding examples that might work in their particular town, they design new programs to fit unique community needs, and they consider such factors as costs, leakage, labor, finance, and local businesses. The process is not easy, and can require much resolution of old disputes and bridging of factions in a community.

A pilot project in Carbondale, Colorado, made the following progress:

- a business-support team to provide advice and a resource library in an effort to keep existing businesses viable;
- a public/private business incentive program to invest in potential new businesses;
- a farmers' market;
- a buy-local campaign;
- low-cost bank loans for energy-efficiency projects;
- an up-to-date and widely distributed list of local health resources; and
- research on a newspaper recycling project.

Associated benefits include

- A public/private rapid assistance team, formed to respond to new business inquiries, scored its first victory a new coffee-processing plant.

- The local Chamber of Commerce increased its membership fourfold after hiring its first full-time director.

- Former adversaries now work together on programs of mutual benefit. For example, although the farmers' market was organized by newcomers, they integrated it into the annual harvest celebration, a tradition of the old-timers.

- The local grocer began to distinctively label and sell locally grown produce.

- People began moving their savings from large city banks into the local bank, despite the loss of one-half point of interest.

RMI is quick to point out that any success is due to the community members' commitment and action. But the Project does provide a flexible outline for community members to fill in according to local conditions and their own preferences. Moreover, the outline builds on success; one success generates others. And the analysis and project development skills the community develops will continue to safeguard the vitality of the community.

In the words of Bob Weiss, director of New Employment for Women, Inc., in Lincoln City, West Virginia, "Everyone talks about what Lincoln County doesn't have, but the [Economic Renewal] workshops helped us appreciate what we do have and helped us find ways to build on our strengths."

Michael Kinsley, director of the Economic Renewal Program, stresses in his article "Development Does Not Equal Growth" (*Pacific Mountain Review* (volume XI, no. 1, 1993), that:

> Though a sound economy requires development, that is, vigorous business activity, it doesn't require growth, that is, increased community size. A community might be compared to a human being. Human growth after maturity is cancer. When a town continues to grow after maturity, its cancer is manifest in many ways—environmental degradation, spiteful controversy, and loss of a sense of community.
>
> But *development* is very different from growth. After reaching physical maturity, we humans can continue to develop in many beneficial ways—learning new skills, gaining deeper wisdom, and much more. Similarly, a community can develop itself without growth. It can create housing and jobs, expand cultural and educational opportunities, improve health, and protect the public safety.

Flexible Manufacturing Networks

Flexible Manufacturing Networks (FMNs) have the potential to address a number of the problems related to work outlined in the introduction to this section. Essentially, an FMN is a group of small (sometimes very small) businesses that come together to create a product none of them could manufacture on their own. A business could potentially be a member of many networks at once, making a diversity of products. An FMN doesn't last forever. Businesses join to manufacture a specific product, and when the job is done, the network dissolves.

Here in the United States, ACEnet (Appalachian Center for Economic Networks) in Athens, Ohio, is on the cutting edge of FMN development. The organization was founded in 1985 as the Worker-Owned Network (WON) to revitalize the economy of Appalachian Ohio and help lower-income people create worker-owned cooperatives. WON grew out of a discussion group started by five women, including the organization's current co-director, June Holley. As June tells the story, "We knew nothing about economics, but we wanted to understand what we could do about the poverty in our area. So we came together to learn about economic justice. After a while we wanted to do something, so we started WON to create worker-owned businesses." This just goes to show that we don't have to be "experts" to bring about change! In 1991, WON became ACEnet to more accurately reflect their work, which includes a small-business incubator and the development of FMNs and the networks to support them.

When ACEnet co-directors June Holley and Roger Wilkins became interested in FMNs as a model for business and job creation in Ohio, they looked to Italy, where the concept has been incredibly successful. In Modena, a city in northern Italy, the number of firms increased from 4,000 in 1950 to 24,000 in 1985 because of FMNs. And the Emilia-Romagna region moved from seventeenth to second in per-capita income from 1970 to 1985. In this region, one in five workers is an owner, and fewer than 2 percent of the manufacturing firms employs more than fifty workers.

Examples of FMNs include a group of five firms in Northern Italy that produce robotic arms; Pro Audio in Denmark is an FMN of electronics manufacturers who produce high-end, custom sound studios; and in Capri, six hundred very small knitwear firms have shared Computer Assisted Deisgn systems on which they prepare sample designs and shared marketing to distribute their sweaters worldwide.

Regional Development Model

Today's technology makes FMNs a practical model for regional economic revitalization. Technological advances—particularly in information processing and dissemination—allow decentralized manufacturing systems to be just as efficient (maybe more so) than the centralized systems that used to be considered essential.

In rural areas, FMNs can link up several small businesses located apart from each other—even in distant communities. People don't have to commute long hours to a large factory, nor do communities need to extend tax breaks and other financial incentives to corporations looking for the best deal in their bid for a new site.

Holley and Wilkins discovered that no two networks are alike. Rather, FMNs are best understood as a *process*. What they all have in common is their use of networks to organize economic activity, to increase flexibility, and to gain a competitive advantage in the marketplace. Such networks have been described as "a set of on-going relationships among autonomous entities...characterized by a set of mostly unconscious rules of behavior." The rules include open sharing of information; a sense that network participants can collectively solve problems and create possibilities; an awareness that the problems may not have final solutions, requiring on-going invention instead; a sense of inclusiveness; and an appreciation of diversity.

Field of Potential

Since FMNs are comprised of many small firms working together, each has a larger pool of creativity from which to draw—what ACEnet calls the "field of potential." For example, the availability of this larger pool solves the problem of having to take on additional debt to produce more goods or new products. Rather than buying new equipment, a business locates another firm with the necessary means, and they find a way of working together.

Workers benefit from FMNs, even if their business isn't worker owned. From their conversations with workers in FMNs and with others involved in the process, Holley and Wilkens concluded that "because they have so many choices in the field of possibility, [workers] still feel like owners of firms." In the Emilia-Romagna region, for example, employees are encouraged to start their own businesses when they have gained enough necessary knowledge. In fact, one out of every three workers in this region starts a new firm each year.

Another important feature of FMNs is they are market-driven, and products are designed in close cooperation with the customer. FMNs create goods for what are called "niche" markets — specialty markets for a small, select group of consumers. FMNs establish direct connections with the intended customer and, because the networks are made up of a group of small firms, most of whom produce more than one product for more than one market, they are able to produce short-run, customized items profitably, with micro-innovations taking place easily between production runs, in a way that larger firms simply cannot match. Therefore, the product meets the customer's needs exactly, which translates into greater customer satisfaction and higher quality, longer-lasting goods.

Putting Ideas into Practice

To determine the viability of the FNM concept in this country, ACEnet initiated a pilot FMN in 1991. They created a for-profit subsidiary called Accessible Designs/Adjustable Systems (AD/AS), which brings together small manufacturing firms from an eleven-county area to produce accessible-housing components for the physically disabled and the elderly. This market niche requires a high level of innovation and customization with a ready market, thanks to the passage of the Americans with Disabilities Act and the Fair Housing Amendments. The network was capitalized mostly with low-interest loans from community supporters.

AD/AS has developed three products so far: an accessible, adjustable kitchen; a wall-mounted, manually adjustable, accessible desk or workstation designed for installation in colleges and universities; and a free-standing adjustable workstation for use in classrooms. About twenty small manufacturing firms have cooperated in the development of these products, including cabinetmakers, design firms, metalworkers, machine shops and electronics firms. Six firms are involved in production, and sales have already been made. Since the network includes cabinetmakers who are craft-oriented rather than production-oriented, the quality of the furniture is superior, with a simple, clean design. Plus, people with disabilities have been involved from the beginning to ensure that the products truly meet their needs.

FMNs as an Ecological Business Model

Of course, the FMN structure can't guarantee ecological integrity, which depends upon the individuals involved, as is true of most decentralized, community-based models. However, the FMN process, with its high degree of innovation and collaboration, lends itself naturally to an ecological perspective regarding problems associated with manufacturing processes, since businesses cooperate to solve problems creatively rather than compete with one another to produce the cheapest product first. (Personally, I would recommend that an FMN have a Standard of Environmental Conduct in writing to which participating businesses would adhere.)

Further, FMNs mimic living organisms. Each network (organism) is comprised of a diversity of businesses (cells). Each of these businesses contributes something vital to the well-being of the network as a whole. And when the network disbands because it has fulfilled its purpose, the individual businesses provide the basis—or nutrients—for future FMNs. Thus the integrity of the individual businesses as well as the larger economy of which they are a part is preserved, just as the natural process of death in an ecosystem makes it possible for the ecosystem to evolve and adapt to change over time. This is a much more natural process than what is practiced by most large businesses and corporations today which expand by taking on huge amounts of debt unsustainably. Expansion can also involve inappropriate development, resulting in environmental and social distress. Once the expansion has taken place, the corporation strives to maintain its size at any cost. Too often, the end result of inappropriate growth is the need to dramatically downsize, with its inevitable hardship for the community and the workers.

Encountering Obstacles

Not everyone is immediately supportive of FMNs. Among the biggest obstacles to network creation are the "bigger is better" and "centralization means efficiency" myths. Traditional businesses tend to expand rather than find ways of cooperating for the common good. Margaret Cheap, Executive Director of the National Cooperative Bank (NCB) Development Corporation, says she has been busy educating fund managers and bankers, including people in her own organization, about the potential of networks. "I usually refer to 'collaboration' rather than 'cooperation'," Cheap says, "since that's something business people know how to talk about." Because competition is seen as essential to success, the idea of cooperating seems counterproductive. "We're watching the evolution of the network concept with keen interest," Cheap notes. "From the point of view of cooperative formation, we're very excited about this trend."

Other obstacles involve traditional financial institutions which need to be educated about the advantages of more egalitarian structures and the FMN process. They simply don't have a way of evaluating such a foreign concept. They are used to loaning money to (or investing in) a single business, not a network of businesses. Another problem is that colleges and universities don't expose business students, lawyers, or accountants to economic alternatives. Consequently, they don't know how to deal with their unique attributes in real life.

ACEnet is tackling these problems in their region by creating the Economic Development Infrastructure (EDI), which consists of existing economic-development groups, banks, and other sources of capital as well as colleges and technical schools. ACEnet has facilitated several meetings to introduce the EDI to FMN strategy and enlist their support.

Because ACEnet is very concerned about economic and social justice for low-income women, people of color, and people with disabilities, they are initiating a process by which a new set of relationships are created in the community, linking FMN firms, nontraditional workers and their communities, and educational institutions. These groups work together to design a multilayered training system to prepare these nontraditional workers for FMN production jobs. ACEnet expects to generate two hundred fifty new jobs in the region by 1995 and a thousand more by 2000.

Successful Hybrids

The good news is businesses are collaborating in many ways to lessen the negative impacts of the current economic climate, although these networks don't necessarily look like pure FMNs (i.e., small businesses collectively producing something that none could otherwise manufacture on their own). Paul Summers, of the Northwest Center for Policy Studies at the University of Washington in Seattle, can rattle off a whole list of businesses around the country in the budding stages of networking, including woodworkers, high-tech firms, the metals industry, hosiery and textile manufactures, and electronics firms. Maine, New Jersey, California, North Carolina, Arkansas, and Washington all have networks, most of which Summers believes began "out of desperation rather than opportunity." Still, they represent the silver lining in the cloud of the depression.

My favorite example is the Food Works Culinary Center in Arcata, California. Cindy Copple, the Center's originator, along with the Arcata Economic Development Center (AEDC), describes Food Works as a "hybrid between FMNs and the incubator model." Their goal is to create a micro-industry to enable small producers to compete in the larger economy without having to grow beyond their means. AEDC constructed a 20,000-square-foot processing incubator. The building was completed in 1992 and houses twelve small businesses.

These companies—ranging in age from one to ten years—include makers of tofu, chocolate truffles, desserts, pasta, sauces, jams, smoked fish, condiments, and the like. They take advantage of economies of scale by jointly purchasing supplies such as jars and pallets. Distribution also is more efficient from the single location. A marketing association is being planned to be supported by dues; decisions will be made collectively by members. In addition, Food Works has a kitchen owned by AEDC that is rented on an hourly basis to tiny businesses just beginning to test the waters. A warehouse with freezer space is leased to businesses outside of the Center as well.

Copple, who has been active in the cooperative movement for years (she started the Arcata Food Co-op twenty years ago), believes that the stability of the economy depends on working with small businesses. "They are here [in our community] because they want to be and have a self-imposed integrity. Rolling out the red carpet to large industry is not the way to go." Yet, certain economies of scale must be achieved if these businesses are to survive in a today's national and international economy. Her vision towards this end is to create a micro-industry by supporting the businesses already in existence. According to Copple, many businesses grow to employ three or four people and get stuck there. Growing to about ten or so is ideal, she feels, especially when businesses join together in networks.

AD/AS is perhaps the most advanced FMN—in a pure sense—in the United States. However, it is obvious that small businesses are looking at various forms of collaboration and networking and adjusting the flexible concept to meet their own needs. As Cindy Copple told me, "We can learn from the relationships [of Italian FMNs], but we don't have the same situation here as in Italy." Therefore we will take what works for us and leave the rest behind.

Community Capital, Community Labor

How can we finance the activities and enterprises that we support in our communities? This section looks at some of the emerging models and strategies communities are using to raise the capital necessary to fund projects such as housing co-ops, small-business incubators, land trusts that keep housing costs affordable, and resident-owned and managed mobile home communities, to name a few. Of course it's tough. It often feels as though there just isn't enough money to go around. Fact is, there is plenty of money out there, it's a matter of changing our priorities and deciding to channel it in more sustainable directions.

If development processes such as that promoted by the Economic Renewal Program are to have the most impact, and flexible manufacturing networks (and other business-based models) are to fufill their community revitalization potential, support for community-based financial institutions must increase. Fortunately, in addition to community-based banks and credit unions, social-investing and social-venture networks, there are a number of extremely creative and exciting smaller-scale (community or neighborhood size) models that range from investor- and donor-supported revolving-loan funds to barter networks to community currencies—all of which help communities keep resources in the region and support the kinds of development community members desire.

Founded in 1967, the Institute for Community Economics (ICE) has become one of the most active and effective organizations working to enable low-income people to participate powerfully in the economic development of their communities. ICE is committed to working for the systemic changes necessary for self-reliance. Its deep belief is that residents of a community must be involved in economic development and be the primary beneficiaries of that development. Toward this end, it provides technical assistance to groups in community organizing, the acquisition of property, legal agreements, and financing. Advice on low-cost housing design, training in appropriate methods of construction, and low-cost skilled labor during the early stages of a project are also services of ICE.

ICE recognized early on that the main obstacle for low- and moderate-income people and organizations is the lack of capital. Without credit or a track record, they find it impossible to obtain financing from more traditional sources, such as banks, credit unions, or even partnerships with investors. Furthermore, high interest payments usually only undermine the success and potential social impact of grassroots projects.

To solve these problems, ICE began to work with two models, the community land trust (CLT) and the revolving-loan fund. The revolving-loan fund (RLF) model is perhaps ICE's best-known work. Their own fund was initiated in 1979 after years of working in community economic development and alternative financing. They saw a need for a bridge between investors and projects in need of capital and recognized that lack of capital often stalled or halted projects. Initially, their fund was established with no endowment, operating for its first three and one-half years entirely with loaned capital. (ICE is currently capitalized at over $11 million, with close to 400 investors supporting the fund.)

ICE's role in providing technical assistance to community groups means that they are skilled evaluators of borrowers, able to accurately assess their needs and capacities. Their excellent technical-assistance team works closely with borrowers, monitoring them and troubleshooting if needed. Their working relationship often extends through the entire loan period. The fund also serves as an intermediary between community groups and local lenders who wish to invest in their communities but do not want to manage loans and projects themselves.

In 1985, ICE sponsored the first National Conference of Community Development Loan Funds. The Conference grew out of ICE's providing technical assistance to community groups wishing to initiate local and regional revolving-loan funds like ICE's. Over thirty funds (those in operation and many in the planning stages) sent representatives, and out of this conference came the National Association of Community Development Loan Funds (NACDLF).

Although the funds support different types of community-development projects, they are all working to address the issue of poverty, the patterns of ownership and control (of housing, land, and business), and the inequitable distribution of capital in our communities. Member funds are committed to "responsible stewardship of investment resources and sound business management." At the end of 1993, there were forty-one member RLFs in the United States.

NACDLF places a high priority on the ability of member funds to leverage capital from new sources into disinvested communities. It also recognizes that poverty and economic disenfranchisement are social and political failings as much as they are economic ones. Therefore, NACDLF measures success not only by economic returns, but also by the extent to which its members help rebuild the civic infrastructure of businesses, voluntary organizations, social services, and housing so essential to community revitalization.

NACDLF has established standards to guide and evaluate the performance of member funds. The organization also conducts "loan fund assessments," rigorous and comprehensive reviews of individual fund's operations and lending. Detailed reports are provided to the reviewed fund along with specific recommendations for improvement. Peer Reviews are another tool by which member funds are evaluated. This process is the most comprehensive evaluation process offered and consists of an on-site consultation and complete financial and management assessment, as well as technical assistance, as needed, to facilitate improvement. In addition, NACDLF offers technical assistance, organizes an annual conference, and is in the process of developing computer software to manage loan funds (which will also be available to nonmembers).

Profiles

Revolving Loan Funds

The New Hampshire
Community Loan Fund (NHCLF)

P.O. Box 800, Concord, NH 03302, (603) 224–6669

The New Hampshire Community Loan Fund, founded in 1983, was the first RLF to be organized on the community loan fund model promoted by ICE. As a founding member of the National Association of Community Development Loan Funds, it has played a major role in shaping the national community-investment movement.

The Fund began with the premise that people are poor, in part, because they lack access to credit and that given the opportunity, people with capital would invest locally for the benefit of lower-income people. Building this bridge guides the Fund as it has since the early days when community-based housing efforts were practically nonexistent in New Hampshire. Since 1983, NHCLF has helped secure more than 1,100 units of affordable housing and has made 133 loans totaling $6.9 million, leveraging $23 million from other sources.

Because there were very few community-based nonprofit housing or community-development organizations in New Hampshire, few programs to support such organizations and very little public awareness of the issues, the Fund's first task was to educate the public, helping them to understand housing problems and introducing community-based solutions such as land trusts and coops.

The Fund's first project, which helped put it on the map, so to speak, was helping a group of mobile-home park residents prevent the loss of their park to a condominium developer. They were assisted in forming the state's first mobile-home park cooperative; then the Fund financed the coop's purchase of the park. Today, twenty-seven New Hampshire mobile-home parks are owned by resident cooperatives (more than in most larger states). Twenty have received financing from NHCLF. Many of the residential co-ops have had long, hard struggles before succeeding in purchasing their parks. For example, it took two years for the South Parrish Road Cooperative in rural Winchester. This fifty-nine–unit park had difficulty obtaining fixed-rate financing. Finally, the Vermont National Bank came through, while the Fund provided the $182,000 down payment. Co-op members put up $62,000 of their own equity. The co-op then began to make some important improvements—first upgrading the septic system, then replacing thirteen leach fields and upgrading old electrical systems. Ed Belisle, treasurer and founding member says, "We're bringing the park up to snuff. It's ours. It belongs to us."

NHCLF coordinates a network of the state's dozen developing and established community land trusts and has helped to nurture land trusts in a several communities. Monthly meetings and ongoing individual networking serve to foster cooperation and information sharing to groups working in isolation in the largely rural state. The Fund has also incubated several of these groups. Concord Area Trust for Community Housing (CATCH) was started with Fund assistance nearly five years ago. This group now provides more than fifty families in the capital city with affordable housing. Like the state's other groups, CATCH is committed to both long-term affordability and resident empowerment and cooperative ownership. In early 1993, CATCH finished construction of the state's first nonprofit housing development, now home to twenty-six low-income families, which is making the transition to cooperative ownership.

The Fund acts as both a responsive and a catalytic agent. For example in 1990, while recovering some properties in Manchester, the state's second largest city, NHCLF became the owner of two apartment buildings. To use this unexpected inheritance most effectively, the Fund consulted key service providers in the city. As a result, Families in Transition was developed to help families recover from homelessness. The need for this service is so great that the organization is becoming an expanded, separate, nonprofit agency serving the community. This new area of housing reaches an even further disenfranchised (and growing) group—homeless families with children.

One story illustrates how the combination of safe, secure housing and supportive services help families move from homelessness to self-sufficiency. Trish came to this transitional housing program from a shelter for battered women, where she was staying with her five-year-old son. After less than a year in the program, Trish graduated and moved into an apartment of her own. She remains active with the community of families at the transitional housing program, has a job as a VISTA volunteer with the New Hampshire Coalition for the Homeless and serves on the board of the Manchester Area Housing Trust.

In 1993, the Fund had $2.6 million in loan capital and is looking to double this amount by 1995. Loan terms as of mid-1993 (contact the Fund for the most updated information):

Loan amount: Minimum of $1,000 ($5,000 or more is helpful)

Interest rate: 0–2% for transitional housing loans; 0–4% for general loans.

Term: Minimum of one year (5–10 years is most helpful)

Impact: A $10,000 loan to the Fund provides the capital needed for 2–4 units of housing and credibility to leverage $30,000 from conventional sources.

Cascadia Revolving Fund

157 Yesler Way, Suite 414, Seattle, WA 98104, (206) 447–9226

Cascadia Revolving Fund (CRF), founded in 1985, is a community-based RLF supported by socially responsible investors. The more than $1 million loaned by CRF has all gone directly to grassroots business expansion and the creation of new jobs for fifty local (Pacific Northwest) organizations that embrace some aspect of the Fund's world vision—environmentally supportive technologies, individual and community empowerment, economic opportunities for women, minorities and the poor. All of Cascadia's borrowers offer services and products or uphold ideals that make an impact on both the community and, in turn, the world. For example, a loan to a Seattle-based women's publishing house helped finance the publication of a book on domestic abuse, which went on to become a bestseller with over 100,000 copies in print and four foreign editions. In the past three years, CRF has initiated three innovative projects that demonstrate the potential of RLFs: a Peer Lending program, a Rural Initiatives program, and a Pollution Preventing Lending program.

The Peer Lending program was initiated in cooperation with the Interim Community Development Association in Seattle, an organization that works to revitialize Seattle's International District. CRF's Peer program began with Southeast Asian refugees partly because their communities are based on mutual assistance, and so they readily understand and embrace the peer-lending concept. In mid-1993, a community grocery store, a food brokerage, a sewing business, and several farms are in the works, headed by Cascadia's first entrepreneurial training class. All members in this class are members of the Hmong or Khumu communities, formerly of Laos and now in King County. New classes start regularly, and both Cascadia and Interim are committed to following through with students who develop plans for businesses.

The Rural Initiatives program works in cooperation with the local economic-development committees in the city of Forks and in Clallam County to finance businesses in the distressed timber communities of Clallam County. Cascadia has also agreed to serve as the fiscal sponsor for a revolving-loan fund, initiated by Headwaters (an environmental organization) and the Rogue Institute for Ecology and Economy, that will benefit southwest Oregon's local communities and displaced timber workers.

The Pollution Prevention program makes loans to small businesses so they can buy equipment to reduce their production of toxins. The emphasis of this project is to eliminate or reduce toxins, not manage them once they are produced.

Loan projects include Rents Due Ranch, an organic farm, to buy the land to cultivate after they were forced from the land they previously leased; Port Townsend Shipwrights Cooperative, a worker-owned cooperative that builds and repairs wooden boats, to build an indoor dry dock; Professionals' Child Care Services, a minority-owned multiracial day-care center, for a construction loan to make the facility wheelchair accessible; Methow Valley Land Trust, to buy land to keep green in perpetuity for wildlife; and Elves and Angels, a rural quality wooden children's toy manufacturer, for working capital.

As of fall 1993, the Fund has $1,250,000 from 180 investors. Loans are screened by a loan review committee for financial viability. Technical assistance is arranged or required when necessary for success. Borrowers must reside in Washington or Oregon and meet the following criteria: produce essential, high-quality goods and services; create family wage jobs; promote ecological sustainability and regional self-reliance; support worker democracy, ownership and safety; be owned by low-income and minority persons; and spring from a vision of social and ethical values. Terms for lenders are negotiated individually. In general, the minimum investment is $500 for at least one year.

Self-Help Association for a Regional Economy (SHARE)

E. F. Schumacher SocietyBox 76A, RD 3, Great Barrington, MA 02139,

Self-Help Association for a Regional Economy (SHARE) is a loan collateralization program supporting small businesses in the Berkshires that are socially and ecologically sustainable. The program works in cooperation with a local bank to provide low-interest loans to individuals and small businesses that meet the following criteria:

> Businesses must be from the region. To the extent possible, they must use local materials and employ local people to produce goods to sell to a local market.

> The goods/services offered must be needed by the regional community. Priority is given to businesses producing food, clothing, shelter, and alternative energy and providing health and transportation services.

> Businesses must use appropriate-scale technology and must not be environmentally damaging.

> Businesses must have responsible relationships with workers and with the community. Priority is given to cooperatives and businesses with a high degree of worker participation.

> Financial criteria include a sound business plan that demonstrates the capacity to repay the loan, good bookkeeping methods, and the inability to qualify for a traditional bank loan.

Loans up to $3,000 are made from SHARE's credit fund. People join the credit fund by opening a ninety-day-notice account and designating it a SHARE account. The depositor agrees that SHARE may use up to 75 percent of the balance as collateral for loans made from the credit fund.

The bank makes the actual loans, based on the decisions of SHARE's directors, and collects the payments. Because the loans are fully collateralized, the bank can make them at rates well below the prime. In line with its basic beliefs, SHARE supports cottage industries, small farmers, and very small businesses. Since SHARE is really a community-based project, its activities include more than simply making loans. SHARE members work together to support the businesses they have decided to back with their accounts. Their support includes word-of-mouth marketing to friends and acquaintances, asking store owners to stock SHARE businesses' products, and moral support. Members receive a monthly newsletter that keeps them informed about SHARE's activities and how businesses are doing.

Recipients of SHARE loans include:

Jim Golden, to build a barn for his two draft horses. (Many farmers prefer draft horses to tractors since they do not damage the land and they can go places big machines cannot.)

Sue and Wayne Sellew, to enable them to upgrade their cheesemaking equipment to meet state guidelines. Although their goat cheese, Monterey Chevre, is excellent, their lack of credit history made a traditional loan difficult.

Kites of Four Winds, so that owners Nick and Sallie Van Sant could take advantage of a 50 percent markdown on fabric offered when a major fabric maker closed. The business nearly doubled profit rates because of the low-cost fabric and paid back the loan in six months.

Bonnie Nordoff, who knits specialty clothing at home. Her first SHARE loan established credit with a wholesaler, while the second upgraded her knitting machine. When she needed a third loan, she was able to receive a traditional bank loan thanks to her credit history with SHARE.

A local Community-Supported Agriculture (CSA), a group of consumers who have banded together to employ one full-time gardener and several part-time helpers to produce biodynamically grown vegetables.

Support within the community has grown consistently over the years, creating a much greater awareness of "what's here and what's not here" as well as discussions about "what kinds of businesses do we want to support?" SHARE is an excellent way to bring community members into the process of choosing their future. And the $100 minimum deposit (subsequent deposits can be for any amount) ensures that virtually anyone in the community can participate.

SHARE is committed to helping other communities develop similar projects. It will furnish a packet of information and legal documents for $10 to those interested in similar projects in their regions.

Working Capital

ICCD, 2500 North River Road, Manchester, NH 03104, (603) 644–3124.

Working Capital, a nonprofit community loan fund, works with community organizations to provide loans to small-business owners in New England. The loans are initially small ($500 or so), however, after the first loan is repaid, loans can increase up to $5,000.

Working Capital has trained twelve organizations in New Hampshire, Massachusetts, and Vermont to run its program in local communities, assuring easy access for business people and local control. Capital for loans is provided by the Meredith Village Savings Bank, Fleet Bank, and the Vermont National Bank's Socially Responsible Banking Fund.

All borrowers must join a business loan group consisting of other "self-employed peers" who are responsible for reviewing and approving loans for each other and making sure the loans are repaid. Members can only apply for larger loans if all group members are up-to-date on their payments.

Although Working Capital is relatively new (since late 1990), it already has an excellent track record. More important, it has made a real difference in the lives of many people. Sample loans include $1,000 to the owner of a cab company in Bellows Falls, Vermont, to purchase a used cab and for auto insurance; $500 to a woman who grows jalapeño peppers in Burlington, Vermont, to develop a logo and label and purchase supplies; $500 to an individual in Massachusetts, who provides word-processing and typing services, for a printer and software.

These kinds of small, unsecured loans are essential to small business persons who need a boost via advertising or additional supplies and especially for single mothers who want to start or expand a home-based business. Working Capital plays a key role in creating sustainable, locally controlled communities.

Unlike the other RLFs described in these pages, Working Capital does not accept direct loans from social investors. However, funds can be deposited in Vermont National Bank's Socially Responsible Banking Fund and targeted toward Working Capital.

Currencies, barter/work exchange

Community Currency

Money was created as a more convenient means of exchange when barter proved inefficient. In those early days, money was itself either a commodity (e.g., iron nails in Scotland, dried cod in Newfoundland, sugar in some West Indies islands, salt in ancient Rome, and corn in Massachusetts in the 1600s), or it was backed by a commodity valued by society. For example, the first Latin coins were stamped with the image of a cow and could be redeemed for cattle. In the 1700s, paper money was invented and backed by gold and silver. These gold and silver standards were abandoned in the 1900s, so today our money is backed by nothing but promises. Even this promised value of our money falls each year, and, in hard economic times, there are fewer dollars to go around—or so it seems.

Jane Jacobs, economist and author of *Cities and the Wealth of Nations* (Random House, 1984) sees the economy of a region as a living entity, and sees regional currency as an appropriate regulator of its life. She writes, "Currencies are powerful carriers of feedback information, and potent triggers of adjustments, but on their own terms. A national currency registers, above all, consolidated information on a nation's international trade."

The feedback information a national currency provides to local communities isn't very helpful in understanding local/regional economic conditions. It wouldn't be accurate to say the information isn't relevant because local economies are a part of the national/international picture, however, it isn't specific enough to translate into meaningful actions on the local/regional level.

Community currency is a tool that can help revitalize local economies by encouraging wealth to stay within a commuity rather than flowing out. It provides valuable information about the community's balance of trade. For example, if a currency is valued only in a certain region, then it cannot be used for goods or services from outside that region (unless the recipient agrees to spend the currency in the region of origin). And local currencies are backed by something tangible that the community agrees has value, as illustrated by the following examples.

Community-based currency isn't new. During the Great Depression, some towns printed scrip that was exchanged for goods and services when federal dollars were scarce. In fact, it wasn't until 1913 that the Federal Reserve Act mandated a central banking system. Before that Act, currency in the United States was based on everything from lumber to land. Today, however, the idea of community currency is novel. Yet more and more towns across the country are developing some version of a community currency for the same reason scrip was used during the Depression. The E. F. Schumacher Society, based in Great Barrington, Massachusetts, which has been at the forefront of community-based economics since it was founded in 1980 to promote the work of E. F. Schumacher (author of *Small is Beautiful*), has been researching and developing practical ways of introducing community currencies for several years.

In 1990, a unique opportunity presented itself. A local deli, well loved by many people in Great Barrington, had to change its location because its lease was running out and a new lease would double the rent. Frank, the owner of the deli, went to several banks to borrow money to move to another location and was turned down. Finally he approached SHARE, the Schumacher Society's loan-collaterialization program. To Frank's surprise, Susan Witt, SHARE's administrator, suggested that he issue his own currency—Deli Dollars—and sell them to his customers to raise the money he needed to renovate the new location. Each note sold for $9 and could buy $10 worth of food, as long as customers waited six months to redeem it.

"I put five hundred notes on sale, and they went in a flash. It was astonishing," Frank says. Before long, Deli Dollars were turning up all over town as people exchanged them instead of federal dollars for goods, services, or debts. In effect these paper notes, which were essentially nothing more than small, short-term loans from customers, became a community currency. They so excited the people of Great Barrington that they were followed by Farm Preserve Notes issued cooperatively by two farms, Taft Farms and the Corn Crib. In this case, because there were two farms involved, SHARE acted as a clearinghouse to equalize the redemption, rather than the farmers working it out. Each farm raised about $3,500 the first year, and the farms reissued notes in 1993. The Monterey General Store and Kintaro (a new Japanese restaurant and sushi bar) have also issued their own script. Together, these businesses raised between $15,000 and $20,000 dollars in two years.

Scrip is a low-cost way to finance a local business. Susan Witt states, "These days, a lot of banks won't touch some of these small loans. They just don't have the money to do it. But if the community is committed to a place, it ought to be able to invest in its future by promising to shop there. The plan also helps us keep our money in our community."

Another innovative project the Schumacher folks initiated is Berkshares, a program that involves local merchants in Great Barrington. For every $10 of purchases customers make at participating stores, they receive one Berkshare, worth $1, which can be redeemed, dollar for dollar for up to half the cost of merchandise. This program was initiated in September, 1992, and was repeated in 1993.

In Mandan and Bismarck, North Dakota, local banks and participating merchants came together to offer zero-percent interest holiday loans up to $1500 with nine months to repay. Participating merchants pay a one-time advertising fee of $50 and borrowers pay a $10 processing fee. This program offers advantages to the customer (increased buying power and no high interest payments for charge card purchases), to the merchant (increased local purchasing power, inexpensive holiday promotion, returning customers, higher volume of business), and to the bank (opportunity to increase good will). While not a community currency, these local loans do keep money in the local community.

Inspired by these programs in North Dakota, the E. F. Schumacher Society has proposed a similar loan program for Great Barrington, only instead of issuing federal dollars, borrowers will receive Berkshares in denominations of 10s, 20s and 50s which must be used by December 25. Merchants will redeem the Berkshares by December 31 for a bank check in the amount of the Berkshares minus a 3% exchange fee.

Finally, in Montpelier, Vermont local merchants issued Flood Bucks after the March, 1992, flood that devastated many local businesses in the downtown area. Customers purchased the Flood Bucks to be used later, like a gift certificate, at any participating store.

Susan Witt sees these programs as part of a larger strategy to strengthen regional economies.

> Basically, we're looking to find the way in which wealth generated in the region can be kept in the region. Our local banks which did a very good

job of that in the past, have now been bought up by larger and larger holding companies. So the deposits, the earnings generated in rural regions and inner cities, become like the wealth generated in Third World areas: It tends to all flow out into a few central, international, urban centers.

A regional currency is ultimately the way that communities can regain independence and begin to unplug from the federal system: to take back their rights to generate their own regional currencies. As our area of Great Barrington gets used to exchanging Berkshire Farm Preserve Notes and Deli Dollars, we hope it will be the beginning of a true, independent, regional currency that's broadly circulated.

According to E. F. Schumacher, "Production from local resources for local needs is the most rational way of economic life, while dependence on imports from afar and the consequent need to produce for export to unknown and distant people is highly uneconomic and justifiable only in exceptional cases and on a small scale." Over time, regional currencies will inevitably lead to more regional production.

These are hard times, and there are no easy answers. But one thing is certain: There will be no magic solution trickling down from our centralized government. The vision, and the energy to realize it, resides within each of us, in our communites. Regional currencies, in whatever form, are an exciting and necessary tool.

Barter/Work exchange

We are all familiar with the often strident cry for Jobs, Jobs, Jobs. For most people, "economic development" should translate into more and better paying jobs than before. There are some important issues to examine, though, before jumping on the jobs bandwagon. According to the United Nations' Development Programme (UNDP), from 1975 to 1990 Gross World Product (GWP) increased by 20% while per-capita employment dropped by 1.2%. Further, UNDP projects that the ratio of jobs to GWP will continue to drop in the future. This means that increased consumption, leading to increased production, no longer leads to more jobs—contrary to popular wisdom and contrary to what governments and corporations tell us.

Robert Gilman, editor and publisher of *In Context*, sees four basic responses to our current (and future) unemployment crisis. The first is to continue to create make-work jobs, which he feels is "fundamentally destructive" and a "waste of lives and...the environment." The second response is to adopt a Social Darwinist approach and "let the unemployed starve." As crass as this sounds, our present treatment of the homeless and, in the not-so-distant future, of people on welfare strongly reeks of this approach. The third response is to adopt a welfare approach in which the employed are taxed to provide an income to the unemployed. Given the current controversy over welfare, this would not be a popular strategy. Finally Gilman proposes a "new ethic," which I feel deserves careful consideration. He suggests that people presently employed work less to provide more jobs for the unemployed. Of course people would have to be paid a decent wage. Someone working a full week for the minimum wage or slightly higher could not afford to work less.

J. W. Smith, author of *World's Wasted Wealth 2: Save Our Wealth, Save Our Environment*, has spent the past forty years trying to understand why industrialized societies are on a "treadmill, seeming to produce more and more but gaining little, and at times even regressing in overall standards of living [while] the rest of the world also seems to be on a permanent treadmill, one of poverty." Essentially what happens is each gain in industrial efficiency leads to increased production, increased wealth for the owners of production, and fewer jobs for workers. (I should note here that increased production also leads to using more resources and increased production of waste.)

It is not the scope of this book to go into all the implications of getting rid of unnecessary jobs and working less. Basically, I believe we'd see fewer unemployed people, less waste (both of money and resources), and, perhaps most important, less-stressed, happier, and more fulfilled people. We'd have more time for our families and to be active, fully participating citizens, and we'd be able to focus on activities that really interest us. I've often felt that we make things so impossibly hard for ourselves. Most of us have, at the very least, toyed with the idea of getting off the treadmill and living a simpler life. Those who have done this are almost always thrilled they did. By rethinking our current notions of jobs and work, we could help move our whole society to a simpler, richer life. It goes without saying this would greatly benefit other societies, cultures, and the Earth as well.

Profile

Local Energy, Electric Currency

by Joel Russ

As a rule, environmentally conscious people living in rural places reduce their dependency on currency to a minimum. However, the need for some remains. Yet this need for currency probably isn't entirely a need for the federally issued "coin of the realm" of whichever nation-state we find ourselves in. In part, it is a need for some common medium with which to make exchanges with others in the neighborhood or community.

There are, of course, noncurrency modes valuable to local economy; even the most cursory study of traditional primal and peasant economic systems brings to light age-old practices such as household production (e.g., growing a vegetable garden or playing music to provide free entertainment for your family) and mutual aid (e.g., helping your neighbor build a fence or looking after your friend's kids).

Mutual aid refers to those valuable things we do simply to assist our friends, neighbors, or relatives without expecting money in return. Barter works on a similar principle but is more explicit, having a bit more of an eye toward ensuring an equitable trade within an understood (usually near-term) time frame. The problem with either barter or mutual aid in its more trusting, altruistic form is that there are usually limits to the skills, knowledge, products, and available time of our close friends and immediate neighbors. Hence, even when what we need can be supplied within the broad local community, we often must rely on monetized exchanges, ones involving currency.

A friend of mine and cofounder of our local LETSystem, Gregoire Lamoureux, has made the observation that a problem with conventional money is that (as part of the vast international market system) it tends to flow to where it makes the most money—usually to the biggest cities, the trade and industrial centers, a good share of it finally coursing into and through the bank accounts of very wealthy weapons and oil peddlers. Such, after all, is the immense scope of The System. But most of us live closer to the other end of the scale, and we voluntary simplicitists can often feel we have too little money for our needs.

Since 1972, I've spent all but a couple of years living in the Slocan, a 67-mile-long valley in the northern drainages of the Columbia River system. We are situated remotely, amid the southern Selkirk Mountains, in southeastern British Columbia. About a year ago, a group in my part (the south) of the Slocan Valley decided to try a new money system—one that is local, theft-proof, and low-cost in terms of federal currency investment. What was needed was a credit system that could enable us to exchange goods and services among a large number of people living within a geographic area about thirty miles long. The Local Employment Trading System (LETS or LETSystem) offers such a means, being one of the latest manifestations of the local-currency idea often advocated as a way to strengthen communities.

Born in British Colombia's Comox Valley in 1983, LETS has spread around the world and is in use, we understand, in close to one hundred communities. We've heard that in Australia alone there are over fifty LETSystems, the largest having five hundred members. It is said that in Ontario, Canada, there are seven functioning LETSystems. The original in the Comox Valley suspended operation for a while, though we've heard it is being reorganized.

Michael Linton, a computer programmer in Courtenay, British Colombia, developed software for an exchange system whose essence has been understood by many people. Linton's LETSystem uses the software to record credits for transactions between individuals. In terms of flexibility, the credits resemble a money system, LETS offering advantages over common one-to-one barter. Barter between two people, which has probably been around about as long as human societies have existed, is still useful in many cases. But because a LETSystem includes many people with varied goods and services to offer, transactions aren't limited in the way that direct barter is.

Here's an example of how LETS transactions work: Tambray sells carrots to Tika for 40 credits, and Tika phones in the transaction to the LETS answering machine. Tambray's 40 credits are added to her account in the LETS computer data files, while Tika's account is debited 40 credits. If Tambray wishes to hire Bob, another LETS member, to fix her pickup truck, she can do so using the credits in her account; if she doesn't have enough credits, she can feel free to go into debt, which we term "going into commitment"—no stigma attached. And credit is interest free.

Transactions can be made partially in credits and partially in dollars, if the people involved in a particular transaction so agree; only the LETS credit portion is recorded in our computer. Within a year, a member could exchange with ten or twenty others, conceivably more. Each member is responsible for his or her own reporting of exchanges to Revenue Canada, if relevant at all.

Every so often, a statement is issued, showing the balance of all members' accounts. Having a negative balance doesn't mean you are "overdrawn," as with a bank account, but simply that you are committed to do work or exchange goods within the community in the reasonable future.

This is the gist of the system. But its details of operation must be tailored to fit the specific community. The LETSystem is in essence a bookkeeping method, and as such it doesn't impose anything on the community. Rather, it ties into the principle of community self-control.

Members control the nature and function of the local version of the LETSystem. General and steering committee meetings are held as often as the group finds appropriate. Also, membership dues or other means of collectively paying the price of an answering machine—as well as photocopying, mailing, and long-distance phone costs—are worked out within each group. For instance, members of our system pay $12 per year to cover these costs (the only real reason for any formal membership).

A LETSystem keeps local energy local, rather than pouring it (in dollar-bill form) out of the community. LETS thus supports a truly local economy. Those who believe in reducing their participation in the standard currency system, thereby contributing to reducing The System's pressure on natural systems, find LETS participation a meaningful ecological gesture.

While there is an advantage to having more than just a few people involved in exchanges—more than, say, two at a time, as in barter—it is very important to keep a local system a manageable size; perhaps seventy-five to one hundred fifty members is optimal. We have heard that if LETSystems grow too large, the face-to-face community aspect can disintegrate, causing a crisis in faith; this has apparently been a contributing factor to the demise of some LETSystems.

Faith is the key to the operation of any currency system. No exception, a LETSystem is like a bicycle on which riders can ride without falling only if pedaling and moving forward. We've all seen tandem bicycles. Imagine a bicycle for eighty! Everybody should be pedaling, that is, supplying the needed faith element by continuing to participate.

Our LETS group is called the Southern Slocan Valley Community Exchange (SSVCE). After a year and a half, we are still refining some functional details. Our unit of credit is the Clam. I believe this name was chosen because people liked the sound of "That'll cost ya twenty Clams." (One of our members does claim Slocan Lake is home to some freshwater clams, though I can't recall ever finding any.) We now have some eighty members, whose households represent maybe two hundred fifty people). We would like to increase this formal membership to around one hundred. We publish a revised services directory and newsletter every time we sign up ten new members.

So far, the range of exchanges has included (among many other things) chimney repair, bedding plants, chainsaw maintenance, t'ai chi lessons, haircuts, computer work, shiatsu, electrical work, farm products, help with household moving, sewing, child care, help with deer fencing, tool rental, firewood bucking, auto repair, help with manual excavation, massage, renovation carpentry, dog sitting, and help with concrete work. In September, 1993 we held our first Fall Fair, welcoming everybody but offering a situation in which people could exchange using Clams, and in which people new to the LETS idea could learn about the SSVCE.

The North American economic system is ailing these days, it's true. But it hasn't collapsed. At present, no one here in the Valley regards the SSVCE as anything but a component of general economic life—that is, economic life in the broad, ethnographer's sense. If we give the Clam an equivalence with the Canadian dollar (as some people do, in their thinking), in 1993 Clams may represent as much as 5 percent of some people's incomes.

Of course, we have hopes that Clams can replace a greater percentage of yearly expenditures; we're just getting started. In the first year of our system's operation, it took three months or more for things to really get rolling at all. We needed to build up membership and familiarity with how the system works.

We envision possibilities. Imagine making one's cash income go much further—for instance, effectively adding 10–20 percent to one's income per year. That would be significant! Some people imagine that LETS could become the predominant medium of exchange in their lives in the future, once their mortgage is paid off and major tools are bought, to mention only two major expenses. Who knows?

Even now, however, using the LETSystem feels good in a way that cash earning and spending often don't, because Clams are community currency. Related to this, the SSVCE is expanding people's spheres of acquaintance and friendship, offering a way for both old and new Valley residents to meet and interact.

Readers who feel computers are depersonalizing technological contrivances should realize the computer operates unobtrusively and that a LETSystem is primarily a social institution that embodies only as many good vibes as people invest in it. (LETS-type bookkeeping could even be done without the computer, I'm sure.)

In addition to household production, we now have a multi dimensional exchange reality in the Slocan Valley, including barter, mutual aid, Clams, and conventional money. Different households balance these modalities in different ways, as suits their needs. The Southern Slocan Valley Community Exchange holds the potential to function well so long as the membership is composed of people who are stable in the community, that is, so long as they "stay home," to use Gary Snyder's phrase.

We still have some unanswered questions. For instance, will our high Clam accumulators always find services or goods they wish to buy? Will low Clam accumulators feel sufficient incentive to learn new skills, so as to have more to offer that the community actually wants? Will members generally tend to trade with nearby neighbors?

In response to an article I wrote for *Case Study*, a Vancouver journal of "the new economics," SSVCE was contacted by a David Weston of Nanaimo, British Colombia I had mentioned the LETSystem as one possible dimension of a sustainable, community-based economics. David, whose enclosures indicated he had studied economics at Oxford, commented on LETSystems in general—not in any disparagingly critical way, since he believes in the usefulness of such systems, but in a constructively cautionary way.

David's three suggestions were 1) Set a credit limit so that people can't go irresponsibly "into commitment"; 2) "De-link" from the national currency as the meaningful scale of value for transactions; that is, don't make an equivalence between ordinary wages or prices in the local currency unit (Clams, in our case) and the national dollar. 3) Keep the system service-oriented rather than goods-oriented.

These each warrant a bit of comment.

First, when the SSVCE was getting started, a member suggested a credit limit (in light of the fact that LETSystems such as the original in the Comox Valley had been bedeviled by heavy debts). However, not wishing to be distrustful, our founding SSVCE membership rejected a credit limit. It was felt peer pressure should be sufficient to curb any member's slide toward irresponsibility. However, after a year we had had some problems due to transiency within the community. We have now instituted a 300-Clam credit limit for the first year of membership, and 500 thereafter; a member can apply to the steering committee for a special waiver if more credit is needed and s/he is a good risk.

Second, the "de-linkage" idea was brought up and discussed briefly in the dialogue circle at one of our meetings. While nothing was put forward in terms of policy, some members expressed that they were already thinking in terms other than a straight dollars-to-Clams translation of the value of a service or item. Other people felt such a mental translation could be useful for a time, until people get a good feel for making exchanges.

Third, David's reasons for recommending that the system be kept service- rather than goods-oriented are these: In some alternative-exchange systems, when people have gone into heavy debt (or "commitment") they've sometimes simply tried to rent the use of their capital goods (things they own). David cites this as frequently the case when an indebted member has more possessions than other members generally do; but this is a problem, he says, because such an individual then may feel that s/he need not offer his or her energy and skills to the membership, and energy and skills are often what the members really need most and what make them equals in the community. For people who own more than others to rent their capital goods is the beginning of a class structure (haves and have-nots).

This is an issue we haven't yet come to grips with as a group, although it would appear we haven't run into any problem of this sort. But it also begs the question of what constitutes a member's property and what is rather in the end a product of his or her labor (for instance, a home-built compost shredder)

At present, our actual experience with our system is quite encouraging overall. We look forward to more exchanges and an enriched community life.

Unlike many systems in operation, we are using computer software written by David Badke of Silverton, British Colombia. People interested in the operation and history of LETSystems, or in obtaining the LETS software packages that Michael Linton sells, can contact Michael at 375 Johnston Avenue, Courteney, British Colombia V9N 2Y2, Canada. It might be a good idea to send, $5 to defray the cost of photocopying and mailing. (Michael is one of us, and isn't getting rich at this.)

Profile

Womanshare

Womanshare is a time/credit program that recognizes time as a limited resource and our real wealth. It was envisioned by two women, Diana McCourt and Jane Wilson, who wanted to find a way to establish an economy that encourages friendship while valuing women's work. All hours of work are valued equally, (i.e., a dentist's hour is worth just as much as a babysitter's). The basic principles that guide Womanshare are a caring community, simple living and ecological mindfulness, diversity, linking, trust, joyous living and empowerment.

Women join the program by committing themselves to the principles, paying membership dues (a combination of cash to pay out-of-pocket expenses, based on ability to pay, and time) and providing a list of skills she'd like to offer along with a list of service requests. She receives the newsletter, the skills list of all members and monthly mailings that include invitations to membership meetings and other communications to encourage trading and community building. Exchanges are made by members directly, usually by phone. Once the job is done, the provider sends a postcard to Womanshare, recording both credits spent and credits earned. Credits can be spent on services provided by any member.

In less than two years, Womanshare grew to its desired size of seventy, attracting women from age 22 to 72, from the Upper West Side of New York City, downtown, and Brooklyn, offering a wide diversity of skills (over two hundred in mid-1993). In addition to trading skills within the network, members are offered workshops (members can teach at least sixty subjects!), and at times Womanshare sponsors special presentations, such as the time members met with representatives of Japan's Seikatsu Club Consumers' Cooperative. (Seikatsu, which means "way of life" in Japanese, was started in 1965 by two women who wanted to provide healthier food for their families. It became a movement that now has 250,000 member families, with over one hundred worker-owned cooperatives producing ecologically sound products and services as well as an extensive mutual aid program.)

While Womanshare is relatively small, it operates within a network of many work-exchange systems growing throughout the world. It is "an antidote to underemployment and limited cash, and broadens oppportunities for all participants to be actively involved in an innovative concept of earning power" (from Womanshare literature).

Profile

Ithaca HOURS

*by Paul Glover**

Here in Ithaca, New York, we've begun to gain control of the social and environmental effects of commerce by issuing over $45,000 of our own local currency, to over 800 participants, since 1991. Thousands of purchases and many new friendships have been made with our money, and hundreds of thousands of dollars of local trading has been added to what we call our Grassroots National Product.

We printed our own money because we watched the Federal dollars come to town, shake a few hands, then leave to buy rainforest lumber and fight wars. Ithaca's HOURS, by contrast, stay in our region to help us hire each other. While dollars make us increasingly dependent on multinational corporations and bankers, HOURS reinforce community trading and expand commerce, which is more accountable to our concern for ecology and social justice.

Here's how it works: the Ithaca HOUR is Ithaca's $10.00 bill, because ten dollars is the average hourly wage in Tompkins County, New York. Ithaca HOURS notes, printed in four denominations, buy plumbing, carpentry, electrical work, roofing, nursing, chiropractic, child care, car and bike repair, food, eyeglasses, firewood, gifts, and thousands of other goods and services. Our credit union accepts them for mortgage and loan fees. People pay rent with HOURS. The best restaurants in town take them, as do movie theaters, bowling alleys, two large locally owned grocery stores, and thirty farmer's market vendors.

Ithaca's new HOURly minimum lifts the lowest paid up without knocking down higher wages. For example, several of Ithaca's organic farmers are paying the highest farm labor wages in the Western Hemisphere: $10.00 of spending power per HOUR.

---

*Paul Glover created the HOUR system; Paul is a community economist, ecological urban designer, and author of *Los Angele: A History of the Future,* who holds a degree in management. The article, "Heck, Make Your Own Money!" is reprinted with permission from *The Boycott Quarterly* (Spring 1994).

These farmers benefit by the HOURS' loyalty to local agriculture. On the other hand, dentists, massage therapists and lawyers charging more than the $10.00 average per hour are permitted to collect several HOURS hourly. But increasingly we hear of professional services being provided at our equitable wage.

Everyone who agrees to accept HOURS is paid four HOURS ($40.00) for being listed in our newsletter *Ithaca Money*. Every eight months they may apply to be paid an additional two HOURS, as a reward for continuing their participation. This is how we gradually and carefully increase the per capita supply of our money.

Ithaca Money's 1,200 listings, rivalling the *Yellow Pages*, are a portrait of our community's capability, bringing into the marketplace time and skills not employed by the conventional market. Residents are proud of income gained by doing work they enjoy. We encounter each other as fellow Ithacans, rather than as winners and losers scrambling for dollars.

The Success Stories of participants published in *Ithaca Money* testify to the acts of generosity and community that our system prompts. We're making a community while making a living. As we do so, we relieve the social desperation which has led to compulsive shopping and wasted resources.

At the same time Ithaca's locally owned stores, which keep more wealth local, make sales and get spending power they otherwise would not have. And over $3,800 of local currency has been donated to 20 community organizations so far by the Barter Potluck, our wide-open governing body.

The Potluck, meeting twice monthly, acts as our "Municipal Reserve Board," making decisions about the printing, denominations, manner of issue, and grants and loans of HOURS, while sharing a good meal. It's more democratic and fiscally responsible than the Federal Reserve Board.

As we discover new ways to provide for each other, we reduce dependence on imports. At the same time, our greater self-reliance, rather than isolating Ithaca, gives us more potential to reach outward with ecological export industries. We can capitalize new businesses with loans of our own cash.

We regard Ithaca's HOURS as real money, backed by real people, real time, real skills and real tools. Dollars, by contrast, are funny money, backed no longer by gold or silver, but by less than nothing—$4.3 trillion of national debt.

The designs of Ithaca HOURS honors local features we respect, like native flowers, powerful waterfalls, crafts, farms and our children. The designs of Federal dollars, on the other hand, honor slave holders (Washington, Jefferson, Hamilton, Jackson) and the monuments of corporate government. Multi-colored HOURS, some printed on locally made watermarked cattail (marsh reed) paper, all with serial numbers, are harder to counterfeit than dollars.

Local currency is a lot of fun, and it's legal. HOURS must be used within state lines (they may not compete with dollars as interstate currency) and denominations must be at least $1.00 (no "fractional currency"). They must be designed so that it is obvious that they are *not* dollars. And note that HOURS are taxable income when traded for professional goods or services.

Local currency is also lots of work and responsibility. To give other communities a boost, we've been providing a *Hometown Money Starter Kit*. The Kit explains step-by-step start-up and maintenance of an HOURS system, and includes forms, laws, articles, procedures, insights, samples of Ithaca's HOURS, and past and future issues of *Ithaca Money*. We've sent the Kit to over 150 communities in 41 states so far, and our example is becoming national. To get one, send $25.00 (2.5 HOURS option in NY) to Ithaca Money, Box 6578, Ithaca, NY, 14851.

Stories of Success (exerpted from *Ithaca Money*)

Danny is an electrician who has used HOURS for upholstery, food and restaurant meals. His wife, a musician, spent HOURS for publicity photos. "Spending money locally keeps it here for us, helping Ithaca rather than enriching multinational corporations. Half the things we buy come from corporations that rape the Earth and pocket the profit. We need to think about the ways we live and the products we consume."

Ed provides opthalmology (eye doctor) services for HOURS, most of which he's spent for food. "For many years I've had a sign on my wall stating that I'm willing to negotiate for my services: no one should lack medical care because they lack dollars." He says that "HOURS and barter are a segment of this solution to health care needs. HOURS says that everyone's time is important, and I like that."

Michael provides alternative energy consulting, permaculture design, graphic design of bumper stickers, and has done phone calling for HOURS. He spends HOURS for meals, housecleaning, chiropractor and rent. "HOURS are the best thing to hit town since sliced bread. We're keeping the money system on a local level where it's supposed to be. We're creating a bioregional system, producing locally rather than enriching distant corporations by importing tens of thousands of mile away."

Eileen has received HOURS as donations for wildlife rehabilitation. When looking for a babysitter on the list she "met the most wonderful person. She does child care in exchange for house and garden work." This allowed Eileen to pursue her college degree. "Without Ithaca Money, 1992 would have been much more difficult. Being able to trade makes life easier, and it's fun. I've given away Quarter HOURS to friends who are fascinated with the idea. I've even bought Girl Scout cookies with HOURS, from a scout who needed them for music lessons."

NINE

Economics of Place

Decommodifying Land: The Challenge and the Opportunity

by Susan Witt, E. F. Schumacher Society

> We abuse the land because we regard it as a commodity belonging to us. When we see land as a community to which we belong, we may begin to use it with love and respect.
>
> —Aldo Leopold, *A Sand County Almanac*

Aldo Leopold presented a bold challenge to environmentalists: If we are to foster a culture of love and respect for land, land can no longer be an item to buy and sell on the market. Leopold was describing not merely a new land ethic but a transformation of our relationship with land in fact and deed. The American people are by-in-large doers, not thinkers. Nothing short of a fundamental change in the economic treatment of land can affect our American psyche; nothing short of a radical overhauling of an established system of land law can hope to achieve the results Aldo Leopold envisioned.

Over the last ten years the environmental movement has learned that it is not enough to say no to the developer of the site down the street without saying yes to some other form of appropriate economic livelihood for our neighbors; the protection of one piece of land with conservation restrictions only places higher value on the adjoining lands and raises their potential for inappropriate development. Reactive techniques are limited in scope. It is a time for action of a broad and populist nature with common cause and common consent, action that is bold and affirmative, with beneficial consequences for all. Future generations deserve nothing less. We can and must meet Aldo Leopold's challenge.

Centralized planning of state-owned land has proven to be a great failure, as has the almost totally unregulated exchange of land on the open market. How shall we begin to remove all land from the open market and create a new system of allocation and land use that is fair to all and ecologically sound? What could such a system look like?

In "The Possessional Problem," a chapter from economist Ralph Borsodi's book *The Seventeen Problems of Man and Society*, Borsodi distinguishes between those things that can be legally owned and thus traded and those that are more appropriately in the realm of "trusteeship," to use Gandhi's term. The items that an individual creates as a result of labor applied to land—such as the harvest from a garden, the home built of wood from the forest, the cloth spun from flax in the field—are all appropriately private property and may rightfully be traded as commodities. Borsodi suggests, however, that the land itself and its resources, which are Earth-given and of limited supply, should be held in trusteeship, their use allocated on a limited basis for present and future generations. When an individual is allowed private ownership of such a limited resources, then that individual has an unfair economic advantage. The scarcity of arable land coupled with a growing demand for its use results in an increase in the value of the land through no merit of the landowner. The potential for speculative gain fostered in the present system of land ownership places tremendous pressure on the landowner to maximize the economic value of the land through its development. The use of zoning regulations and conservation easements and restrictions is a small and increasingly costly method to reduce the trend of land exploitation.

A further result of the ability to commoditize land is that the wealth generated by a community will flow first to investment in land for which high gains are anticipated rather than into new small businesses. When a region has excess capital, that capital can work to draw out the imaginative and entrepreneurial skills of its people and thus generate new businesses producing goods and services once imported from other regions. This freed investment capital can facilitate increased regional production and therefore create greater regional insulation from fluctuations in the world economy. When capital is tied up in land, however, the local economy chokes up. Credit for the small-business owner tightens. The region loses its diversity, which is the basis of a more sustainable economy and of a more environmentally responsible business sector.

In the Berkshires (Massachusetts), during the height of the spending spree of the 1980s, a weekend pastime was to put a "For Sale" sign in the front yard and offer the property to any inquirer at a highly inflated price to see if there were any takers. It was a form of gambling with the land at stake. The possibility of "hitting the jackpot" is very seductive to working people who have seen their savings account grow only too slowly even after years and years of hard work. The ever-present possibility of selling the land at a gain and then moving on to greener pastures erodes the commitment to community and place that is ultimately the safeguard of our mutually inherited rivers, lakes and wild lands.

(This piece was adapted, with permission, from a longer article published by the E.F. Schumacher Society.)

Housing

Access to decent, affordable housing is the goal of many community organizations; lack of such housing is one of our nation's most pressing social problems. The American dream of home ownership is often just that—a dream. Even renting is becoming more difficult as gentrification overtakes whole neighborhoods. Displacement, often resulting in homelessness, is a reality for millions of Americans, many of them families who have fallen on hard times—job loss, illness, or injury—than ever before. Two ways of meeting these challenges are cooperative housing and cohousing.

Cooperative Housing

Some communities are turning to housing cooperatives to enable low- and moderate-income people to own homes at a reasonable cost. In a housing cooperative, the building is owned by the cooperative corporation and the resident members own shares proportional to the value of the unit they occupy. In a market cooperative, members can sell their shares for full market value. In a limited-equity cooperative, the resale value of each share is held below market value to ensure that the housing will continue to be affordable. Co-ops can be started by individuals, organizations, or local governments. Often residents of a neighborhood get together and, with some technical assistance from an advocacy organization and financial backing, organize to purchase a building themselves. Most cooperatives in existence today were funded with complex packages of grants, loans and sometimes sweat equity. Some government programs like HOME and HOPE (which are HUD programs) promote limited-equity co-ops as a preferred model for affordable housing. The National Cooperative Bank, headquartered in Washington, D.C., was created by Congress in the late 1970s specifically to serve cooperative ventures. The Bank can make loans, which unfortunately have to be at market rates of interest, to housing cooperatives. So far the Bank has loaned or invested $987 million in housing cooperatives.

All cooperative residents have a long-term lease on a unit and vote on policy and decisions for the whole development. "This is not just selling a person a home and hoping it works out," says Barry Zigas, former president of the National Low-Income Housing Coalition, in Washington, D.C. "When people ban together in a cooperative, they have to be—cooperative. They're getting into a long-term relationship with their neighbors." Success, therefore, requires ongoing, substantial training in management, operations, and leadership development.

Cooperatives often increase the strength of a community as the participants work together for common goals, develop their skills, share what they already know, and support each other through the inevitable rough times. Chuck Matthei, founder and past director of the Institute for Community Economics (ICE), observes that while many cooperatives begin as "partnerships of convenience," members typically find a high level of companionship, mutual aid and "social security" during the process of development, organization, and management.

Cohousing

Cohousing, the English translation of a Danish word that means "living communities," had its start over twenty years ago in Denmark after single mothers who wanted to improve their lives put a few ads in the paper; their goal was to share living space as well as their lives. Today there over one hundred cohousing communities in Denmark, and they are fast becoming a mainstream way of dealing with housing across Europe. While the movement is less than ten years old in the United States, there are well over one hundred groups in the United States, forty of them in the Northeast. Not all have actually started a "living community," however, since this takes time as well as personal and financial commitment.

Cohousing is an effort to rebuild the lost structures of community and reweave a social fabric to create neighborhoods that are people-friendly and Earth-sensible. Instead of letting banks and land developers plan residential communities, the residents-to-be actually come together themselves to design their neighborhood and physical environment. The way we build our space around us effects our social and cultural life. If we look to traditional cultures we see interrelated buildings. Cohousing is about rethinking how we build in our space.

How might this look? People have private homes, but these are smaller because many facilities are shared. Common facilities, which are placed in a central location, may include laundry rooms, a large kitchen and dining area for shared meals, bulk food storage areas, and space for processing and storing crops, as well as places for children and teenagers, guest rooms, and workshops for wood, fiber, autos, and so on. Physical structures are built to encourage social interaction. Cars, which so easily separate people, may be kept at the periphery of the community, an arrangement that allows the area around the living spaces to fill up with pedestrians and the stuff of interaction: gardens, walkways, bikes, sandboxes, quiet sitting areas and open commons. Homes are clustered together in a more sociable atmosphere, rather than with great expanses of private lawn and one driveway each. Through the environment it builds, the community honors the individual's need for privacy quite well.

Finding models that protect individuals and the integrity of groups and that are also bankable is a major challenge for cohousing practitioners. In California and out West people are looking toward using a condominium model as legal structure. In New England groups are looking toward being cooperative corporations. Cohousing groups also need to look at land ownership issues. The potential here for the land trust model is very exciting. Financial issues on the personal level are also a challenge for cohousing groups. Fact is, housing is simply not affordable for most people anymore; and cohousing doesn't necessarily make it more affordable, initially. However, you do get more for your money. And needs such as laundry facilities, garden space, and equipment for gardening—even transportation, depending on the group—are jointly owned, so you don't have to buy them by yourself. You are placing yourself in an environment that is more conducive to living a healthy life, physically, socially, and culturally.

Cohousing faces design challenges and potentials as well. For architects, working with a cohousing group can be time consuming because so many clients are involved in the process. However, it can also be rewarding, as Peter Kitchell, an architect working with a cohousing group in Amherst, notes, "The people who want to do this...are looking for a very rich life. They are singles and pairs and all kinds of sexual preferences and ages. It leads to some original and very valid new expressions of living together that we have to translate into buildings."

Local zoning and planning officials need to be educated since zoning ordinances often prohibit designs (e.g., cluster housing) most conducive to the creation of "living communities." For example, less than 10 percent of Massachusett's 351 towns and cities have zoning laws that allow cohousing to be built without a variance. Bob Engler, a Cambridge development consultant who works with cohousing groups, explains, "People want to put their houses closer together than the normal law allows, they want a community building and a child-safe area. And that's breaking a lot of local zoning laws. Most zoning laws don't allow that flexibility." The challenge is to provide new images of what it's like to live differently. In addition, there is exciting potential for cohousing with regard to technologies for treating our water, dealing with waste, and exploring alternative energy production once we begin designing in terms of systems instead of for single homes.

Many cohousing advocates feel the biggest challenge—and potential—is the social aspect. This is especially true of groups who follow the consensus decision-making model, which is very different from democracy (one person, one vote, majority wins). Consensus decision making promises to take care of all the needs of people involved. It takes more time, diligence, patience, and a striving to be at once objective and compassionate. It also requires an incredible awareness of the balance between process and task work.

Lynne Hadley, a cohousing pioneer in Brattleboro, Vermont talks about the "joys of accountability" inherent in cohousing. She says, "These two words aren't used together in United States. We have fears of living together. People are afraid of having their rights as individuals taken away. Building trust is the hardest part. Cohousing provides an opportunity for people to interact with each other through the phases of their lives, especially for elders to be a vital part of the community. When we begin to call a place home and get a sense of place, that's the root of political activity

The Pioneer Valley Cohousing Group (PVCG) in Amherst, Massachusetts, had its beginnings in 1989 after a couple placed an ad in the local paper ("Couple seeks others to buy land and build a community"). Today the group is ready to break ground on twenty-five acres purchased from the Town of Amherst. PVCG will be a resident-designed community of thirty-two households using a cluster model that enhances social interaction. Each household will have a small, private dwelling supported by a common house with shared amenities. Building will be limited to six acres, leaving the rest, which includes woods and a wetland, undeveloped

Before purchasing land, PVCG met regularly to develop their decision-making process and build the relationships that are as important to a community—some would say more important—as actually having land to build on. As one member put it before the land was purchased, "We have created our community. We just need a place to put it now.

PVCG makes decisions by consensus and will call in an outside mediator to assist if necessary. Five of their proposed thirty-two units are set aside for people of color. They do not yet have a racially diverse membership, but it is an important part of the group's vision for the future. Units will cost between $65,000 and $140,000, depending on size and specifications. There is a certain amount of flexibility regarding down payments and monthly payments, and the group will work with individuals to find a plan that works; however, low-income people (and even some of moderate income) will find it difficult to afford cohousing without outside help in the form of "soft" loans.

(Special thanks to Lynne Hadley for her help with this piece. Parts of this section are based on Lynne's presentation at a Catalyst-sponsored conference in 1992: "Economics as if Vermont Really Mattered.")

Reconnecting People & the Land: The Promise of Community Land Trusts

The only way to make possible a truly good life for mankind is to utterly abolish the principle of absolute ownership of land and other natural resources, and completely replace it with agreements of tenure in trust. No amount of legalization can provide an honest title to any portion of the Earth.

—Ralph Borsodi, developer (with Robert Swann), of the Community Land Trust model

In the country and city alike, the majority of people find themselves estranged from the land. Land is the basis, the foundation not only for our homes, but for the whole of our lives. The answer to the question, "Who owns and controls the land?" provides much of the information necessary to understand the staggering inequities in our society. More and more land is owned and controlled by fewer and fewer people resulting in homelessness and generational cycles of poverty that shatter people's lives.

The CLT is a practical model for bringing people and the land together. Not so coincidentally, CLTs can also be instrumental in healing people's relationships with each other as they work together to transform their community into a place their children, and their children's children, can call "home." I will paint a snapshot of a few CLTs to give you a sense of how they work and of their potential.

Keep in mind any single model or strategy is only one piece of the community development puzzle. Successful community development is a process involving the members of a community in building their own future.

How often have we seen well-intentioned people or organizations come into a community with a grand scheme for what they think the community needs? They bring all the resources and even have the funding to get things off the ground. But the community being "done unto" doesn't feel connected to the project. A few years down the road, the project fails. Not only is this a waste of resources, it weakens the heart of the community. If this process is repeated over and over, through no fault of its own the community is deemed "hopeless" and can be abandoned, even by its own residents.

We do not need to be "experts" to take on projects that may seem daunting, such as affordable housing, co-ops, or business development. We do need passion, commitment and willingness to work with lots of different kinds of people. We need to know when and who to ask for help, and we need plenty of patience.

Community Land Trusts

The purpose of a CLT is to strike a fair balance between individual and community interests, combining features of both private and community ownership. The trust is a nonprofit corporation with open membership and an elected board that typically includes residents of trust-owned lands, other community residents, and public-interest representatives.

The trust acquires land in perpetuity through purchase or donation, thus removing land from the speculative real estate market. The trust then leases the land on a long-term or lifetime basis. Leaseholders (which may include families, individuals, businesses, cooperatives, and community organizations) pay a regular lease fee based on "use value" rather than "full market value."

While leaseholders do not own the land they use, they may own buildings and other improvements. CLTs often help the leaseholders obtain ownership of buildings by arranging affordable financing. An agreement is usually signed between homeowners and the trust that provides for the terms under which a home may be sold. The agreement generally includes a "limited equity" provision which restricts the amount of appreciation a seller may receive. Limited equity serves to keep housing affordable over time.

Today, CLTs are serving the needs of people in rural and urban communities alike. According to the Institute for Community Economics (which pioneered the development of the CLT model beginning in the 1970s), there were 70 operating CLTs in the U.S. and 31 in development (meaning a working group has formed) in 1993. (In 1983 there were only 15 CLTs.) Almost half of the CLTs are in urban areas; the remaining CLTs are evenly divided between rural areas and towns and small cities. Each CLT has its own unique story. Some are small, holding one or two tracts of land, others are large and impact the lives of hundreds of people. Wherever the CLT, members must work with a broad range of agencies and institutions to obtain land, build, or rehabilitate housing and help residents with financing. Community organizing skills are essential, not only to get things going, but also to keep the CLT vital and alive over time.

Profiles

Rural and Urban Community Land Trusts

H.O.M.E. and the Covenant Community Land Trust

Homeowners Organized for More Employment (H.O.M.E.) was founded by Lucy Poulin, then a Carmelite nun, in 1970. Poulin grew up in rural Maine and, as the eighth of eleven children, was no stranger to poverty. After graduating from high school and then running the family farm for ten years, Poulin joined a Carmelite convent in Plainfield, New Hampshire. She was reassigned to a Carmelite house near Orland, a tiny town in Maine haunted by poverty, when the New Hampshire convent was closed. H.O.M.E. had its beginnings when a woman knocked on the convent door wanting help selling her quilts. A public meeting was arranged, and a large group of people showed up. The first thing they did was purchase a farmhouse on twenty-three acres of land that was used for everything: sales, retail, offices, and inventory. "It was a success from the start, and as we sold crafts, more people brought more crafts to sell," Poulin says.

As the craft aspect of H.O.M.E. grew, other needs became apparent. For example, many people couldn't read, and they needed a larger store as well as a place people could come to learn crafts. Poulin explains,

> We needed a store. We needed a school. Both needs were critical. So we started to build the school, and we started to build ourselves a store. Maybe that doesn't make sense to start two such major projects at the same time when we hardly knew if we could finish one of them. But in terms of need, it was the right thing to do. We started an awful lot at once, and it was very difficult. But people came to help and we did it. We finished both of them.

In 1978, H.O.M.E. initiated the Covenant Community Land Trust in response to a desperate need for affordable housing. People involved with the Trust learned the best way to put a project together and created relationships with funding sources, including the Maine State Housing Authority. In 1988, H.O.M.E. began an outreach program to help start other CLTs in Maine and, in 1989, played a key role in the creation of an omnibus affordable-housing bill, which was approved by the legislature, and a $5 million bond referendum approved by the voters. H.O.M.E. now provides technical assistance to new projects in Main.

In addition to conversion of existing buildings, H.O.M.E.'s CLT has produced more than thirteen single-family houses and three two-family houses to date. The construction of these solid, wood-shingled, energy-efficient (wood-heated) homes is done largely by volunteers, using lumber that H.O.M.E. cuts on its land and mills itself. Because of this and because the homes are part of the land trust (people purchase only the house and the right to use the land), these homes cost about $35,000. H.O.M.E. works with a local bank to arrange affordable mortgages.

A belief that people's needs deserve to be responded to and the faith that a way will be found despite overwhelming odds, has guided H.O.M.E. consistently over the years. Need dictates the expansion of existing projects and the implementation of new ones. For example, Project Woodstove began when one of the staff discovered an elderly woman trying to keep warm burning charcoal briquets in her kitchen cook stove. Now H.O.M.E. harvests, cuts and delivers emergency firewood free to people who have no other way to get it. Today, H.O.M.E. operates a lumber and shingle mill, a cobbler's shop, a day care, an auto repair shop, a flea market, and a food store that distributes free government surplus foods and sells a limited selection of vegetables (from H.O.M.E.'s garden), grain for animals, seedlings and plants. H.O.M.E. also maintains several shelters for the homeless, for battered women and children and for the elderly, and hires and trains many of the destitute people who come to them for shelter providing much needed jobs.

H.O.M.E. is much more than a CLT, yet the CLT is essential to the organization's overall success. H.O.M.E. demonstrates how projects evolve as they respond to people's needs and it proves you don't have to be an expert to make things happen. Says Poulin, "I have to believe that we human beings don't know our limits."

Dudley Street Neighborhood Initiative (DSNI)

One of the most inspiring examples of community organizing I've encountered in a long time, DSNI describes itself as "a multi-racial membership organization whose aim is one of community controlled revitalization of a neighborhood which is at once one of Boston's most depressed areas, as well as one of the most sought after by speculators and developers." Dudley Neighbors, Inc., is the organization's CLT component.

Dudley Street is a racially diverse neighborhood less than two miles southwest of downtown Boston in Roxbury. It is home to approximately 15,000 African-Americans, Hispanics, Cape Verdeans, and a few whites. For the past twenty-five years or so, the community has been literally sucked dry. Money poured out and ill-conceived housing projects fell into disrepair. Resulting despair brought its attendant woes—drugs, rising poverty, shattered families, and violence. During the 1970s, as real-estate prices plummeted and buildings were abandoned, fires raged through the neighborhood, often set by owners to collect insurance rather than pay taxes on deteriorating buildings. When the fires stopped, more than 20 percent of the neighborhood lots were vacant, about 1,300 of them—the largest single concentration of vacant land in the city.

Organizations, agencies, and developers made empty promises; some haphazard projects were undertaken, but the result left residents feeling disillusioned and abandoned. The neighborhood was "redlined" (denied loans) by the banks and the vacant lots became unofficial city dumps, places to avoid because of crime. (While banks denied accusations of racism, the Boston Redevelopment Authority reported that between 1981 and 1987, whites were three times as likely as economically similar blacks to receive mortages in Boston—and the neighborhood with the worst mortgage lending rate was Dudley).

In 1985 Nelson Merced, director of La Alianza Hispana (a community human-services organization in Roxbury), and Robert Holmes, a corporate attorney and an officer of the Riley Foundation (a charitable trust) invited Dudley Street residents to a meeting to "work to take charge" of their future. This was the culmination of months of work on the part of the Riley Foundation and representatives of human-service and community-development organizations, who met several times to figure out what to do about Dudley. These folks put together a whole plan for the revitalization of the neighborhood and incorporated as DSNI.

But as luck would have it, when they presented their plan to the residents who attended the meeting, they were met with exasperation and questions such as, "Who the hell is Riley?" Clearly these people had had enough of outsiders thinking they knew what was best. Merced explains, "Residents felt under siege by crime, and they were discouraged about all this vacant land. Now here comes the steamroller with a new plan for what to do with their community. They resented the fact that once again they had not been involved from the very first. And they were right."

The plan was discarded, and DSNI reorganized to include residents such as Fadilah Muhammed and Che Madyun, a single mother who became president of the board, and met regularly with City officials and lawyers: "People respected what everyone else was saying. I had never been in that position before." A storefront office was opened by the end of 1985, and a broad vision had been defined: to "create a neighborhood," a place that includes stores and light industry, playgrounds, day-care centers and recreational facilities, as well as decent, affordable housing.

This is where the fun begins. Rather than wait for the City to come to them, DSNI decided to get its attention and invite it to join them. The first step was to clean up the vacant lots, which meant the City needed to close two illegal trash-transfer stations. Demonstrations were held at the worst sites with media in attendance, and some DSNI activists threatened to dump trash on City Hall. They succeeded and were even provided with rakes and trucks to aid in cleanup.

In 1987, DSNI released its comprehensive plan for neighborhood development, which calls for the creation of a "village commons" with housing, stores, and open space. In addition, the plan calls for two thousand units of housing, half from existing rehabilitated buildings, the rest new buildings on vacant lots. The problem was obtaining possession of those vacant lots. As luck would have it, the City's Public Facilities Department (PFD) was conducting a survey of all city-owned land vacant land with an eye toward figuring out how much affordable housing could be built; the largest concentration was in the Dudley neighborhood. Residents educated themselves about business and politics by seeking help from lawyers, activists, and experienced community developers. At the same time, they began meeting with Lisa Chapnick, PFD's director. Chapnick says, "It was so impressive to see people who have every right to be angry or in despair come in with a concrete plan and vision for the future. It was a train you wanted to get on. It would have been immoral not to."

DSNI's master plan called for the consolidation of all public and private vacant lots. A piecemeal approach would defeat their overall vision of a real neighborhood. Amazingly, in 1988 DSNI was granted eminent domain authority over vacant land by the Boston Redevelopment Authority, which allowed them to take thirty acres of land, referred to as the "Dudley Triangle" (including fifteen acres of private property). This was the first time a nonprofit was granted land-taking powers! That it happened underscores the importance of bringing people most affected by a situation to the table, working together, building trust, creating a vision and a viable strategy to get there, doing your homework, working with other agencies and organizations (including the government), and keeping the lines of communication open between all concerned. And under it all lies commitment and passion.

Dudley Neighbors, Inc. (DNI) was created in 1988 to hold the land in trust acquired either through negotiation with existing owners or taken through eminent domain. The trust is paying for the initial land with a $2 million loan from the Ford Foundation. The first housing project—Winthrop Estates, a $5.6 million development consisting of thirty-eight homes (3-4 bedrooms, 1 1/2 baths, basement,

2-car driveway, and fenced yard)—broke ground in the spring of 1993, and residents began moving in during the fall. Thirty-three of these homes will be affordable to families in the $18,000 to $37,500 income range.

Well over one hundred potential home buyers have taken DSNI's home-ownership classes, which will qualify them for reduced rate mortgages. As Maydun explains, "It's not about just building the houses—it's about having people who live here ready to be able to access them....We build not only housing, but people, too."

Today, people continue to move into Winthrop Estates. Stafford Heights, a 45-unit limited-equity housing co-op is underway, and plans for the town commons and additional apartment rehabilitation are moving forward. It often feels like change comes too slowly, even (or especially) while you're in the midst of trying to make it happen. Successful community-organizing initiatives such as DSNI offer encouragement. For years very little change was visible in Dudley, except for less trash. Yet change was bubbling under the surface as people gained skills and confidence. As Madyun proudly declared at Winthrop Estate's open house in the fall of 1993, "This has been ten hard years, but we have arrived. We're building up the community, taking a stand, making a difference."

North Camden Land Trust*

The City of Camden is cut in two by a major highway that funnels New Jersey traffic over the Ben Franklin Bridge into downtown Philadelphia. North of the highway lies the North Camden neighborhood. Camden as a whole is an economically depressed city. North Camden could be described as economically abandoned. But the people who live there have not abandoned it; they have been struggling for years to save and revitalize their neighborhood, and they are making progress. The North Camden Land Trust (NCLT) has become a crucial part of this effort.

Background

NCLT Administrator Luis Galindez describes Camden as having once been "a city of opportunity, with good housing, jobs, a beautiful environment." But by the 1960s local conditions were changing. Businesses and more affluent residents were moving out. Housing was deteriorating. Increasing numbers of low-income people moved into the city, including Hispanic farm workers who came first for the winters, then settled permanently. By the early '70s, the population of North Camden consisted primarily of low-income Hispanic and African American people for whom economic opportunities were extremely limited.

*The North Camden Land Trust provides an excellent example of how the land trust model, with support from other community organizations and funding from a community-development, revolving-loan fund can build a community from the ground up, providing housing, jobs, and hope for the future. This article, written by Kirby White, is reprinted with permission from *Community Economics* (Spring 1993).

In 1972 and 1973, North Camden was torn by riots. Luis Galindez says, "People started fighting each other, taking over property, burning buildings." Lillian Ubarry, an organizer for Concerned Citizens of North Camden and a lifelong neighborhood resident, says, "After the riots, businesses and anybody with a little bit of money just packed up and left, because they were scared. So things got really rough in North Camden. There was nothing happening. The City didn't want to pick up the trash; they didn't want to do anything.

At that point, Lillian says, "A group of people started talking and said we need to bring this neighborhood back up, and they decided to form an organization, which they named Concerned Citizens of North Camden." An experienced organizer, Tom Knoche, was contacted and agreed to help. With foundation support, several local activists, including Lillian, were hired and trained as organizers.

One of CCNC's early initiatives was a board-up program. Neighborhood residents cleaned up and boarded about 300 abandoned City-owned buildings. As they did so, they identified houses that were in relatively sound and habitable condition. CCNC then organized a squatting program, helping local families to move into abandoned houses and fix them up. Lillian says, "We called the first 13 families the 13 pioneers, the first people brave enough to go into the houses. The City didn't know anything about this at first. We told the families just move right on in and start doing whatever you can to get the house up to code. We had workshops, with electricians and plumbers and heating men to come and teach the people the skills. And some folks had some of those skills, and they would trade off and help each other."

To prepare for the City's reaction, CCNC organized local residents to defend the program. Lillian says, "One day a squatter moved into a block where a City Councilwoman lived, and she wanted that house for a friend, so she called the cops. When we found out that the cops were coming we got all our people together on the porch and just started screaming, 'No eviction or arrest!' When the cops came we said we wanted to talk to people from the City because we wanted a housing program." By this time, City officials knew that CCNC had become a force in the neighborhood, and a meeting with the Mayor and other officials was arranged. Luis Galindez says, "The Mayor had just been elected, so it was just at the right time, and it worked. We got our program."

With the cooperation of the City, CCNC was able to match 142 families with vacant homes needing modest repairs. By 1984, most of the better buildings had been occupied. Those that remained would be more expensive to rehabilitate. The program was expected to continue, but in 1984 the City cut its funding.

At this time CCNC was involved in a struggle to prevent the construction of a prison on the North Camden waterfront near the Ben Franklin Bridge. Lillian says, "One reason the City cut the housing program was because we weren't supporters of them. We were fighting against that prison so hard that they decided they were going to pull our program, thinking that would close us. That's when we decided that North Camden Land Trust was the best way to go."

Development of the Land Trust

The land trust concept appealed to CCNC for several reasons. The prison battle was eventually lost, but important lessons were learned. The group knew that if they were going to improve conditions in the neighborhood they would need greater long-term control over the community's land base. Bounded on three sides by the Delaware and Cooper Rivers, the land had potential value for various outside interests. Luis says, "People were coming to Camden with the idea that they could buy properties near the waterfront, sit on them for two or three years and then make money out of them. People in the neighborhood were scared, wondering if they were going to lose their houses. So we wanted the land trust to stabilize the neighborhood.

The land trust made particular sense to CCNC as it planned to rehabilitate more housing. Luis says, "We sat down and said, the housing stock that is available needs major repairs. If we're going to save that housing, we're going to make an organization to keep it affordable for the people who live here—an organization where the community has control over the housing stock." At the same time, the land trust was seen as a way to build community. "We have people now who are land trust homeowners," Luis says, "who come to meetings and make decisions for the community's sake. And it's a way to build community-at-large—we have both African American and Hispanic people in the organization." (NCLT meetings are conducted in both Spanish and English.)

The North Camden Land Trust was incorporated in December, 1984. The first project involved two buildings acquired from the City, to be rehabilitated with sweat equity labor. Financial resources were limited, and as the work proceeded, NCLT needed to borrow money to complete the project. Tom Knoche contacted the recently established Delaware Valley Community Reinvestment Fund (DVCRF) to explore the possibility of a loan.

Most lenders would not even have considered a loan to a grassroots group for a sweat equity project in this neighborhood, but DVCRF got involved, helped the group refine its plans for the project, and then made a loan that allowed completion of the project. It was one of the first loans made by DVCRF, and the beginning of a long-term relationship that would provide both continued financing and technical assistance for NCLT (and would help to shape DVCRF's own program).

With limited public subsidies but with support from DVCRF, NCLT continued its sweat equity rehab program, completing a total of ten homes between 1986 and 1988. In 1989, development accelerated when NCLT joined forces with another nonprofit organization, Camden Lutheran Housing Corporation. In this partnership, NCLT has concentrated on initial planning, selecting and working with residents, and developing its own rehab crew, while Camden Lutheran Housing has worked with municipal and state funding sources and packaged financing for projects. Since 1989, the two organizations have developed 23 homes and are now beginning another ten -unit project, involving new homes on vacant lots as well as rehab.

The first ten homes were sold to local families, with financing through NCLT, which retains the title to the land. However, NCLT found that arranging transfer of a title when a homeowner wanted to sell was difficult and expensive. The land trust also wanted to be sure that the rehabbed homes were adequately maintained over the long term. For these reasons, NCLT now retains ownership of the homes it develops but allows residents to build equity as members of what is, in effect, a coop. Monthly payments are $265 or $285, depending on the size of the home (compared to rents of $375 for a one bedroom apartment). The portion of the payment that is used to retire the mortgage principal is credited to the resident's account, to be paid if the family moves after having lived in the home for at least five years.

Betsy Phillips, Director of Camden Lutheran Housing, says, "The coop model gives all the families an interest in everybody else's property, though there's still a sense of ownership of each property by the family." Lerenda Matthews, who is President of NCLT and a resident says, "We all have something to say about it, and that has a lot to do with the way the houses are maintained.

In addition to developing 33 family homes, NCLT has worked with Leavenhouse, which operates a community soup kitchen, to develop 22 units of permanent single-room-occupancy housing for homeless people. Helen Smith House, opened in 1989, includes 11 units, and Casa Rainbow, opened at the end of 1992, also provides 11 units.

The Rehab Crew: Community Jobs

The housing produced by these efforts is only one part of what has been achieved. The housing program has brought money into a capital-starved neighborhood, and the land trust has made sure that the neighborhood receives the greatest possible benefit from this infusion of capital. Ernie Boyd, NCLT Resource Coordinator, says, "The way all the other nonprofits in Camden work is that they get some government money and it passes through their office into the hands of a contractor, who is almost always a non-Camden contractor, with non-Camden workers. They do the housing, but the wages, benefits, and skill development go outside the city. What we've done here is assemble a rehab crew made up entirely of neighborhood residents. All the money stays in the neighborhood, the skills stay in the neighborhood."

NCLT's rehab crew is coordinated by Nick Montes, a North Camden native. It currently employs about ten local people, who do virtually all of the rehab work on NCLT projects. With the cooperation of a semi-retired electrician and licensed plumber, they are able to do plumbing, heating and electrical work, as well as construction. The program provides valuable on-the-job training for crew members, while completing projects on time and on schedule—something that other organizations with similar programs have found difficult to achieve.

This approach to rehab has also provided important side-benefits. Ernie Boyd says, "People see their friends and acquaintances working on the buildings. We have considerably lower loss rates than most contractors. People in the neighborhood sort of look out for our work in progress. There are a bunch of people in the winter who hang out and need something to stay warm with, so when we do demo work the lumber that we can't salvage for anything else we give to them, which helps to knit us into the neighborhood.

NCLT also makes a point of purchasing materials from suppliers in the city. Luis Galindez says, "The main thing is to get community people involved, so when there is a new piece to be added to the puzzle we say, 'Can we get it here so we don't have to go out there and get it—can we keep it here in the community?'"

Neighborhood Planning

Rebuilding a neighborhood is indeed a matter of fitting many pieces into a complicated puzzle so that the over-all pattern will benefit local people. Often the process also requires rejecting pieces that outside interests are trying to force into the picture. Several years after the first prison was built on North Camden's waterfront, another site in the neighborhood was proposed for a second large prison. This time, CCNC and the other neighborhood organizations were well prepared to resist the plan. The campaign they organized drew widespread support, and the prison proposal was defeated.

The community also rallied against another proposal that threatened to increase its social and economic isolation. Rutgers University, which has a branch campus south of the approach to the Ben Franklin Bridge, wanted to close one of the few local streets that cross the highway to connect North Camden with the rest of the city. Again the community managed to defeat a plan that would have further distorted its infrastructure to serve the interests of others.

But local residents knew they needed more than a defensive strategy. They needed to make their own plans to guide future development. They needed to decide what *should* happen to their waterfront, and what types of development would bring the desired services and economic opportunities to the neighborhood. And, as the land trust continued to acquire property, they needed to decide where the next rehab efforts should be concentrated, where new housing should be built on vacant land, and where vacant land should be committed to other uses.

To promote appropriate uses of waterfront land and prevent inappropriate uses, CCNC and other community organizations formed a coalition known as Save Our Waterfront. In 1992, to consolidate these and other planning efforts, the North Camden Planning Project was initiated, with support from the DVCRF, and the Camden Redevelopment Agency, and with the cooperation of local churches, community organizations, businesses, and residents. The project has held a series of meetings to gather detailed input from neighborhood people on a block-by-block basis.

Some exciting developments are projected. On one site, a police substation and a Police Athletic League center are to be opened. An adjacent section of the waterfront will become a new park. Nearby, the Black Peoples' United Movement, a nonprofit organization, plans to develop a food distribution center and has agreed to commit 100 of the jobs developed at the site to residents of North Camden. In another portion of the neighborhood, the Redevelopment Agency plans to develop a shopping center with a supermarket (there is only one supermarket in the entire city).

These pieces are not yet in place. There is still much work to be done in North Camden, but the people who have been working for more than a decade to put the pieces together will go on working. They have roots here, and they are, as Luis points out, a young community (median age in Camden is 18). Recently, three members of the staff of the U.S. Senate Banking Committee were brought to North Camden by the National Association of Community Development Loan Funds. Luis gave them a tour of the neighborhood. He says one of their first questions was, "How can you stand to live here?" Luis told them, "We can live here because we are a young community, we have energy, and we have hope."

Putting Models Together in Vermont

Vermont has several programs related to land and housing that compliment each other nicely, providing an excellent example of how a range of land trust and financing models can work together to address a diversity of needs. These programs include the Vermont Land Trust, the Vermont Housing & Conservation Board, the Vermont Community Loan Fund, and CLTs such as the Burlington CLT and the Central Vermont CLT.

The Vermont Land Trust (VLT) is a conservation trust that in its sixteen-year history, has permanently protected 54,500 acres of farm and forest land in one hundred towns. The VLT creates opportunities for farmers to purchase farms and additional cropland at prices that reflect the land's agricultural value, not its development value. While the Trust accepts donations of land, it operates primarily by accepting donations of conservation easements from landowners who wish to voluntarily conserve their lands or by purchasing the development rights outright. In exchange for the gift (or sale) of development rights, the owner receives a tax deduction in the amount equal to the difference between the fair market value of the property, with and without the restrictions.

For example last year, the elder Kayharts sold the development rights on 443 acres of farmland to the VLT. In addition to pasture and wooded acreage, the land includes wetlands and an important nesting spot for migrating water fowl. In the fall of 1993, more than 15,000 snow geese landed here during their southerly migration. Now the next generation of Kayharts, who have been managing the productive dairy farm for their parents, will be able to acquire the farm at its agricultural value. This is one working dairy farm that won't be lost to development! (Vermont has lost 1,248 dairy farms since 1980—almost one third.)

The Burlington CLT, founded in 1984, buys land and buildings, holds the land in trust, and sells the buildings to low- and moderate-income people, tenant cooperatives, and community organizations. BCLT has a wide variety of services including rental housing, single-family homes, condominiums, tenant-owned cooperatives, family shelter, transitional housing, the Community Health Center, and the Sarah Cole House, a community home for formerly homeless women. The trust currently leases 46 single-family homes, 36 units of co-op housing, and two student co-ops consisting of 22 single rooms. It has covenants with 83 owners of condominiums; manages 83 units of rental housing (most of which has been substantially rehabbed); and provides housing for 12 formerly homeless women and 15 people with special needs. The Trust has recently gotten involved with providing facilities for nonprofit agencies and is also concerned with conserving open space in the city. (The Central Vermont CLT, based in Montpelier, functions in a similar fashion as BCLT, although its holdings aren't as extensive.)

Financing the acquisition of land or development rights can often present an obstacle to community-based organizations; in Vermont we have some help. The Vermont Housing & Conservation Board (VHCB) was established by the Vermont General Assembly in 1987 to both create affordable housing for Vermonters and to conserve and protect agricultural land, historic properties, and important natural areas. It administers the Vermont Housing & Conservation Trust Fund to provide grants and loans to nonprofit housing providers and for the protection of important natural resources. This state program is unique, and the funds it makes available make a big difference to housing and conservation efforts in the state.

The Vermont Community Loan Fund (VCLF), based in Montpelier, makes below-market rate loans to nonprofit community-development organizations (such as land trusts or housing co-ops) that provide housing to low- and moderate-income people. Revolving-loan funds (RLFs) are an important model that helps keep money in local communities and provides residents with a measure of control over development. (See "Community Labor," Chapter Eight).

These separate programs could probably benefit by working together more intentionally. Still, they offer the seeds of a comprehensive land and housing strategy for Vermont that other states could follow.

Localizing Food Systems
by *Kenneth A. Dahlberg**

Until recently, we have been blind to the importance of food in local and regional environments and economies, but the growing sustainability movement is starting to seek genuine, long-term, localized approaches to our food systems. With vision, we can do this in a way that will empower families and neighborhoods and make our communities healthier, more self-reliant and more equitable.

---

*Excerpted from *The Neighborhood Works* (February/March, 1994). Kenneth A. Dahlberg is a professor of political science and environmental studies at Western Michigan University, Kalamazoo, Michigan.

Current agriculture (nationally and internationally) needs restructuring. Not only does it impose extremely high health, social and environmental costs, but it is highly fossil-fuel dependent. In the United States it takes roughly 10 energy calories to deliver one food calorie on our plates. As fossil fuel prices rise, there will be a huge multiplier effect on food prices. We can either wait until things collapse or start building the necessary local and regional food systems now.

Most people are unaware of how dependent their cities are upon distant national and international systems for food or how vulnerable those systems are. Neither are they aware of the extent and complexity of their local food system, much less its potential; the annual value of produce from all U.S. gardens is roughly equal to that of the annual U.S. corn crop, about $18 billion a year. What's more, agricultural, horticultural and food-related activities constitute between 20 percent and 25 percent of a local economy.

Defining Local Systems

What then is a local food system? The local part starts at the household level and expands to neighborhood, municipal and regional levels. At each level there are different cycles, issues, problems and possibilities. The food part includes all the various social, symbolic, health, power, access and equity dimensions (imagine all the facets of personal and corporate efforets to provide the hungry and homeless with "real" Thanksgiving dinners). "Systems" include not just the production aspects of food but also issues of processing, distribution, access, use, food recycling and waste. Besides social, economic and environmental issues, each of these points also involves a number of ethical and value questions.

Why localize? Sustainable agriculturalists have called for localization to increase environmental sustainability. Developing local markets reduces dependence upon distant (and often erratic) supply. Localizing food systems and growing more food locally and regionally also opens new opportunities for dealing with problems of hunger, joblessness, urban decay and environmental degradation. Such a vision includes:

Providing both long-term food security and better health for all local residents by making a variety of safe and nutritious food available to all;

Creating a cushion of self-reliance against transport strikes, major storms and disasters and rising prices resulting from oligopolies and/or rising fossil fuel prices and their multiplier effects;

Providing continuing employment for local farmers, horticulturalists and food workers;

Making households and neighborhoods more self-reliant by making more land, work and employment available throughout the food system;

Freeing up more local dollars for local development by increasing the energy and resource efficiency of local food systems, especially by reducing energy costs and putting organic wastes into productive use rather than expensive landfills;

Creating a healthier, more diverse and more pleasant environment by cleaning up air, water and soil systems; creating more green spaces and more diverse rural landscapes; and reducing health costs and pollution clean up costs; and

Reducing dependence on emergency hunger and feeding programs by moving toward hunger prevention programs.

Food Policy Councils

How do we do this? At a personal level we can grow, process and preserve more of our own food. We can buy local food from farmers markets and u-picks. We can join a community supported agriculture organization. As citizens, we can support innovative neighborhood and municipal programs and organizations. One example includes the growing popularity of food policy councils which form to address a given community's food system.

The issues addressed by these citizen advisory boards are critical and need to be investigated by local governments, nonprofits and the general population. They include:

Production: promoting household and community gardens; seeking to preserve local farmers and farmland; promoting community supported agriculture;

Processing: encouraging local food processing plants, as well as household and community canning programs;

Distribution and access: promoting co-ops, buying clubs and full use of available government programs; coordinating emergency feeding systems; ensuring availability of inner-city supermarkets; encouraging local farmers markets;

Use: promoting food safety and handling, and nutritious diets;

Food recycling: promoting gleaning, food banks, pantries and soup kitchens; and

Waste stream: using creative approaches to waste reduction, recycling and composting in each stage of the system.

Letting the Community Support the Farm
by Patti Wolter*

For the past five years, Dan Guenthner has traveled between his home in Minneapolis' Seward neighborhood and Common Harvest Farm, 18 miles away,

*Excerpted from *The Neighborhood Works* (February/March, 1994), where Patti Wolter is an editor.

where he grows organic produce for the 120 families who support the farm financially.

The system is called community supported agriculture—and it comes in many forms, but the basic model has a farmer growing fruits and vegetables for a set group of consumers who have bought "shares" in the farm or contribute to it financially in exchange for fresh produce. When Guenthner started his farm in 1989, there were less than 100 such farms in the United States. Now, he says, there are about 400.

"It's a way to connect the consumer or citizen to their food source," Guenthner explains. "People supporting us feel connected to us. They know where their food comes from, who grows it and how it's grown."

In a world of 24-hour, coupon-driven, super-duper markets, that's a rare thing. But as more and more people live in urban or suburban environments, Guenthner believes people are looking for new ways to "get back to the land," as well as do something about their concerns for the environment. Small CSA farms, by nature of their size and crop diversity, tend to use more environmentally responsible methods of farming; most, but not all, use organic methods, which means they do not farm with pesticides or herbicides.

"It's so easy to talk about global envrionmental issues, but they're vague—like ozone. But getting a bag of organic vegetables on your doorstep achieves a very personal connection with doing something good for the environment," Guenthner says.

Community supported agriculture is also a different approach to saving valuable farmland on the edges of metropolitan areas. As cities grow out, property values go up, and small farmers cannot afford to stay. With CSA, because an entire community or group of consumers are directly giving money in return for produce, the farmer can survive financially and retain the land.

"Instead of getting 3 percent of the food dollar [as with corporate agriculture], we get 100 percent, and we sell to people who like real tomatoes that have taste," explains Leland Eikermann, a self-described agroecology consultant who runs a 500-acre "hybrid" CSA farm about 60 miles from St. Louis. Eikermann, who ran a 3,000-acre corn and soybean farm for almost 15 years, explains that instead of growing cheap raw materials for food processors, he direct markets to restaurants and health food stores along with the families who subscribe to the farm.

For Eikermann, the issue is one of survival—both for the small family farmer and for the entire food system. As corporations have taken over farms and food processing and tapped into international markets for cheap produce, actual food production has become a concentrated process. Few regions actually produce all the items needed for one well-balanced meal. From seed to dinner plate, the food on your plate could have travelled thousands of miles. Which, Eikermann points out, means the U.S. food system is really a transportation system, "based on fuel, not on food."

His solution? The same as Guenthner's: Decentralize the food system, get back to a more locally grown, seasonal diet ("You don't need strawberries in January"), revive traditions of canning and freezing, and join a community supported farm.

By and large, however, the sustainable agriculture movement, and especially the organic food movement, is perceived to be accessible only to its white, middle- and upper-class constituents. Organic produce is generally more expensive than regular produce, due to scales of production. To some degree, these perceptions are accurate, but examples of CSA farms exist where customers come from a variety of income backgrounds and pay what they can.

Guenthner argues that the cooperative nature of CSA makes it well-suited to a variety of consumers. Ten percent of his members are low-income families, and their shares are paid for though a scholarship fund for which he solicits grants and donations. He has also made connections with area churches and social service providers who have purchased subscriptions which they then distribute. His goal is to supply as much of his customers' entire food supply as possible throughout the year, through canning, freezing and other techniques.

But as he and other CSA farmers continue to work out the kinks (only a handful have even moved beyond season-to-season financial stability), they remain optimistic about CSA's potential. "Food is a very passionate, personal thing in people's lives," Guenthner says. "The farm draws a strong connection between neighbors and their food. I've been working with local food pantries, and a group getting food to people with AIDS. I've discovered that food becomes a vehicle to reach a wide group of people."

Natural Resources:
The Potential of Sustainable Forestry

The Pacific Northwest of the United States, British Columbia, and Alaska are facing an economic and ecological crisis that is causing divisions in communities and even violence. At issue is forest destruction and what to do about it. Less than 10 percent (some say less than 5 percent) of this continent's original old-growth forests remains. For years, environmentalists and activists have fought for the protection of the remaining ancient forests. While the forest industry blames the spotted owl and environmentalists for the loss of logging and milling jobs, the truth is more jobs have been lost to technology, the export of whole logs mostly to Japan, and overcutting of the 1980s.

Money talks louder than trees, and the timber industry's pleas of economic hard times, using fearful workers and forest-dependent communities as pawns, along with empty promises to be more responsible in the future continue to rule the day. Neither government nor industry is going to to embrace changes threatening to the status quo. Therefore, people working to save and restore Earth's forests and the economies of forest-based communities are challenged to learn the how-tos of living with healthy forests and to find a balance that provides for the health and vitality of working forests and wilderness alike. Utilizing the concepts and models discussed in this book to build healthy forest-based communities offers the greatest source of hope for both workers *and* forests. Despite obstacles, the emerging sustainable-forestry movement has the potential to heal the economic and ecological wounds perpetuated by the profit-hungry forest industry.

Sustainable forestry places primary importance on healthy, biodiverse forests of all types. Industrial forest-management practices such as clearcutting, monoculture planting, use of chemicals, exporting raw logs (and jobs), plantations in the place of natural forests, and other common, destructive practices are not acceptable. Sustainable forest managers do cut trees, however, they do not cut the biggest and the best (high-grading). Nor do they cut all trees of a certain age (even-age management), leaving just the young ones. The forest as an ecosystem, home to a diversity of plants, animals, and fungi, is respected—and paramount. Degraded forests are managed in such a way that diversity and vitality can be restored over time, and old growth is off-limits.

Herb Hammond is a Certified Forest Ecologist in British Columbia with twenty years' experience as an industrial forester. His firm, Silva Ecosystem Consultants, works with indignous communities in Canada. He has developed what he calls "wholistic forest management," which involves long-term planning (hundreds of years into the future, not just five or ten), forest-use zoning, citizen community forestry boards, and consensus-based decision making. In his excellent book, *Seeing the Forest among the Trees*, Hammond explains,

> This approach does not mean a poorer economy or less jobs. Indeed, because of the need for better planning, more labor-intensive forest sensitive practices, and value-added manufacturing, protected landscape networks and wholistic forest-use zones will mean more diverse, stable employment than is currently generated by the increasingly mechanized logging and milling industries. Another economic point to emphasize is meaningful employment rather than short-term jobs. Restoring thousands of hectares of degraded forests in British Columbia and using remaining natural forests in ways that maintain fully functioning forests requires skilled, dedicated people capable of solving problems with finesse rather than with larger machines.

Specifically, sustainable community-based economic development in forest-dependent communities involves such things as processing logs locally, thereby keeping jobs and money in the region. Milling operations can make a point of producing goods needed by people in the region, rather than ones that are primarily sold to places farther away. While national and international trade do play a role in a diverse economy, providing for as many of our needs as possible from as close to home as possible is a primary value of community-based economics.

While trees can be considered a renewable resource, forests aren't. For sustainable forestry to have the most impact, we'll have to make the best use of the wood that is cut, and use wood for those things that truly require it. Paper, for example, can be made from recycled paper, kenaf, and hemp. Many building materials, too, can be made from recycled wood or paper, or agricultural products such as straw or hemp, or a mixture of wood and recycled products. Burning wood in biomass plants to produce electricity is increasingly common, especially in northern New England, and extraordinarily destructive to forest ecosystems since every part, even the roots, can be mined. Instead, we can invest in renewable energy sources such as wind and solar rather than turn our forests into factories for electricity.

Can sustainable forestry work in practice—economically as well as ecologically? It sure can! Sustainable or well-managed operations, in North America and elsewhere, including the tropics, do exist—and their numbers are growing rapidly. (Well-managed means working towards sustainability. It can take a few years to convert, just as when switching from using chemicals in farming to organic growing.)

Certification

Growing along with the sustainable-forestry movement—and integral to it—is certification, a process by which a reliable, independent, accredited organization with expertise in forest ecology, harvesting methods, and social issues related to native and forest-based communities certifies that a forest is being sustainably managed. The two most well-known certifiers so far are Rainforest Alliance's Smart Wood Program and Scientific Certification Systems (SCS), based in California. Other certification organizations are the Institute for Sustainable Forestry, based in Redway, California which focuses on community-based development, the Rogue Institute for Ecology and Economy in Ashland, Oregon; Forest Trust in Santa Fe, New Mexico; Silva Ecosystem Consultants in Winlaw, British Columbia; and two organizations in the United Kingdom, The Soil Association and Ecological Trading Company.

While all certifiers have some values in common, there are differences made manifest both in the criteria used to assess forest practices and in the assessment process itself. In order to lend credibility to certification, the Forest Stewardship Council was formed to promote sound forest practices and to acredit the certifiers. The FSC's "Principles of Sound Forest Management" include requiring written forest management plans, ensuring local rights (especially those of indigenous and long-settled forest dependent communities) are respected and maintained and that local communities directly benefit from forest operations; minimizing environmental impact, ensuring that the cost of a product accurately reflects the true cost of management and production; and discouraging replacement of natural forests with plantations. The FSC's logo will be displayed along with the certifier's to indicate to the consumer that the certifier meets FSC's standards.

The FSC, and the certification movement as a whole, have a few issues to resolve, among them the role of large timber corporations. Scientific Certification Systems, for example, is talking to companies such as Boise Cascade, Georgia-Pacific, and Louisiana Pacific and is reportedly considering certifying a parcel managed by Boise Cascade. Certifying an operation, however small, of a corporation known for its otherwise destructive forest practices has the potential to discredit the nascent movement and confuse consumers. Another issue concerns the certifiers' rating schemes. Scientific Certification System's evaluation process focuses on "timber resource sustainability," "forest ecosystem maintenance" and "community benefits." Performance is measured on a 100 point scale, like tests in school; 60 or above consitutes a passing grade. As you can imagine, there is a big difference between a 65 and an 85, which makes a big difference on the ground. The other certifiers, on the other hand, have a pass/fail rating system which is clearer and easier to understand.

The process of certication itself also needs to stand up to scrutiny. For example Richard Miller, of The Forest Partnership in Burlington, Vermont, and a former logger, points out that there is a big difference between forest managment plans (which may look good on paper) and what actually happens to a forest being logged. When certifiers go into a forest and approve it, they are seeing it at one point in time. Miller believes that for a seal to mean anything, certifiers should visit a forest at least every couple of weeks during harvest to ensure that the approved plan is actually being carried out. Yearly visits don't have the same effect, Miller insists.

Putting it all together

Using sustainable forestry as a tool for community-based economic development is not just a pipe dream (although it is in its infancy). Forest-based economies today are between the proverbial rock and hard place. If we modify industrial forest practices to take fewer trees and increase tree planting (which turns forests into plantations), we might end up with enough trees for industry (eventually), but the forests will be gone. The implications of forest loss to the vitality of the planet and our own future as a species are immense. Practically speaking, this option isn't viable.

We have to take better care of the forests if the forests are to take care of us. We need to completely rethink how we use wood and how we as a people relate to forests. Integrating business and community development with ecological processes is leading-edge work. At this point in time, there are very few individuals or organizations that know how to do this. According to

Double Green Policy: Toward Environmental and Economic Prosperity, we need to "pursue comprehensive integration of economic and environmental goals, not favoring one over the other." We need new institutions that are "entrepreneurial in nature, locally controlled, self-sustaining, adaptive to new information, and committed to long-term progress."

While we are learning more each day about forest ecology, we actually know very little. Computer models and forcasts are based on projections into the future based on current data. It's hard to anticipate unknown factors; we can plug in assumptions to change the scenario, but we still can't determine, with certainty, what will happen in the end. I see the integration of Earth's reality into our human planning as a weaving process. We will need to be constantly going back and forth between hard facts and the volatile process of natural systems and cycles. We will need to be flexible and open to surprises. At the foundation of this is a deep knowing of ourselves as part of the forest, and thus we can bring our intuition—our hearts and souls—into the planning process. To put it simply, we need to love the forest and allow our love to guide us.

Profile

The Menominee

In *Dreamers Without Power* by George Spindler and Louise Spindler, this dictum is said to have been given by nineteenth-century chiefs and headmen: "Start with the rising sun and work toward the setting sun, but take only the mature trees, the sick trees, and the trees that have fallen. When you reach the end of the reservation, turn and cut from the setting sun to the rising sun and the trees will last forever."

The Menominee Indian Reservation in Wisconsin provides an excellent model of sustainable forestry. Even though it is one of the United States' largest operations, and the forest has been sustainably managed for one hundred fifty years. The Menominee demonstrate the potential for the future as more working forests are sustainably managed and forests grow over generations. The Menominee reservation consists of 234,000 acres, 95 percent of which is forested, which is home to about 4,000 Menominee.

The Menominee forest is extremely diverse, containing eleven of the sixteen major types of forest habitat in Wisconsin and more than twenty-five tree species. All the species originally found in this forest still flourish here, with the exception of elm. And yet the forest is managed intensively for both hardwood and softwood. The Menominee harvest about thirty million board feet of timber every year—more than two billion board feet since cutting began in 1865. The most recent forest inventory indicates a higher volume and quality of wood now than when the land was first surveyed.

Menominee forestry differs from industrial forestry in several ways. Perhaps one of the major differences is they cut the worst trees, not the best. They operate in summer, fall, and winter, with a lengthy shutdown during spring breakup, when the snow melts and the ground thaws. Only small skidders with rubber tires are allowed in the woods. To minimize damage, tree-length skidding is prohibited, and loggers are required to use permanent skid trails, a rarity in production forests. Loggers can be fined as much as $250 for cutting a green, unmarked tree, and all contractors are required to attend training sessions during the spring shutdown.

Menominee Tribal Enterprises (MTE) is the organization that manages the forestry operations. Run by an elected board of directors and employing 105 hourly and twenty salaried workers, the president receives $45,000, or just over three times as much as the lowest-paid worker. Long tenure in the mill is the rule, although people move from one position to another with some regularity—95 percent of tribal members in the mill have never worked anywhere else. People retain rights to the forest to hunt, fish, make maple sugar, and gather berries, medicines, ginseng, and firewood. Conflicts between timber and nontimber users of the forest are infrequent, but when they arise they are dealt with using the informal methods that kinship-based communities use to hold members accountable to shared values.

Even though there are other enterprises on the reservation, the tribe's economy is forest-based. "MTE is something to be proud of," notes Edward Teller, who teaches the Menominee language and cultural studies at the high school. "It represents self-sufficiency." The land is the center of the Menominee world, the integrity of the forest signifies the health of the Menominee people. Thanks to careful management, the tribe's forest will probably look the same in five hundred years as it does today. Not only that, David Grignon, a tribal planner, says that "The forest today is what it was two hundred years ago when the Old Ones looked at it. Sometimes I go to just sit there and look around, and I know that."

Tanizul Timber

An interview with Chief Ed John by John Kosek*

Tanizul Timber was set up by the community for the community. The shareholders are our community. The board of directors, appointed by the

*Chief Ed John is president of Tanizul Timber in British Columbia, one of the few First Nation lumber companies to gain a tree-farm license, a 25-year authorization to harvest trees on government land. Tanizul Timber was created about eleven years ago to create jobs for the Tla'tzen people, who had an unemployment rate of 80 to 90 percent. They wanted to be involved in an enterprise the people already knew and felt comfortable with and so chose forestry. Ten years after the company's inception, Chief John talked with John Kosek about the dilemmas that come with trying to balance economics and traditional values and ways of

community and held accountable by the community, oversee the development of the company for the people. The board is also responsible for setting up land-management and other management practices that will best advocate the objectives we have set out for ourselves. We talk through issues, and we follow the course.

Although this operation is community-owned, we treat it as a business to make it viable for tomorrow and for the future as well. First and foremost, Tanizul Timber has to be viable economically. Over the 10 years since Tanizul started, we have provided jobs for our people. We have also generated about $45 to $50 million in revenue. This money stays in the community, and we use it to buy goods and services and to support the local economy. It isn't a lot of money, but it's revenue we never had before.

We are in a fluid position and must make milestone decisions on matters that are important for our future—matters related to history, matters related to fisheries, matters related to hunting. Those practices sustained our people for hundreds of generations. Today, we look at sustaining our community by extracting resources. Can we do that if we're to live according to the philosophies of our own people?

We are moving away from our traditional lifestyles into a new way of using the land, but we must remember we can't abandon the past in exchange for what this new resource development will do for us. We can make all sorts of rationalizations about what First Nations brings to forestry, but the fact of the matter is that we are also getting involved in a type of development that, in some ways, conflicts with our values. Yes, we can bring more sensitive consideration into the use of the land and the resources, but there is a conflict of values. If we are going be involved in forestry, we have to make some decisions as to how we are going to do it, how to recognize certain situations, and how far we are prepared to compromise. These are decisions the community has to make, and they are important issues to deal with.

Our people survived for many years in forestry, but the industry is changing. We are talking about the traditional territories of my people, and more and more we see the timber companies exploiting our territories. We see the change, but do we like it? Our communities are taking into consideration the alarming rate at which this exploitation is happening. It is a huge dilemma. In the past, we put up blockades against industry and government for how they handled our land and our resources.

We live on the land and that affects how we treat it. Fishing and hunting are important to us. Water helps sustain the fish that feed the rivers—it must be clean for the fish to spawn. In a lot of places in our province, the salmon are being rapidly depleted because of contamination due to erosion after logging. In some cases, the salmon have disappeared. The salmon resource has been good at feeding our people far longer than forestry has, and we won't jeopardize that.

When we look at timber resources, we look at them from a different perspective from other timber companies. That land is our land; it is our traditional territory. That

living. This interview is edited from a longer interview by John Kosek, "Ethics, Economics, and Ecosystems," published in *Cultural Survival Quarterly* (Spring, 1993).

land and the resources within that territory have sustained our people for hundreds of generations. And they must sustain us into the future for as many hundreds of generations.

To us, the moose, the bear, the berries in the forest are as important as the timber we take out. Our philosophy teaches us to treat the animals in that forest with as much respect as we treat each other. We give thanks for every animal we take from the forest and for every bird, every fish because that allows us to survive. That is a part of our philosophy and teaching."

Creating Healthy Cities
by Stephen Wheeler*

Imagine living in an urban community in which you could walk to stores, restaurants, and offices, in which parks, restored creeks, and garden space were also close to home, in which trains and trolleys could take you anywhere you needed to go, in which women and children felt safe in public places, in which different racial and economic groups lived near one another, and, last but not least, in which most people knew their neighbors and looked out for them. Sound impossible? Today such an ideal seems far from reality. But in the long run it is even more unlikely that current patterns of suburban sprawl and central city decline can continue.

Since a great many environmental and social problems are tied to the ways we build and maintain our communities, creating a sustainable society will mean embarking on a new path of ecological urban development, literally redesigning our cities and towns. No existing city or region provides a perfect model. Yet many examples of good urban design can be found, and all over the world citizens and local governments are exploring new approaches. Moreover, in recent years the word "sustainability" has begun to enter the vocabulary of city planners. Seattle, Portland, Olympia, and San Jose are among the American cities officially embarked on sustainable-city programs. Such efforts often focus primarily on recycling and energy conservation. However, deeper underlying questions of land use, housing, transportation, and social justice are also beginning to be addressed. A wide range of economic mechanisms for healthier urban development is also beginning to come

*Stephen Wheeler is a board member of Urban Ecology, Inc., an nonprofit membership group in Berkeley, California seeking to bring about ecologically and socially sustainable cities. He is editor of the group's quarterly journal *The Urban Ecologist*, which was nominated for an *Utne Reader* Alternative Press Award in 1993. He is a graduate of Dartmouth College and is pursuing graduate study in sustainable urban development at the Department of City and Regional Planning at the University of California at Berkeley. Within the San Francisco Bay Area, he has led efforts to oppose freeway construction and to provide better bicycle and public transit alternatives.

of age, ranging from higher parking charges to discourage automobile use to community-development loans to help rebuild inner-city areas. In the long run, new models of urban community will emerge in which cities and towns are far more connected to natural ecosystems, and are also much pleasanter, safer, more equitable, and more community oriented.

Transportation

Traffic congestion and over-reliance on the automobile are main features of our current cities and towns. In the United States the number of motor vehicle miles traveled per capita tripled between 1950 and 1990, from 3,000 miles to just under 9,000[1], largely as the result of suburban patterns of land use and the decline of public transit. Americans burn up about 1.4 billion gallons of fuel annually just sitting in traffic, and waste 12 billion hours.[2] Congestion is also growing around European cities and in Third World nations, as the rest of the world follows the U.S. model of automobile dependency. In South Korea, for example, traffic volumes are rising by as much as 25 percent a year, while a high rate of accidents led to 11,640 fatalities and 325,943 serious injuries in 1992.[3]

Over the past fifty years our communities have been designed more to accommodate automobiles than to meet the needs of people.[4] Many suburban neighborhoods don't even have sidewalks. Busy streets, wide intersections and vast distances between destinations in suburbia discourage walking, bicycling, or human interaction. Meanwhile, automobile-oriented planning has effectively gutted many big-city downtowns. Oakland, California, for example, has gone out of its way to promote automobile travel for decades. In the 1950s and 1960s large freeways destroyed residential neighborhoods east, west, and north of the central business district, while in the downtown area many streets were converted into three- or four-lane, one-way funnels for traffic. The city is now easy to drive through, but the new roads simply help carry people to suburbs and outlying shopping centers, while the city's downtown streets are not pleasant for people to be on. Pedestrians have stayed away, businesses have closed, and many downtown storefronts are permanently empty.

Grim though this pattern may be, the age of the automobile may be ending. One hopeful sign is that a growing number of U.S. cities are seeking to rebuild the rail transit networks they scrapped fifty years ago. Since 1980, new rail systems have been opened in nine U.S. cities, including Baltimore, San Diego, San Jose, and Sacramento. Existing rail lines are being expanded in Washington, D.C., the San Francisco Bay Area, and elsewhere. Fourteen additional cities are planning rail transit systems. Portland, Oregon is planning three more routes in addition to its successful MAX trolley, and is considering an innovative proposal called the LUTRAQ (Land Use, Transportation and Air Quality) alternative, which would promote development around transit stations as an alternative to building a freeway. Even Los Angeles, capital of the automobile culture, is spending tens of billions of dollars creating an ambitious rail network, which includes four subway lines, nine light-rail lines, and five commuter lines. The city is also developing a coordinated land use/transportation policy that would cluster future development around this rail network.[5] Over the next fifty or one hundred years, such policies could fundamentally reshape this city and others.

Many communities are also seeking ways to make their streets "bicycle friendly." Phoenix, Arizona, is creating an ambitious 110-mile bikeway network and has added racks on the front of buses to allow cyclists to take their bikes with them everywhere in the city. Arlington, Virginia, and Palo Alto, California, now require showers and lockers for cyclists in new commercial buildings of above a certain size, making it easier for people to bicycle to work. Seattle spends more than $100,000 a year upgrading its bike facilities and has one hundred police officers traveling by mountain bike instead of patrol car.

A more far-reaching movement to retake streets from the automobile has been underway in Europe since the early 1980s. Efforts at "traffic-calming" began simultaneously in German and Dutch cities, as residents fed up with traffic demanded local government action. One Dutch neighborhood literally took the law into its own hands, creating speed humps on its street and then defending them when the city sent bulldozers to clear the obstructions away. By the early 1990s most major European cities had created downtown car-free zones. Throngs of people filled streets formerly occupied by automobiles. Although local businesses often worried at first, eliminating cars from the central city has usually proved beneficial to retailers.

As the world's foremost bastion of the automobile, the United States has yet to seriously embrace traffic-calming in its cities. However, a few small steps have been taken. Portland, Oregon, has a small pedestrian and transit-only area in its downtown and is embarking on an Arterial Traffic-Calming Program as well as a Skinny Streets Program, narrowing residential streets to slow traffic.[6] Cities such as Oakland and Berkeley, California, are adding speed humps to residential streets to slow traffic. Neighborhood associations in the latter community have requested humps on 128 streets in addition to the city's existing traffic-diverter system and demonstration slow street.

Although progress is slow, efforts are also underway in the United States to reorient economic incentives to favor public transit, bicycling, or walking rather than automobiles. Many cities have raised downtown parking charges, and are encouraging employers to subsidize their employees' transit expenses rather than giving free parking as a perk. Gas taxes and tolls are slowly rising. The Union of Concerned Scientists and other groups have developed innovative proposals for traffic-reducing incentives such as "pay-as-you-drive" insurance, in which people would pay for their car insurance through a tax at the gas pump, thus providing a strong economic impetus to drive less.[7] Eventually, through a combination of economic incentives, improved alternatives, and better land-use planning, automobile use can be substantially reduced.

Land Use and Housing

Land use patterns change even more slowly than transportation systems, but here there is hope as well. The basic need is to move away from low-density suburban sprawl, which leads to loss of open space and agricultural land, destruction of natural ecosystems, dependency on the automobile, high fuel and materials consumption, air and water pollution, isolated land uses, and the segregation of racial and economic groups from one another. Instead, the need is to develop compact cities and towns that are both more dense and far more livable than most current U.S. communities.

Many cities are adopting policies aimed at promoting mixed-use development and transit-oriented development, which offer an alternative to low-density sprawl. "Mixed-use development" simply means placing homes, shops and workplaces near one another, rather than far apart as under traditional U.S. zoning. This reduces automobile use and helps create more vibrant, pedestrian-oriented communities. "Transit-oriented development" takes the process one step further, clustering communities around stops on a transit network. In recent years the Washington, D.C. area, for example, has seen large amounts of mixed-use development around stations of its Metro system. Seattle is also considering an ambitious "urban village" strategy in which a number of compact, mixed-use urban centers served by public transit would be created within the broader city.

Progressive planners such as Peter Calthorpe, Andres Duany, and Elizabeth Plater-Zyberk are developing proposals for transit-oriented communities with the look and feel of traditional small towns.[8] Although some of these are relatively suburban in nature and are being built on formerly rural land—such as Calthorpe's Laguna West development near Sacramento and Duany/Plater-Zyberk's new Florida town of Seaside—others are infill projects on underused land within existing urban areas. Given the need to restrain the growth of cities and preserve remaining open space and farmland, infill projects represent an important strategy for the future.

Various sorts of intentional communities provide alternatives to traditional housing patterns that are higher density, more neighborly, and better suited to today's wide diversity of household types. Cohousing is one such model, a movement has been going strong in Denmark for more than twenty years, with more than 20,000 people living in several hundred communities, and is now catching on rapidly in the United States. In cohousing communities, the future residents get together and design for themselves a cluster of living units and common facilities, usually with the help of architects or a professional facilitator. Although each living unit typically has its own kitchen and a small outdoor area, residents often cook and eat together in a central dining room, and frequently share responsibilities for child care, gardening, and maintenance.[9] Muir Commons in Davis, California, was the first U.S. cohousing project to be built. Completed in 1990, it sits in the midst of a traditional suburban subdivision, whose large single family homes march stiffly in rows across the landscape. Yet the lush gardens, heavily used common facilities, and twenty-six modest townhouses of Muir Commons offer a totally different impression, one of a creative, vibrant community with a feeling of life that the traditional subdivision lacks.

A wide range of economic incentives can help reorient land use in the United States and provide affordable, livable housing within urban areas. Mechanisms to removing housing units from the speculative market, such as limited-equity co-ops, are important since these help keep homes affordable in the long run. Nonprofit housing developers and community development corporations are also essential to build the lower-income housing that profit-oriented developers won't touch. Tax breaks and preferences can help reduce pressures to develop agricultural land, and give incentives for rehabilitation of existing housing. Individuals can help finance housing and community development by encouraging institutions such as churches, pension funds, and banks to invest in these areas, and by putting their own money to work through progressive financial institutions. South Shore Bank in Chicago, for example, has lent primarily to five Chicago communities of color since 1972. Its 7,500 borrowers have amassed a cumulative repayment rate of 98 percent, and the bank's lending has helped rehabilitate more than 10,000 rental housing units.

Ecological Restoration and Urban Greening

People have been moving to suburbia for some good reasons, and one of them is that many cities and towns currently do not offer a pleasant, green, safe environment in which to live. This situation can be remedied in part through measures such as calming traffic and improving housing design. But one of the most fundamental steps toward making cities livable will be to bring nature back into the city.

Municipalities have traditionally sprinkled a few small parks here and there for their residents. These are fine, but much more is needed. One current approach is to create greenways—long corridors of natural land that intersect to form a network. Greenways can support a much greater variety of wildlife than isolated parks; they also offer far greater recreational opportunities for walkers or bicyclists. The city of Toronto, Canada, for example, is planning an ambitious greenway network following natural watercourses,[10] and Los Angeles is considering one along rail corridors. Abandoned railway lines make ideal greenways; the Rails-to-Trails Conservancy, based in Washington, D.C., has helped convert more than five hundred such lines near U.S. cities to recreational use.

Creek restoration is another way to bring nature back into the city. Most urban streams were channelized or put into culverts over the past century. However, a growing number of cities are seeking to bring them back. Portions of creeks in the California municipalities of Berkeley, Richmond and San Luis Obispo now run in reconstructed natural beds, and additional creek restorations are planned in Santa Rosa, Palo Alto and Walnut Creek. Various forms of watershed planning, wetlands restoration, and shoreline reclamation are also catching on, often due to the efforts of volunteer community groups. For example, the Anacostia Watershed Society in Washington, D.C., has taken it upon itself to care for the Anacostia River and its tributaries. Using 2,440 volunteers, the group has removed 65 tons of debris and 1,820 tires from the river's banks, and has planted more than 4,000 trees.

Urban gardening and farming is a further means for urban dwellers to regain touch with the natural world. Agriculture can be viable on surprisingly small plots of land within cities, even on a commercial basis. Kona Kai Farms in Berkeley, California, has grown as much as $250,000 worth of lettuce and greens per year on a quarter-acre city lot. (Greenhouse agriculture is common in Dutch cities.) Networks of community gardeners are to be found in most urban areas in the United States; the San Francisco League of Urban Gardeners, for example, has created more than fourteen community gardens in various parts of that city. Boston Urban Gardeners has developed gardens used by 3,000 individuals each year. By literally getting their hands dirty and producing some of their own food, residents of urban areas can maintain a sense of connection with the ecosystem of which they are a part.

Energy and Materials

One of the main problems with current patterns of human settlement is that they are very wasteful of resources and create many pollutants and wastes. Changing the actual form of the city can help—for example, residents in a compact, mixed-use neighborhood will drive far less, on average, than residents of a standard suburb, saving gasoline and reducing air pollution. Good building design and use of ecologically appropriate materials can help as well. Lastly, programs for reusing and recycling materials are essential. Such programs have already been begun in most cities, but can be further improved.

Perhaps the most progress is being made in the area of energy conservation. Today's houses are far more energy efficient than ten or twenty years ago because they are better insulated, have energy-saving doors and windows, and have more energy-efficient appliances. Many of these improvements have come about as the result of specific state or federal requirements, such as California's Title 24 energy-efficiency standards for new-home construction. Other energy-saving measures have been promoted by utilities, who have come to realize that is often cheaper to offer incentives for energy-efficient construction and lighting than to build new power plants. Large utilities such as Consolidated Edison in the New York metropolitan area have literally given away tens of thousands of energy-saving compact fluorescent light bulbs to customers, and have spent millions in consumer rebates for purchase of more efficient refrigerators, air conditioners, and industrial motors.

Solar hot-water heating, wind energy, and photovoltaic technologies are making slow but steady progress and will eventually play a leading role in community energy self-sufficiency. Meanwhile, passive solar design is slowly infiltrating architecture, as architects realize the enormous energy savings that can result simply from having a home facing south with windows catching winter sunlight for heating. Architects and builders are also beginning to use more ecologically appropriate materials in the construction of homes, such as lumber made from 100 percent recycled plastic, wallboard made from recycled cellulose fiber, and less toxic paints. By these and other means cities of the future will reduce their drain on the Earth's resources.

Social Justice

Communities cannot be healthy in the long run if they allow great inequities between different racial, economic, or ethnic groups. An important part of creating livable cities will be to address the injustices that are built into our physical environment and that are present in government policy. This challenge has been one of the most difficult areas for our society to come to grips with.

The environmental justice-movement of recent years has pointed out to urban leaders and mainstream environmentalists that incinerators, toxic wastes, and polluting industries have been placed disproportionately in communities of color and lower-income neighborhoods. In one study of Houston, Texas, researcher Robert Bullard found that all five of the city's garbage dumps were located in mostly African-American neighborhoods, while seven out of eight of its incinerators were sited in communities of color. The solution is not to relocate such facilities elsewhere, but to recognize that no community should be exposed to them and to see more environmentally-appropriate alternatives. [11]

Equally damaging has been the neglect of the physical environment of inner cities, which are home to many communities of color and lower-income groups. Housing, schools, and public facilities are often in bad repair. Few parks and natural areas enliven the landscape. Freeways and heavily trafficked arterials have often destroyed neighborhoods. Past urban-redevelopment efforts have often simply made the situation worse by replacing functioning neighborhoods with grim public-housing projects.

Bringing social justice into our cities and towns means pursuing a wide variety of programs to end this state of affairs. Since building freeways and automobile infrastructure has historically favored white suburbia, it is time to build rail networks for existing central cities instead. Since federal housing policy has subsidized suburban, detached, single-family housing, it is time to give equivalent support to affordable-housing developers in urban areas and innovative multifamily designs. Revenue-sharing between inner cities and suburbs could help as well by evening the tax base between jurisdictions within metropolitan regions. A variety of community-development corporations and other nonprofit groups could help carry out improvements and implement a social-justice agenda on the local level.

Planning for Women, Children, and other Human Beings

We live in cities and towns that by and large have been designed by men, for men, according to male values. These values do not necessarily create environments that are friendly or comfortable for women or children, or even for many males. Because of prevailing patterns of transportation, land use, and urban design, it is difficult or unsafe for women and children to walk around in many areas. Mothers spend much of their time chauffeuring children from one place to another, and older children have little mobility. In one study cited by Peter Calthorpe, children in a traditional Vermont town—in which houses were relatively near one another on a grid of quiet streets with stores nearby—were found to have three times the mobility of children living on cul-de-sacs in southern California's Orange County, while the Californian kids, stuck in their homes, watched four times as much television.

Safety is another major concern, especially for women. In few communities do women feel safe walking alone after dark. While the roots of this problem go deep, the nature of the physical environment itself can help improve or undermine safety. Basically, a relatively dense, pedestrian-oriented, mixed-use neighborhood is likely to be much safer than low-density, single-use areas whose streets are deserted. Other changes, such as removing sexist billboards and advertising, banning guns, and implementing social-justice initiatives, can help create a public environment that is more friendly towards women.[12]

Ever since the time of the ancient Greeks, women's space has been defined as the home, which is usually isolated from public spaces and the broader community. Public spaces have in turn been men's space, and have often been designed according to male tastes. The grand public avenues and buildings of Paris and Washington, D.C., for example, embody a sort of male bravado (they were originally designed for military parades), while the large glass-and-steel office buildings of modernist architecture are products of an impersonal design aesthetic, which is more male than female

The antidote is to humanize the public environment, creating buildings and spaces that are designed for people rather than show, that promote human interaction, and that are safe and inviting for children as well. Playful touches are important, as is color and greenery. Common-sense innovations such as placing child-care centers near workplaces and diaper-changing areas in public restrooms can help a great deal.

Reinventing the City

All of this may seem a blueprint for a utopian society. Yet many efforts at improving urban environments are already underway, from the rebuilding of transit systems to the restoration of natural environments and the creation of community development financial institutions. Although it is easy to think that our current patterns of urban and suburban development are hopelessly entrenched, they are in fact very recent. Most of what we see around us has been built in the last fifty years. If we keep on with these patterns of development for the next fifty years, we are in trouble as a society, but if we develop new models of healthy cities, towns and neighborhoods, we can begin to effectively address a whole range of social and environmental problems.

What is needed most of all is a sense of collective commitment to improving our urban environment, rather than continued patterns of escape to suburbia and isolated single-family homes. We need to focus on public concerns and public values—the urban commons, if you will—rather than continue on private, individualistic needs. We also need to reintegrate our communities with the Earth, and with the needs of a global society. By seeking innovative new ways to create healthy cities, we can help solve global problems and at the same time bring about better homes and neighborhoods for ourselves.

Notes

1. James J. KacKenzie et al., *The Going Rate: What It Really Costs to Drive* (Washington, D.C.: World Resources Institute, 1992) 3.

2. Marcia D. Lowe, "Reinventing Transport," in Lester R. Brown et al., *State of the World 1994* (New York: W.W. Norton & Co., 1994) 84.

3. *Baedel Update* (Taejon City, South Korea: Baedel Eco-Society, 1993) 4.

4. For a good description of how automobiles have affected our cities and towns and possible alternatives, see David Engwicht, *Reclaiming Our Cities & Towns: Better Living With Less Traffic* (Philadelphia: New Society Publishers, 1993).

5. City of Los Angeles Planning Department, *Draft Land Use/Transportation Policy* (March, 1993).

6. *The Urban Ecologist* (Winter, 1994): 15.

7. For further information on economic incentives for reducing automobile use, see Deborah Gordon, *Steering a New Course: Transportation, Energy and the Environment* (New York: W.W. Norton, 1990).

8. See Peter Calthorpe, *The Next American Metropolis: Ecology, Community and the American Dream* (Princeton, N.J.: Princeton Architectural Press, 1993).

9. For more information on cohousing, see Kathryn McCamant and Charles Durrett, *Cohousing: A Contemporary Approach to Housing Ourselves*, 2nd Ed., (Berkeley, Calif.: Ten Speed Press, 1994).

10. Metropolitan Planning Department, *The Livable Metropolis: Draft Metropolitan Toronto Official Plan* (Toronto, Canada: Municipality of Toronto, 1992).

11. For a good introduction to the theory and philosophy behind the environmental-justice movement, see Richard Hofrichter, ed., *Toxic Struggles: The Theory and Practice of Environmental Justice* (Philadelphia: New Society Publishers, 1993).

12. See Dolores Hayden, *Redesigning the American Dream: The Future of Housing, Work, and Family Life* (New York: W.W. Norton, 1984).

TEN

Economics of Culture

ONE OF THE biggest challenges we face is reconnecting our economics with culture, place, and local traditions. A sustainable economy simply cannot exist outside of these aspects of community life.

Several years ago I attended a conference organized by the Seventh Generation Fund called "Investing in Our People and Land." The purpose of the conference was to develop ways of building economic self-reliance for Native Americans living on their lands. The vast majority of participants were already working on their reservations on projects of various sorts, ranging from agriculture to small-business development to dealing with the intricate relationships and failed communication between Native Americans, their tribal councils, the Bureau of Indian Affairs (BIA), and the federal government. Most participants recognized that the solutions will not come from the U.S. government, the BIA, "experts," non-Indian consultants, or corporate America. These routes have already been tried and have usually failed miserably. Instead, the participants focused on developing systems and models that work with traditional culture and spirituality: "Our values are the foundations of our economies. If we are guided by spirituality, then as individuals we carry that: We walk with a clear mind, in honesty, compassion, and respect. The economic systems we build will reflect this."

The participants reaffirmed their connections with their land, history, and community and the importance of using these connections to develop

195

critical thinking, to draw from local assets, and to begin appropriate-scale projects:

> This process starts with problem solving…and includes recognizing and identifying our own skills, knowledge and capacities…our local resources of all kinds, and determining how we can help ourselves and each other to meet our basic needs for self-reliant, meaningful, diverse and enriching lives.…This process is inherently respectful of the Earth and all our relatives.

My goal in this section is to give you a sense of the thinking and activity simmering in Native communities and in Native people who may not be living on their reservations, but are still actively involved in their culture. I am not Native, so I rely on friends who are, personal contacts in the indigenous economic-development community, works written by Native people I respect, and my own sense of what feels right.

It is not my intention in this section to use indigenous models as a prescription for Western woes. Nor do I want to perpetuate a paternalistic, colonial mind-set that says "We have to preserve these cultures because of all they can teach us." Instead I want to show how Native peoples are integrating traditional values with the practical realities of economic development and marketplace economics.

For example, indigenous communities involved with sustainable forestry are very aware of the complexities and contradictions of trying to combine their traditional values, ways of living with the Earth, the pressure for increased production, and the need for profits. What is crucial is that they are aware of the complexities, are discussing them, and are discovering and trying creative solutions.

Ideally, community development would involve the *entire Earth community* in all deliberations and applications. This means the forests, mountains, rivers, oceans, deserts, and all the myriad species living in these ecosystems would "have a voice." Further, spiritual and cultural traditions, including the sacredness of particular places, would be honored and respected without question. The costs to future generations would be considered, and no act would impinge on the integrity of the environment in the future. It will be quite some time before this development process exists in our culture—if it ever does. However, Native communities are leading the way toward such wholistic development that honors life and the sacred. It's not perfect and it never will be. But they are moving forward into unknown and promising territory.

The Fourth World

Typically, economic development aims to eliminate poverty and raise the standard of living of people in impoverished communities. But our ideas about poverty and wealth are not universally applicable. There are people who live a self-sufficient lifestyle—who grow their own food, make their clothing, use locally available materials for buildings and the like. Such groups may look poor to Western visitors because they don't have a lot of consumer goods. What they often have instead are strong, intact families and communities—including enough food, clothing and homes for everyone—and a rich heritage of cultural and spiritual traditions. This too is a kind of wealth, a kind many in the West long for.

Western technology and notions of progress and wealth undermine traditional cultures and replace local systems and institutions developed over generations with centralized, impersonal systems. Economies that prospered using primarily barter and other forms of noncash exchange are rendered obsolete by the monetized international market economy.

There is hope, however. And the seeds of this hope are being sown by an increasing number of indigenous peoples in the Americas and elsewhere who seek a different kind of economic development—a development that is informed by a peoples' place-based traditions. First Nations Development Institute, profiled later in this chapter calls this "values-centered" development. It begins with the recognition that values and traditions are the starting point for success.

To gain further understanding, I spoke with José Barreiro, an activist in Native-American affairs for many years and editor-in-chief of the *Akwe:non Journal* (formerly the *Northeast Indian Quarterly*). He distinguishes between Third World and Fourth World peoples:

> Fourth World identifies peoples from tribal communities across the various hemispheres—people from aboriginal or indigenous cultures—who still have a memory of their culture, language, and religion, and a sense of the history of their relationships to particular places of the Earth, people whose ways of living are primarily in relationship to the natural world that surrounds them.
>
> These people, whom you call "tribal" or "aboriginal," and who have been called Native Americans in the Western hemisphere, organize their systems of human habitation on the logic of the ecological systems they live in, in order to keep the balance. Their main needs as human beings—shelter, food, and so on—are met within one or two ecosystems. There is an awareness they are going to be there for a long time, have been there a long time.
>
> They also share an understanding that humanity is full of diversity. There is more of a recognition in Native culture than in Western cultures of other systems, other peoples, and other species.
>
> There is a unity of principle among Native people, which is why we refer to the Fourth World. The Fourth World includes the Inuit of the northern Arctic, the Mayan in the jungle valleys of Central America, the peoples in the jungles of the Amazon: millions of people around the world.

We in the Fourth World are beginning to recognize each other and communicate directly with each other, to exchange information and delegations and so forth. Numerous meetings have taken place on an international level since the late 1960s and early 1970s. First steps were taken to break down the barriers between these Indigenous peoples. And some lasting friendships were made, like between the Mayan people and Iroquois people. They are beginning to create common ground and common definitions.

These definitions are based on the concept of the Fourth World—the other side of the Third World—which hasn't been totally colonized culturally. The Third World can be defined more as the people who have been colonized so thoroughly culturally that despite the economic oppression they suffer, they still try to be like Second and First World people who colonized them. The Fourth World is saying, "We want to be left alone. You are all wrong; Come this way."

The Fourth World offers the circle. In the First and Second World you have conflict, antagonism, materialism. In the Fourth World you have the circle. You have the harmonious concept.

The Fourth World is the basis. That's what was here. The First World is missing a true ethic of human inhabitation in the Earth. It has forgotten the first lesson. The Fourth World has a memory, a memory most of mankind no longer has. This ethic of human inhabitation cannot be remade; it has already been made. In the natural world systems of humanity, tribal peoples are the elders of the human family. There is a cosmology that is the very basis of many of the Native religions and cultures, as well as a symbology that transfers. The most common of these symbols is the bisected circle—the circle divided in four by the four directions.

When asked, How can people in the First World help in a culturally appropriate way? José responded:

It's important to see the way Native peoples greet each other themselves. There is respect for the ancient knowledge, for the locality of the people who are coming in from the outside, and for the local people who are living on their ground. Guests recognize no matter how much learning they bring with them, they won't understand the culture they are visiting in a day or a year or even in twenty years. So they relax. They let themselves be guided and they try to pay attention to the things their hosts pay attention to among themselves.

Among the most important elements is respect for specificity; respect for the situation as it is seen in a community. This includes the specifics of language and of place; these are deeply ingrained in tribal cultures. They have their roots in the specific awe and respect given to the nature of the place—of a specific waterfall or riverbed or mountain range—and the powers that this may have to the people and the meanings that it may have to the people. It is one of the first things destroyed in the mind of the cultures of the Native peoples by the West, by Christianity, and by the belief, often held by those trained in First World values, that there is no specific spiritual quality to places. This is at the root of some of the misunderstandings between the cultures.

This ability to acknowledge and hear the voice of a place—its energy or spirit—is critical to creating new relationships and learning how to reinhabit the Earth. What is appropriate in one place may not be in another. And this has as much to do with the spirit of the place as it does with the physical limitations of the land and climate and the culture of the people living there.

Indian Economic Development: The U.S. Experience of an Evolving Indian Sovereignty

by John C. Mohawk

The destruction of American Indian economies was one of the most significant impacts visited upon Indian tribes during the invasion of America by Western Europeans...The creation of the reservation system by itself would have been devastating enough...but [t]he practice adopted by the young nation in Indian affairs established federal domination over every aspect of Indian life.

—Donald R. Wharton,
statement to Senate Select Committee, October 25, 1989

Around 1968, American Indians across the United States began protesting what they termed unfair domination by the United States government through its administrative bureaucracies—the Bureau of Indian Affairs (BIA), the Bureau of Land Management (BLM), and a host of smaller, less well-known agencies that had regulated Indian land, water, and lives for well over a century.[1] Federal (and in some cases state) domination over Indian communities was so complete that Indians had practically no power of ownership over their assets and no authority or ability to mobilize capital and labor—the primary ingredients that make development possible.

The contemporary history of Indian development begins, therefore, with the Indian movement for political and economic rights, which included the occupation of Alcatraz Island, the struggle for Indian fishing rights on the Columbia River, the Pit River Indians' struggle for land rights, the Trail of Broken Treaties, the occupation of Wounded Knee in 1973, and a number of other events. The result of these incidents was a widespread consensus in Indian country that power over policy decisions involving Indian resources and development directions must be wrested away from the non-Indian bureaucracies and relocated among the Indian peoples and communities.[2]

Indian communities are among the poorest in the United States, suffering abnormally high unemployment rates and the social ills associated with Third World underdevelopment.[3] The foundation for this state of affairs can be traced to nineteenth-century theories of scientific racism, which proposed that American Indians were racially inferior and in effect "minors" in the sense that they were not competent to make decisions for themselves. This theory coincided rather conveniently with the ambitions of the time to transfer the wealth of the Indians into the hands of others. The idea of Indian incompetence evolved to a practice that required that decisions must be made for Indians, and the institutions that evolved to this task were the various agencies of the War Department and the Bureau of Indian Affairs. It is not accidental that these institutions were not seriously challenged until the 1960s, when theories of racial superiority and inferiority were generally in decline during the United States civil rights movement. This theory of Indians as mentally and socially incompetent because of their biological and cultural traits continues to be practiced in a number of nation states in the Western Hemisphere, notably Brazil.

The American Indian movement of the 1960s and 1970s established a militancy among a younger generation of Indians who refused to continue to be addressed as wards of the Bureau of Indian Affairs and refused to agree that the reservation assets of their grandfathers was somehow transferred to the hands of the United States. The 1970s and 1980s became decades of political development in Indian country, which saw some communities seize control of their own resources and develop those resources with their own goals and objectives and their own control of both the nature of development and the designated beneficiaries.

A number of conditions preclude successful economic development on Indian reservations and require at least a short historic evaluation. Indian nations and communities differ from other Americans primarily in the group nature of the communities. Most immigrants and their descendants exist largely as individuals in American society. The Indians exist as distinct groups and have existed as such since time immemorial. The United States and most modern industrialized states have a tradition of rights of individuals but little tradition of group rights, and even today Indian rights are poorly defined and poorly understood in otherwise "enlightened" countries.

Immigrants and settlers were largely defined by their value to society as laborers. African and African-American slaves were likewise brought to the United States (and formerly Britain's American colonies) as laborers. Alone among English-speaking North America's ethnic identities, the Indians were not valued for their labor but for their land.

After the land was seized, the Indians were supposed to vanish. Banished to (often remote) reservations, Indians presumably languished out of the mainstream's sight and out of mind under the tutelage of federal bureaucracies. When, during the 1960s, other ethnic groups generated demands, those demands focused on redistribution of access to rights within American society. Among Indians, however, as one looks back over the increasingly activist Indian politics of the post-War years, what is striking is the persistent salience of goals which have little to due directly with the common American vision of success. Again and again three intimately related concerns emerge: tribal sovereignty, treaty rights, land. All have to do fundamentally with the maintenance and protection of peoplehood, of community....It has been a politics of national survival.[4]

Economic development is a social process that involves the ability to organize to reach for goals and the power to take action to achieve those goals. Indian economic development may be less about creating wealth than it is about creating the conditions for political power in the context of socially responsible choices for the continued existence and cohesion of the group, (i.e., the Indian nation).

Economic development in the Indian country has been a byproduct of an Indian movement toward sovereignty, and sovereignty has meant being able to do what the Indian government decides to do, thus rendering the decisions of the United States federal courts, which had largely ignored the idea of Indian sovereignty as providing the Indians with any real political power, as close to irrelevant in the real world as possible.

Several case studies of successful Indian political power evolving into economic power, which in turn enhances political power, are now available. The Mescalero Apache, the Cochiti Pueblo, and White Mountain Apache are Indian nations that have dramatically wrested power over their land and resources from the federal bureaucracy and moved diligently to generate employment and tribal wealth from their resources. Other examples, with varying degrees of solvency, include:

- the Cherokee of Oklahoma own and operate an electronics manufacturing plant;

- the Quinault, Lummi, Swinomish and several other tribes in the Northwest and Alaska own and operate fish canneries;

- the Blackfeet of Montana are a major player in the market for writing instruments;

- the Oneidas of Wisconsin, the Gilas of Arizona, and several other tribes own and operate office and industrial parks serving major metropolitan areas;

- the Warm Springs reservation in Oregon owns and operates a major sawmill and a large tourist resort;

- more than one hundred tribes operate bingo casinos, with seating capacities often in the thousands and jackpots approaching the millions; and

- the Choctaw of Mississippi own and operate a factory specializing in electrical wire harnesses for the auto industry, as well as a greeting-card company.[5]

It was long an article of faith of American policy makers that the reason for the failure of the Indian to be successful in "modern" society was that Indian cultures were backward. Policies therefore sought to acculturate Indians, to bring them to Christianity and modernity and thereupon to fruitful economic life. All manner of acculturation was tried, from captivities such as the Bosque Redondo to sending Christian missionaries to Indian reservations as Indian agents. At one point many Indian reservations were dramatically reduced in size and the land distributed to settlers. At mid-twentieth century, the United States Bureau of Indian Affairs was relocating as many Indians as possible to urban areas in an effort to solve the Indian "problem."[6] The new movement toward self-determination has illustrated that one of the ingredients of poverty on Indian reservations is the culture of enforced powerlessness, which has historically characterized United States Indian policy.

Since 1968 it has become increasingly clear that culture has less to do with economic success than does access to political power.[7] Cochiti Pueblo, one of the successful Indian development stories, maintains its traditional Indian form of government. The probability of economic success for an Indian community is greatly enhanced in an environment of fairness and access to opportunity. Fairness, in this context, refers to both the internal decision making and dispute-resolution processes adopted by the Indians and their ability to gain equal treatment at the marketplace in terms of credit and an environment of fair competition.

Traditional forms of government operated by very conservative (i.e., traditionalist) Indian polities have been successful, as have tribal business councils. This is a significant observation because for two centuries apologists for the failure of United States Indian policy have asserted that the primary cause of Indian poverty is the culture of the Indians. The proposal that Indian culture causes poverty completely ignores the fact that the essential ingredients to economic growth—access to means and opportunity—have been forcefully absent in Indian life.

Indians are discovering that the several requirements of effective political organization can be woven into the fabric of their culture. The first requirement for successful development strategies is that the leadership refrain from the activity of "rent seeking" or other opportunistic behavior.[8] In the jargon of Indian economic development, "rent seeking" occurs when a public official uses the powers of his/her office for personal gain, either directly or indirectly; but opportunistic behavior need not be limited to individual rent seekers. Tribal councils sometimes seek to change the rules after investors have assets in place. The same kind of behavior can go a long way toward discouraging Indians from investing their resources in their own businesses and has historically discouraged people from supporting the Indian governments in the United States.

A second requirement, closely related to and perhaps indistinguishable from the first, is that there must be an independent judiciary designed and empowered to render impartial judgments in cases involving conflict between the tribal government and others, including tribal members. The idea that tribal councils must create independent judiciaries and subject themselves to their judgments sounds counter-sovereign (to coin a phrase), but since most people (including tribal members) won't invest their time or money in ventures in which they fear they will be treated unfairly in the event of a conflict, independent judiciaries are emerging as a necessary cornerstone of the evolution of effective Indian development.

Another requirement is that Indians must create institutions that can act effectively. It is a crucial step from having a dream to having a plan to acting on the plan in an organized and efficient manner. As we have seen, before such institutions can be successful in Indian country, the necessary environments must be created in the form of Indian governments conducive to proactive institutions and empowered to take action. In some parts of the Indian country the prospect of sharing responsibility, creating a separate and independent judiciary, and restraining "rent seeking" among some Indian leaders will be extremely challenging.[9]

There must also be planning that allows for some economic pluralism. The number of options for growth are fairly limited: federal (BIA does the planning and implementation), tribal (the tribe does it), entrepreneurial (individuals or small investment groups from within the community do it), and external (when investment and management are provided by external private capital). The first and last choices have become increasingly unpopular among United States Indian nations, partly because these are not sovereignty enhancing and partly because Indian nationalism leans strongly against these choices in many places.

There is one other possible choice: to do nothing. Doing nothing, increasingly, is not a choice at all, and may be a choice toward cultural extinction. Most of the development on Indian reservations, predictably, will be that owned and operated by the Indian nations and entrepreneurial ventures of Indian members. The job of the Indian governments will be twofold. First, they will need to be able to operate with business skills, choosing how much to invest in what and when, just as other business leaders must do. In addition, they will need to make decisions about overall economic development consistent with the goals and ambitions of their people. When economic and political environments permit, successful Indian governments will create environments that sustain and support the kinds of entrepreneurial initiatives consistent with the goals of the group.

Indian sovereignty is being redefined according to what an Indian nation can actually do. It is no longer limited to discussions about state or provincial versus Indian jurisdiction but, rather, it includes material issues and strategies designated by the Indian population and carried out by increasingly able Indian legal entities. The social implications are enormous. If Indian peoples have the power to make decisions about their future they can choose educational paths that allow their languages, history, arts, and culture to survive and therefore can perpetuate the very elements which define them as distinct peoples.

Notes

1. Vine Deloria, Jr. traces the origins of the Indian movement to the Poor Peoples' March organized by Dr. Martin Luther King, Jr. in 1968. The march preceded a bridge blockade at Cornwall Island (near Massena, New York) by Mohawks, the founding of Akwesasne Notes, and the founding of the American Indian Movement in Minneapolis the same year. See Vine Deloria, Jr., *Behind the Trail of Broken Treaties* (New York: Delta Press, 1974) 33–41.
2. These are major elements, though by no means the only elements, that Indians have argued, demonstrated, and fought for in the years since 1968. For several views of the problems of Indian management of resources, please see Anthropology Resource Center's "Native Americans and Energy

Resource Development 11" and also John C. Mohawk, "BIA Senate Hearing: Witch Hunt for A Straw Man," *Daybreak Magazine* (Spring, 1989): 26, 27.

3. See Michael McNally, "Economic Welfare in Indian Country A Consideration of History 1868–1968," in *The Harvard Project on American Indian Economic Development* (May, 1989): 30.

4. Stephen Cornell and Joseph Kalt, "Assessing the Causes and Consequences of Economic Development on American Indian Reservations: An Introduction to the Harvard Project on American Indian Economic Development" (Cambridge, Mass.: The Harvard Project on American Indian Economic Development, 1988): 2.

5. Stephen Cornell, "American Indians, American Dreams, and the Meaning of Success" (Cambridge, Mass.: Harvard Project on American Indian Economic Development, 1987): 3–4. The list in the text included a cement factory owned by the Passamaquoddy Tribe of Maine that has since been sold, and the Mescalero Apache.

6. Some interesting general readings on this subject include Philip Weeks, *The American Indian Experience, a Profile: 1524 to the Present* (Arlington Heights, Ill.: Forum Press, 1988) and Angie Debo, *A History of the Indians of the United States* (Norman, Okla.: University of Oklahoma Press, 1970).

7. This is not to argue that culture has no influence on economic success, but rather that its influence has been historically overwhelmed by policies that denied Indians any opportunity to make decisions over their own lives. Indeed, Stephen Cornell has posited this interesting hypothesis: "Those tribes, in which Indigenous groups of intellectuals—guardians of the deeper meanings of group membership, whose task in part is to think about and exemplify what it means, culturally, to be a member of the group—have survived and continue to play a major role in tribal affairs, will have the potential for more powerful community mobilization and, therefore, for more effective development than those where such groups no longer significantly function." See Stephen Cornell, "Indian Reservation Economic Development: Some Preliminary Hypotheses," (Cambridge, Mass.: The Harvard Project on American India Economic Development, 1987): 21.

8. "From Latin America to an excessively litigious U.S society, rent-seeking can destroy or divert resources fron productive use. The key to shutting down rent-seeking lies in the creation of definitive rules of law—definitive property rights to action and resources....Rules of law are fundamentally a problem of enforcement, and enforcement in a relationship between leaders and their constituents."

9. The literature on the quality of Indian political life is scanty, at best. An interesting book that charges election irregularities and corruption on the Rosebud Reservation in South Dakota, written at the beginning of the American Indian self-determination period, is Robert Bernette, *The Tortured Americans* (Englewood Cliffs, N.J.: Prentice Hall Press, 1971).

Profile

First Nations Development Institute
69 Kelley Road, Falmouth, VA 22405, (703) 371–5615

We cannot educate our children, we cannot preserve their health, we cannot protect their well-being, we cannot promote their mental development if our livelihood is dependent on others. Without the capacity to control the economic future of their reservation, tribes will remain in their current cycle of social disintegration.

—Rebecca Adamson, president of First Nations

First Nations Development Institute (FNDI) was founded in 1979 as a nonprofit organization to help tribes gain control of their resources and develop healthy economies on their reservations consistent with traditional values and culture. The project combines direct, on-site work between the tribes and Native American organizations with national policy development and advocacy. It works with the existing skills, resources, and talents on the reservations and helps its clients use them to the fullest.

The Institute aims to reduce tribal dependence on federal funds and to increase business and development capacity on the reservations. "To understand the First Nations Development Institute, you must realize that we are a national strategy for moving reservation development forward. The synergism for such a strategic approach is quite significant," explains Vice President Sherry Salway Black. The components of the strategy include technical assistance, a research and data bank, a marketing program, the national policy and advocacy arm, and the Tribal Commerce and Enterprise Management Program. The latter is a collaborative project between FNDI and the University of Minnesota that provides tribal leaders with the skills necessary to make culturally appropriate financial decisions. FNDI's technical assistance program provides hands-on work at development sites; the other components provide information, capital, marketing expertise, training, and education and assistance, including legal work on sensitive national policy issues. The project's Oweesta Program assists tribes in capital fund formation by setting up reservation-based, microenterprise loan funds; establishes trust fund management projects; and encourages local savings and provision of credit for tribal members.

These components enable FNDI to assist and guide a business or project from its inception to self-sufficiency by working with their clients throughout the entire process. FNDI looks for community involvement and commitment when working with reservation groups. The Institute also expects tribes or organizations to provide at least one staff person to work with First Nations' field staff to ensure that the knowledge and skills demonstrated are transferred to the tribe. The tribe or organization must agree to share what they have learned with other Native American groups working in similar areas.

From the time of its first $25,000 grant ten years ago, First Nations has grown more than a hundred-fold, with an operating budget of $1.2 million and another $1.8 million in loan capital deposited in socially responsible and Indian-owned financial institutions. FNDI has a core staff of twelve, the majority of whome are Indian, and has worked on nineteen sites, devoting an average of two to five years at each site.

With the help of FNDI, the Saginaw Chippewa of Michigan have implemented a tribal investment plan to overcome federal dependency and to create viable options for self-sufficiency. In 1984, the Indian Land Claims Commission awarded the tribe $10 million as compensation for lands improperly taken. (An earlier award of $16 million was paid out by the BIA as per-capita grants to tribal members and descendents, many of whom had no present-day connection to the reservation. The Saginaw Chippewa now have nothing to show for that settlement. According to one tribal member, "It just made a few used-car salesmen rich.") The tribe wanted to invest this $10 million in themselves to build the economic self-reliance of the reservation by generating internal capital. Despite the BIA's opposition, First Nations and the tribe approached Congress and won the right to keep the award as a tribal asset (rather than having it divided among members) and to invest the funds itself (rather than entrusting it to the BIA). They were the first Native Nation in the United States to accomplish this.

First Nations conducted an eighteen-month training course and provided technical assistance to help the tribe determine investment priorities and choose investment managers. Today, the tribe works in partnership with two local banks to rebuild the reservation. They have built a health center, a teen center, housing, and renovated the tribal gambling facilities. In addition, they have backed tribal members' home loans for more than $750,000.

Thanks to their success with the Saginaw tribe, First Nations is actively involved in helping other tribes become involved in the management of their trust funds. This work led to the discovery of massive mismanagement that went beyond the BIA's trust fund management to include the overall trust land and mineral program. Mismanagement within the Minerals Management Service, Bureau of Land Management, Treasury Department and other federal government entities was also revealed. First Nations and others provided testimony in August, 1992, and is reviewing the possibility of a settlement-fund mechanism for dealing with lost and mismanaged funds.

First Nations is working on formulating policy that grants Native American nations the right to use their trust funds for economic development on reservations. This could have great impact on the economic health of reservations, since the BIA currently holds over $2 billion in trust funds for about two hundred tribes. With the models that First Nations is developing in business, marketing, and finance, the implications of tribes gaining direct control over their money are incredible!

First Nations also works to unravel land-tenure problems, helping nations gain access to resources on their own lands. They are identifying problems requiring solutions at the federal level, including BIA regulation changes. Since the problems are identified at the grassroots, their definition will emerge from the field, not from Washington.

FNDI's work with the Confederated Tribes of the Umatilla Indian Reservation (CTUIR) in Oregon provides an example of how complicated land-tenure issues can be. The Institute began working with CTUIR in 1988 to assist in the development of the Tribal Farm Enterprise (TFE) into a self-sustaining economic venture. The problem of fractionated land was made obvious in short order since a land base is essential for a self-sustaining tribal economy. Three tribes, the Umatilla, Cayuse and Walla Walla (with a total population of about 1,600) live on 172,000 acres located on the Columbia Plateau of northeastern Oregon. The tribes' origional territory was 6 million acres. What happened? A treaty in 1855 reduced the land to 245,000 acres and in 1885 the Slater Allotment Act divided the land into small parcels because the federal government decided that communal land ownership was bad. Indians were given parcels of between forty and eighty acres, and the rest was opened up to non-Indians. These parcels were further divided over the generations as pieces were given to heirs. Today, as many as one hundred people can own forty acres.

First Nations conducted a land study to document the costs of maintaining the land in its fractionated state and projected the results into the next generation. This study formed the basis of FNDI's testimony for the Indian Land Fractionation Hearings in 1992, held before the Senate Select Committee on Indian Affairs. In addition, the Institute is developing a model for the consolidation of land and an acquisition financing mechanism that allows individual tribal members to purchase fractionated interests. The CTUIR is concentrating its first aquisition efforts on land that can help them make a living. Antone Minthorn, chairman of the tribe's general council says, "We want to put this reservation back together. We've lost so much, but we're building. We're building this economy. We're building sovereignty."

The White Earth Land Recovery Project is another example of Native people rebuilding their tribal base. The Project grew out the White Earth Chippewa tribe's land-claims work. Between its treaty in 1867 and 1930, the tribe lost 90 percent of its land. The goal of the Project is to build the tribal economy by supporting traditional land-based activities. White Earth's strategy inlcudes legislation, donation, and purchase. Bonnie Raitt and Lyle Lovett have given benefit concerts, and donations are sought from foundations and individuals. Already the publicity has resulted in two land donations on the reservation. "(We) are committed to protecting the Earth, using renewable resources, and promoting skill development."

Other projects

Ramah Navajo Weavers:

First Nations began working with Ramah Navajo Weavers in 1985, before they were formally organized. After the formation of the Ramah Navajo Weavers Association, research was begun into marketing outlets and ways of diversifying their products to include pillows, handbags, and other woven goods. The project aims to increase income from the weavers' work by improving the conduct of the business and eliminating middlemen, and to prove that traditional skills such as rug weaving can provide a viable livelihood that ensures the survival of traditional ways.

At first the Weavers Association focused only upon improving the quality of local rugs and increasing the markets for them. Today, the association has become a central force in the community, fostering good land stewardship through gardening and reclamation techniques and building cooperative networks to increase self-sufficiency. Katie Heino, one of the founders who chairs the policy committee, sees hope for the future thanks to the association: "Now there is an awareness in the younger people of the value of good weaving. When they have money, they buy rugs. There will be a new generation of weavers, including my own grandchildren. They stand and ask questions, and they watch me."

Porcupine Health Clinic:

Located in Porcupine, South Dakota, on the Pine Ridge Reservation, the Porcupine Health Clinic was created in response to the dangerously inadequate medical care provided by the Indian Health Service (IHS). In 1981 five volunteers, vowing to build a health clinic, formed the Brotherhood Community Health Board after a nineteen-year-old girl bled to death thirty-one miles from the nearest hospital at Pine Ridge. The first clinic was held in an open field with lunch provided from the back of a car. Finally, IHS agreed to a clinic and a 7,140-square-foot, solar-heated clinic complete with examination rooms, a pharmacy, ambulance garage and dentist chairs, which was completed in 1989. However, two months after the clinic was completed, the IHS notified the community they would not use it, claiming budget shortages. (It is generally believed, however, that the real reason may have more to do with the IHS's desire to monopolize Indian health care than money issues.) It was at this point that First Nations came on board to help with negotiations with IHS, informational assistance, and fund-raising. The clinic celebrated its official opening in July, 1992, and has received certification from the state to collect Medicare/Medicaid reimbursements. Times are still hard, but people remain committed to quality health care and serving the needs of the people at Pine Ridge.

First Nations Arts:

First Nations Arts (FNA) is a subsidiary of FNDI that markets (wholesale) one-of-a-kind, distinctive artwork created by a rich cross-section of American Indian artists. Profits support the reservation work of the Institute. FNA provides Indian artists with access to mainstream markets with the goal of helping each artist develop sound business practices and marketing skills. FNA has access to more than two thousand craftspeople and artisans on three hundred reservations and can fill a wide variety of customer needs—from the most traditional to contemporary. Their full-color catalog offers jerky and sausage from farm-raised venison and buffalo, smoked and canned seafood, wild rice products, American Indian herbal teas, dried vegetables for soups and stews, jewelry of all kinds (bead and quill work, sterling, stone and feathers), fetishes, clay vessels, prints, quilting, baskets (grass, twig and bark), dreamcatchers, traditional dolls, ceremonial items (incense, pipes, painted skulls), birch-bark products, and much more. Inquiries from wholesalers are always welcome.

FNDI's perspective on development is summed up beautifully by David Lester, a Creek Indian who has spent twenty years working on tribal development and observing what works and what fails. He says,

> A tribe must look a different definition of development, a more living, organic concept that comes from within rather than a mechanical approach of bringing the outside in. I can see it in the form of maybe a pine tree. It grows in width and height. It has to have a root system, which is embedded in a rich medium. In my view, that medium is our spiritual values. In that context, development takes on a whole different character. It is no longer about money. That is not to say that an economy can succeed if its elements are not profitable. To be true development, tribal development must come from the deeper human motivation to express oneself, economically, politically and culturally. The tribal economy and the political institutions must reflect those deeper values. For growth and development to come from within, people have to learn to trust their own wisdom rather than relying upon the outside world, no matter how well meaning.

Profile

The Lakota Fund
P.O. Box 340, Kyle, SD 57752, (605) 455–2500

The Lakota Fund, founded in 1987, is located on the Pine Ridge Reservation in southwestern South Dakota. According to Fund literature, its purpose is to "facilitate economic and human development through lending programs for small and micro-enterprises, while taking into consideration the unique culture and traditions of the people." Initiated as a project of the First Nation's Development Institute, the Fund is now a community-owned, Lakota, not-for-profit organization, and the first Revolving Loan Fund (RLF) run by and for Native people.

The Oglala Lakota (Sioux) who live in Shannon County, in the heart of the Pine Ridge Reservation, are among the poorest people in the United States. In 1986, per-capita income in Shannon County was $3,244, with an unemployment rate of 85 percent (national per capita income was $12,508). At the time the fund was organized, Pine Ridge had fewer than forty small businesses in an area with a population of about 18,000. Many were owned by non-Indians. Most of the money coming into the reservation was from federal sources, and it would flow right out of the reservation to neighboring towns because of the lack of a private sector. There are no banks on the reservation, and others are hesitant to lend to the reservation because of problems collecting bad debts.

Elsie Meeks, the Fund's Executive Director, says,

> These are not easy problems to solve. But the one thing we find out…is the most effective method for building an economy on the community level is for people to start their own businesses. [D]evelopment has to start with each person. Welfare only makes people poorer and dependent, slaves to the system, and as time goes on this is going to grow worse. Building factories is not the answer, either. It has to come from within each of us. As people start putting their skills to work in a business, they begin a process of learning.

There were needs for two types of business loans at Pine Ridge—small-business loans for individuals operating or starting a formal business, which can be up to $25,000, and microenterprise loans. In 1988, the board and staff of the Fund began looking into peer-group lending, and in 1989, two representatives of the Fund traveled to Bangladesh to visit the pioneer of peer-group lending, the Grameen Bank. While there they studied, firsthand, the conditions in the country and how the central office of the bank worked. They were able to travel the countryside with the bank workers, meet with some of the borrowers to learn how the process worked, and pick up some techniques to best deliver loans to the poor.

After this visit, the Fund concluded that the peer-group lending process would work at Pine Ridge, and the staff worked to adapt the Grameen Bank's model to the culture of the Lakota people. The Circle Banking Project was the result.

Four to six people join together in a peer-lending group (they cannot be immediate family members).

After five training sessions, the Circle is certified. Once certified, up to two members may borrow.

If loans are current for six weeks, then two more members may borrow. No new loans are granted if any are delinquent. Members often help each other meet deadlines through fund-raisers such as raffles, bake sales, or dances.

Loans are up to $400 initially, then $800 and $1000.

A small percentage goes into a group fund for projects and emergencies.

Members put $5 of their own money into a personal savings account every two weeks.

Members who successfully complete their circle find it goes on indefinitely. They can receive additional loans, and it establishes their own line of credit.

A loan as small as $400 might not sound like much, but it can make a huge impact. For example, a seventy-six-year-old woman living on a small pension after her husband died was able to turn her quilting skills into a microenterprise after forming a Circle and obtaining her first loan. She says, "I like [Circle Banking] because it helps me finance my business. [But] the most important thing I learned is how to talk and cooperate with others." Another woman, a recovering alcoholic and mother of five children, borrowed $250 to start a small beading business, which is helping her get off welfare. And, with the support of her Circle, she has been able to stay sober for over two years and is the chairperson of the Circle.

Other businesses the Fund has loaned to include two hair salons, several video rental shops, a restaurant, numerous contractors, a floral shop, a pawn shop, and a buffalo-raising operation. About 65 percent of the Fund's clients are arts and crafts producers.

The Lakota Fund is gets its funding from foundations, socially responsible corporations, individuals, and religious organizations. Individuals can make low-interest loans (3 percent or lower) or tax-deductible contributions.

Living the New Story

The Earth speaks in different languages in different places. Desert language is different from arctic language; the voices of a tropical forest are not the same as the voices in a temperate forest. Indigenous peoples listened to the voices of Earth in their place and thus evolved traditions, rituals, celebrations and taboos, as well as specific knowledge regarding food (hunting, gathering, farming) and healing. Political, social, and economic systems evolved over time, fully integrated with (and directly derived from) a people's relationship with the natural world. This

Earth-based way of life was passed on to the next generation and so on through stories and myth. When children asked where they came from or why something was done one way and not another, they were told a story.

Their stories were often mythic. They wove words around essential truths. Different cultures had different stories, yet the basic truths remained the same. Stories also helped people know what was expected of them, how to behave in certain circumstances, and how to relate to their places. In short, they taught right relationship—with self, other, and Earth. The stories were not human-centered. Rather, they placed the human *in* the cosmos—one strand in a magnificent web of living consciousness.

Our stories have changed. Today in popular culture, science is the master storyteller, and the main character is the human; everything else revolves around us. The universe and the Earth are the "sets" and other species are the "extras." To make matters worse, science has exiled mystery and magic from our stories. To quote Brian Swimme (co-author with Thomas Berry of *The Universe Story*), "Why tell the story of the Sun as a God when we knew the sun was a locus of thermonuclear reactions? We attached ourselves to scientific law and relegated story and myth to the nurseries, tribes, and asylums."

According to Swimme, in addition to holding the tribal community together and teaching lessons, the ritual of storytelling played a key role in regenerating the universe: "The ritual of telling the story is understood as a cosmic event. For unless the story is sung and danced, the universe suffers from decay and fatigue. Everything depends on telling the story—the health of the people, the health of the soil, the health of the sun, the health of the soul, the health of the sky." He challenges us to "keep this tribal perspective in mind" as we seek ways of healing ourselves and the Earth in modern times.

Swimme describes an imaginary future event: A "cosmic storyteller"—an elder grandmother—and a small group of children are gathered around a fire in a meadow. The Old One tells how we are all a part of rock, ocean, mountain, air, fire. That "every rock is a symphony, but the music of soil soars beyond capture in human language," and that our destiny is that of the stars. She concludes: "We do not know what mystery awaits us in the very next moment. But we can be sure we will be astonished and enchanted. This entire universe sprang from a single numinous speck. Our origin is mystery, our destiny is intimate communion with all that is, and our common species aim is to celebrate the Great Joy that has drawn us into itself." Children growing up with these as stories in their hearts will, according to Swimme, enable us to become Earthlings, "evoking out of the depths of the human psyche those qualities enabling our transformation from disease to health." And the best place to start listening for and sharing Earth's stories is where we live—home.

There is a small, but strong and growing, movement B. Swimme quotes from called bioregionalism that is, in essence, about recreating our culture by knowing home. I define "bioregionalism" simply as "living where we live." This translates into producing as many of our needs as possible as close to home as possible and letting go of wasteful and unnecessary consumption. The corollary of living where we live is that other people get to live where they live, too. As we begin to know our home, our bioregion, the stories we tell our children will take on a whole different perspective. We will no longer be able to separate ourselves as people from our place or from the Earth as a whole. We will feel a sense of community, not only with other people but with all of life. Magic, and hope, will be part of our living experience once again.

David Haenke, in *Ecological Politics and Bioregionalism*, describes it this way:

> The power of natural law runs the Earth, and nothing on this planet exists outside of its ultimate control. The Earth is organized, controlled, and governed bioregionally, whether we choose to acknowledge it or not. However, to accept this direction, and to work within this knowledge, is an extraordinarily powerful thing.

A bioregion is not defined by political borders; rather, it is defined naturally by mountain ranges, rivers, watersheds, the climate, and the people living there. Since the goal is to create self-reliant, ecologically sustainable communities able to provide opportunity and creativity for members, a bioregional perspective includes all aspects of society.

Bioregionalists would agree, I believe, on the sacredness and value of all life. Today, humanity is wrestling with this very issue. Assigning varying degrees of value, usually determined by usefulness to humans, has gotten us to where we are now—a time when the whole of life itself is threatened. Bioregionalists would also agree that the basic sustaining, self-organizing laws of nature can be applied to such human systems as agriculture, technology, energy and resource use, economics, land issues, health, education, and politics.

Observing how natural law plays itself out in nature's systems, reflecting on the meaning this has, and discovering ways to apply what we learn to our lives is an incredible challenge and opportunity. We have tried figuring out Nature, finding ways of taming her to suit our needs. We have looked upon the Earth as a warehouse full of goodies for the taking. And for quite some time we have been assuming that somehow our technology will solve our problems in time to save us. This is not going to work. It is time now to listen to the Earth, to pay attention to what she has to say.

The models and strategies that comprise this book are pieces of a puzzle. It's up to us to put them together—to create a picture. Trouble is, there is no preset picture to go by. We have to listen to our places, our cultures, ourselves, and piece together what we know and sense.

Practically speaking, we have a huge struggle facing us. The people and organizations working for change are small and underfunded. The corporate grip is big and powerful. It's easy to feel discouraged; I know sometimes I do.

Yet, I can feel the change—like electrical current just under the surface. I can sense the power in seemingly small ventures. I can envision communities and regions teeming with activity. I see co-ops and small businesses run by local people serving their communities. I see production factories that don't pollute. I see foresters who love the woods and show it. I see kids active and involved in communities. I see whole nations of indigenous peoples governing themselves on their lands, their cultures and economies strong and vibrant. I see clean rivers, clear blue skys and forests of old growth protected and revered—saved for all time. I see healing forests, oceans coming back to life, and salmon jumping in crystal-clear rivers.

I know this future is possible. I can feel it in my bones. I know plenty of others who feel the same. My knowing is not because I think people can do such extraordinary things—although we can. My knowing exists because of my faith in the great mystery and magic of life itself. Science can explain many things, yet the more it explains the more questions we have. There's plenty of room for hope and faith in the vast unknown. I learned this firsthand thanks to my sister's car accident. When MJ was healing from her brain injury, my faith in her recovery was based on what science *didn't* know, not on what it did. If my family had listened to her doctors we would have given up—and the doctor's predictions might have come true.

Like many of us, I lived through those hard times, as I live through these, by envisioning a better way and by telling myself, and whoever will listen, my own version of a new story. My story is shared by countless others who are learning, by trial and error, by inspiration and hard work, how to respectfully inhabit the place on Earth that is our home—which is really what this book is all about. I have attempted to weave a sense of magic and inspiration with the practical how-tos, while not glossing over or minimizing the very real problems and hardships we face. We not only need to tell a new story, we need to live it.

Resources

W HILE THIS LIST may appear comprehensive, it is far from complete. I have attempted to include those organizations I feel can connect you to more localized grassroots projects in their areas of focus as well as those with the most readily available sources of additional information. There's a lot of work to do, and there are thousands of groups and organizations doing pieces of it (and numerous "little" newsletters, too!). This list can get you started.

Bibliography

Alperovitz, Gar, and Jeff Faux. *Rebuilding America: A Blueprint for the New Economy*. Pantheon Books, 1984.

Bado, J., ed. *Case for Ownership: Ohio Case Studies*. Northeast Ohio Employee Ownership Center, Kent Popular Press, Kent, Ohio.

Benello, George C.. *From the Ground Up*. South End Press, 1992.

Berry, Thomas. *Dream of the Earth*. Sierra Club Books, 1988.

Berry, Thomas. *The Universe Story*. HarperSan Francisco, 1992.

Berthold-Bond, Annie. *Clean & Green*. Ceres Press, 1990. A complete guide to natural cleaning.

Bruyn, Severyn T. and James Meehan, eds. *Beyond the Market & the State: New Directions in Community Development*. Temple Univ. Press, 1987.

Calthorpe, Peter. *Next American Metropolis: Ecology, Community, and the American Dream*. Princeton Architectural Press, 1993.

Center for Neighborhood Technology. *Working Neighborhoods: Taking Charge of Your Local Economy*. 1986.

Churchill, Ward. *Struggle for the Land*. Common Courage Press, 1993.

Cisneros, Henry, ed. *Interwoven Destinies: Cities and the Nation*. Norton, 1993.

Co-op America. *National Green Pages.* published annually. Directory of "green" businesses and organizations. Listings include descriptions of goods and services with contact information.

Community Information Exchange. *Case Studies in Successful Home Ownership for Low- and Moderate-Income First-Time Buyers.* Twenty-five case studies.

Community Information Exchange. *Capital and Communities: A Community Guide to Financial Institutions,* 1990.

Community Information Exchange. *Lending for Community Economic Development: A Guide for Small Town and Rural Lenders,* 1992.

Community Information Exchange. *Building Your Community Organization,* 1990.

Community Information Exchange. *Getting Media Attention,* 1992.

Community Information Exchange. *Founding Your Community Organization,* 1990.

Community Information Exchange. *Grassroots Fundraising Workbook,* 1992.

Community Information Exchange. *Alternative Investing in Community Development,* 1987.

Community Information Exchange. *Linking Development Benefits to Neighborhoods: A Manual of Community-Based Strategies,* 1989.

Context Institute. *Eco-Villages and Sustainable Communities.* PO Box 11470, Bainbridge, WA 98110, 200 pp, 1992.

Cooney, Robert and Helen Michalowski, eds. *Power of the People: Active Nonviolence in the United States.* New Society Publishers, 1987.

Coover, Virginia, et al. *Resource Manual for a Living Revolution.* New Society Publishers, 1985.

Corry, Stephen. *Harvest moonshine taking you for a ride: A critique of the 'rainforest harvest'— its theory and practice (research report).* Survival International, 1993.

Council on Economic Priorities. *Shopping for a Better World.* Published yearly.

Dadd, Debra Lynn. *Nontoxic, Natural & Earthwise.* Jeremy P. Tarcher, 1990.

Dadd-Redalia, Debra. *Sustaining the Earth: Choosing Consumer Products That Are Safe for You, Your Family, and the Earth.* Hearst Books, William Morrow & Co., Inc., 1994.

Daly, Herman E. and John B. Cobb, Jr. *For the Common Good: Redirecting the Economy Toward Community, the Environment, and a Sustainable Future.* Beacon Press, 1989.

Deal, Carl. *Greenpeace Guide to Anti-Environmental Organizations.* Odonian Press, Berkeley, CA (800-REAL-STORY).

Dellinger, David. *From Yale to Jail: The Life Story of a Moral Dissenter.* Pantheon Books, 1993.

Dembo, David and Ward Morehouse. *Joblessness & the Pauperization of Work in America.* Apex Press, 1994.

Dembo, David, et al. *Abuse of Power.* New Horizons Press, 1990.

Directories, Inc., U.S. Environmental. *Directory of National Environmental Organizations,* 1992.

Dominguez, Joe and Vicki Robin. *Your Money or Your Life.* Viking Penguin, 1992.

Douthwaite, Richard. *Growth Illusion.* Council Oak Books, 1993.

Du Bois, Paul Martin and Frances Moore Lappé. *Quickening of America: Rebuilding Our Nation, Remaking Our Lives.* Jossey-Bass Publishers, 1994.

Dyson, Burton and Elizabeth Dyson. *Neighborhood Caretakers: Stories, Strategies and Tools for Healing Urban Community.* Knowledge Systems, 1989.

Engwicht, David. *Reclaiming Our Cities & Towns: Better Living With Less Traffic.* New Society Publishers, 1993.

Environmental Data Research Institute. *Environmental Grantmaking Foundations 1994 Directory.* 1655 Elmwood Ave., Ste. 225, Rochester, NY 14620; 800-724-1857, 1994.

Feldman, Jonathan. *Universities in the Business of Repression.* South End Press, 1989.

Fellowship for Intentional Community. *Directory of Intentional Communities.* 8600 Univ. Blvd., Evansville, IN 47712.

Foreman, Dave and Bill Haywood. *Ecodefense: A Field Guide to Monkeywrenching.* Ned Ludd Books, 1987.

Forsey, Helen, ed. *Circles of Strength: Community Alternatives to Alienation.* New Society Publishers, 1993.

Fromm, Dorit. *Collaborative Communities: Cohousing, Central Living, and Other New Forms of Housing with Shared Facilities.* Van Nostrand Reinhold, 1991.

Goldsmith, Edward. *Great U-Turn: De-industrializing Society.* Bootstrap Press, 1988.

Goldsmith, Edward, Martin Khor, Helena Norbeg-Hodge, Vandana Shiva, et al. *Future of Progress: Reflections on Environment & Development.* International Society and Ecology and Culture, 1992.

Greco, Thomas H., Jr. *New Money for Healthy Communities.* 1994, $15.95 plus $3 shipping and handling from the author, PO Box 42663, Tucson, AZ 85733. Describes equitable and dynamic exchange systems in detail, how-tos for local trading systems, community currencies. Discusses strengths, limitations, looks at ways to tranform good systems and make them even better.

Grossman, Richard and Frank Adams. *Taking Care of Business: Citizenship and the Charter of Incorporation* (booklet). Charter Ink, 1993.

Gunn, Christopher and Hazel Dayton Gunn. *Reclaiming Capital: Democratic Initiatives and Community Development.* Cornell University Press, 1991.

Hammond, Herb. *Seeing the Forest Among the Trees: The Case for Wholistic Forest Use.* Polestar Press Ltd, 1992.

Hart, John. *Saving Cities Saving Money: Environmental Strategies That Work.* Resource Renewal Institute, 1992.

Henderson, Hazel. *Paradigms in Progress: Life Beyond Economics.* Knowledge Systems, Inc., 1991.

Hester, Randolph T., Jr. *Community Design Primer.* Ridge Times Press, 1990.

Holcombe, B.J. and Charmaine Wellington. *Search for Justice.* Stillpoint Publishing, 1992.

Humane Society of the United States and the International Alliance for Sustainable Agriculture, 1993. *Humane Consumer & Producer Guide: Buying and producing farm animal products for a humane sustainable agriculture,* 1993.

In Context. *Designing a Sustainable Future: Buildings, Neighborhoods, Cities,* Spring, 1993.

Institute for Community Economics. *Community Land Trust Handbook.* Rodale Press, 1982.

Institute for Community Economics. *Community Loan Fund Manual.* Institute for Community Economics, 1987. Comprehensive guide for starting or managing a community loan fund. Includes case studies and sample documents.

Institute for Community Economics and Community Media Productions. *Common Ground: An Introduction to Community Land Trusts,* 1984. Twenty-five-minute documentary (video, slide, or tape) on CLTs. Rental $20 from ICE (see org. listing).

Institute for Local Self-Reliance. *Getting from Here to There: Building a Rational Transportation System*, 1992.

Jaimes, Annette M., ed. *State of Native America: Genocide, Colonization and Resistance.* South End Press, 1992.

Kaza, Stephanie. *The Attentive Heart: Conversations with Trees.* Ballantine, 1993.

Kimerling, Judith. *Amazon Crude.* National Resource Defense Council, 1991.

Kinder, Peter K., Steven D. Lydenberg and Amy L. Domini. *Social Investment Almanac.* Henry Holt, 1992.

Labalme, Jenny. *Road to Walk: A Struggle for Environmental Justice.* The Regulator Press, 1987.

Lansky, Mitch. *Beyond the Beauty Strip: Savings What's Left of Our Forests.* Tilbury House Publishers, 1992.

Lowry, Ritchie P. *Good Money: A Guide to Profitable Social Investing in the '90s.* W. W. Norton & Co., 1991.

Makhijani, Arjun. *From Global Capitalism to Economic Justice.* Apex Press, 1992.

Makower, Joel, John Elkington and Julia Hailes. *Green Consumer.* Penguin, 1990.

Mander, Jerry. *In the Absence of the Sacred.* Sierra Club Books, 1991.

Maser, Chris. *Redesigned Forest.* Stoddart Publishing Co. Ltd., 1990.

Mayell, Mark, et al. *Natural Health First-Aid Guide: The Definitive Handbook of Natural Remedies for Treating Minor Emergencies.* Pocket Books, Simon & Schuster, Inc., 1994. This book can help you avoid over-the-counter, chemically-derived pharmaceuticals in your medicine cabinet. Remedies include herbal preparations (and instructions on making your own), flower essenses, homeopathy, acupressure points, nutrition and supplements and common sense. Highly recommended!

McCamant, Kathryn, and Charles Furrett. *Cohousing: A Contemporary Approach to Housing Ourselves.* Ten Speed Press, 1988.

McHarg, Ian L. *Designing with Nature.* John Wiliey & Sons, Inc., revised 1992.

McLenighan, Valjean. *Sustainable Manufacturing: Saving Jobs, Saving the Environment.* Center for Neighborhood Technology, 1990.

Meadows, Donella,, et al. *Beyond the Limits.* Chelsea Green, 1992.

Megalli, Mark and Andy Friedman. *Masks of Deception: Corporate Front Groups in America.* Essential Information, Washington, DC.

Megson, James D., and Michael O'Toole. *Employee Ownership: The Vehicle for Community Development and Local Economic Control.*

Meyer, Christine and Faith Moosang, eds. *Living with the Land: Communities Restoring the Earth.* New Society Publishers, 1992.

Minnesota Green. *Creating Communuity Gardens.* Minnesota State Horticulture Society, 1755 Prior Ave., North, Falcon Heights, St. Paul, MN 55113.

Mogil, Christopher, Anne Slepian and Peter Woodrow. *We Gave Away a Fortune: Stories of People Who Have Devoted Themselves & Their Wealth to Peace, Justice & the Environment.* New Society Publishers, 1992.

Morehouse, Ward, ed. *Building Sustainable Communities: Tools and Concepts for Self-Reliant Economic Change.* Bootstrap Press, 1989.

Morrison, Roy. *We Build the Road as We Travel.* New Society Publishers, 1991.

Moyer, Bill. *Movement Action Plan: Eight Successful Stages of Social Movements.* Social Movement Empowerment Project, 1987. 721 Shrader St., San Francisco, CA 94117.

National Federation of Community Development Credit Unions. "Report to the White House: An Analysis of the Role of Credit Unions in Capital Formation and Investment in Low- and Moderate-Income Communities."

New England Green Alliance. *Earth Day Wall Street Action Handbook*, 1990. Box 703, White River Junction, VT 05001.

Nozick, Marcia. *No Place Like Home: Building Sustainable Communities.* Canadian Council on Social Development. 55 Parkdale Ave., Ottawa, ONT K1Y 4G1, Canada.

Parzen, Julia Ann and Michael Hall Kieschnick. *Credit Where Its Due: Development Banking for Communities.* Temple University Press, 1992.

Plant, Christopher, and Judith Plant, eds. *Green Business: Hope or Hoax? Toward an authentic strategy for restoring the Earth.* New Society Publishers, 1991.

Plant, Judith and Christopher Plant, eds. *Putting Power in its Place: Create Community Control.* New Society Publishers, 1992.

Register, Richard. *Ecocity Berkeley: Building Cities for a Healthy Future.* North Atlantic Press, 1987.

Rifkin, Jeremy and Randy Barber. *North Will Rise Again: Pensions, Politics and Power in the 1980s.* Beacon Press, 1978.

Roberts, Wayne, et al. *Get A Life! A Green Cure for Canada's Economic Blues.* Get A Life Publishing House, Canada, 1993.

Rosen, Corey and Karen Young, eds. *Understanding Employee Ownership.* Cornell University Industrial and Labor Relations Press, 1991.

Ross, David P. and Peter J. Usher. *From the Roots Up: Economic Development as if Community Mattered.* Bootstrap Press, 1986.

Schmookler, Andrew Bard. *Illusion of Choice: How the Market Economy Shapes Our Destiny.* State University of New York Press, 1993.

Schumacher, E. F. *Small is Beautiful: Economics as if People Mattered.* Blond & Briggs Ltd., 1973.

Shavelson, Jeff. *Third Way: A Sourcebook—Innovations in Community-Owned Enterprise.* National Center for Economic Alternatives, 1990.

Shields, Katrina. *In the Tiger's Mouth: An Empowerment Guide for Social Action.* New Society Publishers, 1994.

Shiva, Vandana. *Staying Alive.* Zed Books, 1989.

Shiva, Vandana. *Violence of the Green Revolution.* Zed, 1991.

Shiva, Vandana, ed. *Close to Home: Women Reconnect Ecology, Health, and Development Worldwide.* New Society Publishers, 1994.

Sojourners. *Who Is My Neighbor? Economics as if Values Matter.* 1994. (800) 714-7474. Excellent all-encompassing guide to economic models and strategies that promote social justice. Subjects: consuming, work, land, the courts, and banks woven together by writers who care about people, the Earth, and their work.

Swimme, Brian. *Universe is a Green Dragon: A Cosmic Creation Story.* Bear & Company, 1984.

Tokar, Brian. *Green Alternative: Creating an Ecological Future.* New Society Publishers, 1992.

Urban Ecology. *Report of the First International Ecological City Conference.*

Van der Ryn, Sim and Peter Calthorpe. *Sustainable Communities.* Sierra Club Books, 1986.

Wachtel, Paul. *Poverty of Affluence.* New Society Publishers, 1989.

Walter, Bob, Lois Arkin and Richard Crenshaw, eds. *Sustainable Cities; Concepts and Strategies for Eco-City Development*. Eco-Home Media, 1992. 4344 Russell Ave., Los Angeles, CA 90027.

War Resisters League. *Handbook for Nonviolent Action*. 1989.

Wellner, Pamela and Eugene Dickey. *Wood Users Guide*. Rainforest Action Network, 1991.

Wetherow, David. *Whole Community Catalogue*. Communities, Inc., 1992.

Whaley, Rick with Walter Bresette. *Walleye Warriors: An Effective Alliance Against Racism and for the Earth*. New Society Publishers, 1994.

Wilson, Elizabeth. *Sphinx in the City*. Univeristy of California Press, Berkeley, 1991. Critique of urban planning from a feminist perspective.

Organizations and Publications

20/20 Vision
1000 16th St., NW, Ste. 810, Washington, DC 20036, 202-728-1157.
Letterwriting campaigns and information related to "effective citizen lobbying techniques."

20/20 Vision National Project
1828 Jefferson Pl., NW, Washington, DC 20036, 800-669-1782.
Sends monthly postcards with 20-minute action you can take to make the world a better place.

ACEnet
94 N. Columbus Rd., Athens, OH 45701, 614-592-3854.
Committed to regional economic development. Support for worker-owned business, business incubators and flexible manufacturing networks. Newsletter, publications and technical assistance.

ACORN
739 Eighth Street, SE, Washington, DC 20003, 202-547-9292.
Largest neighborhood-based volunteer membership group in United States—more than 600 chapters nationwide. Organizes on issues of pressing importance to urban, low-income and minority communities. Contact national group for chapter in your area.

Akwe:kon Journal
300 Calwell Hall, Cornell University, Ithaca, NY 14853.
Quarterly journal published by Cornell's American Indian Program.

Akwesasne Notes
Mohawk Nation, Via Roosevelt, NY 13683-0196.
Official bi-monthly newspaper of the Mohawk Nation.

Alliance for a Paving Moratorium
PO Box 4357, Arcata, CA 95521, 707-826-7775.

Alternatives Federal Credit Union
301 West State St., Ithaca, NY 14850, 807-273-4611.
Deposits invested in community through loan programs for affordable housing, energy-efficient cars and minority and women-owned businesses.

American Civil Liberties Union
122 Maryland Ave., NE, Washington, DC 20002, 202-544-1681.
Publishes the *Step-by-Step Guide to Using the Freedom of Information Act*

Amy Belanger
PO Box 7132, Milton, FL 32570.
Contact Amy for current list of community currency projects nationwide (LETS, HOURS, script, other models). Send $1.00 to cover copying and postage costs.

Anawim Fund of the Midwest
517 W. 7th, PO Box 4022, Davenport, IA 52808, 319-324-6632.

Animal Town
PO Box 485, Healdsburg, CA 95448, 800-445-8642.
Family run business that designs and produces cooperative games with social/environmental themes. Free catalog of games, books, tapes, other neat material for kids of all ages.

Annals of Earth
Ocean Arks International, One Locust St., Falmouth, MA 02540.

Appalachian Ohio Public Interest Center
36 Congress St., Athens, OH 45701, 614-593-7490.
Initiated the Rural Regeneration Strategy which incorporates a community-building action process. A document on rural regeneration is available for $5.00.

ARABLE
715 Lincoln St., Eugene, OR 97401, 503-485-7630.

Arctic to Amazonia Alliance
PO Box 73, Strafford, VT 05072, 802-765-4337.
Primary purpose is to facilitate better communication and understanding between indigenous and non-indigenous peoples, particularly regarding the relationships among human rights, economics, social justice and the environment. Publications, resources, conferences.

Association for Enterprise Opportunity
320 North Michigan Ave., Ste. 804, Chicago, IL 60601, 312-357-0177.
Recently formed trade organization for microenterprise programs.

Auro-Sinan Company
PO Box 857, Davis, CA 95617, 916-753-3104.
Paints, woodfinishes, glues that are completely free of petroleum and crude oil. Catalog available.

Bamberton (contact: Guy Dauncey)
#550, 2950 Douglas St., Victoria, BC V8T 4N4, Canada, 604-389-1888.
Bamberton is a proposed planned community on 1560 acres. The vision is "a community which enables its inhabitants to pursue ecologically sustainable lifestyles, and to enjoy a high quality of life and a prosperous post-industrial economy, in harmony with the natural world."

Berakah Alternative Investment Fund
925 S. Mason, Ste. 131, Katy, TX 77540, 713-392-3838.

Bio-Dynamic Farming & Gardening Association
PO Box 550, Kimberton, PA 19442, 215-935-7797.
Promotes biodynamic agriculture and is a national clearinghouse for information on community supported agriculture.

Blackfeet National Bank
PO Box 730, Browning, MT 59417, 406-338-7000.
Owned by Blackfeet Tribe. (See description in main text.)

Boston Community Loan Fund
30 Germania St., Jamacia Plain, MA 02130, 617-522-6768.

Boycott Action News
c/o Co-op America, 1850 M St., NW, Ste. 700, Washington, DC 20036.
Eight-page add-on to the Co-op America Quarterly, provides up-dated basic listings of on-going boycotts. Available with membership to Co-op America.

Boycott Quarterly
Center for Economic Democracy, PO Box 64, Olympia, WA 98507.
Provides news and updates on current boycotts and other economic democracy topics. Extensive listing of ongoing boycotts and the products they make.

Building With Nature
PO Box 369, Gualala, CA 95445, 707-884-4513.
Information on eco-healthy building materials.

Bunny Huggers' Gazette
PO Box 601, Temple, TX 76503.
Bimonthly publication providing an extensive listing of animal rights boycotts.

Business Ethics
52 S. 10th St., #110, Minneapolis, MN 55403, 612-962-4700.
Trends, management ideas, interviews, case studies related to green and socially responsive business.

Businesses for Social Responsibility
1850 M St., NW, Washington, DC 20036, 202-467-5566.

Calvert Group
4550 Montgomery Ave., Bethesda, MD 20814, 800-368-2748.
Calvert offers a large family of socially and environmentally responsible mutual funds. The Calvert Social Investment Fund offers a money market fund, a managed growth fund and equity portfolio and a bond fund. The recently launched the Calvert World Values Fund is the first global socially screened mutual fund in theUnited States.

Capital District Community Loan Fund
340 First St., Albany, NY 12206, 518-436-8586.

Capital Missions
2400 E. Main St., Ste. 103, St. Charles, IL 60174, 708-876-1101.
Venture capital for women's enterprises.

Career Works
PO Box 316, Norwich, VT 05055, 802-649-5650.
Employment agency for socially responsible jobs.

Cascadia Revolving Fund
157 Yesler, Ste. 414, Seattle, WA 98104, 206-447-9226.

Catalyst Group
139 Main Street, Ste. 701, Brattleboro, VT 05301, 802-254-8144.
A networking and consulting company building socially concerned businesses and investment practices. Also connects investors with ecologically responsive businesses needing capital.

Center for Community Change
1000 Wisconsin Ave., NW, Washington, DC 20007, 202-342-0567.
Technical assistance for groups interested in community reinvestment.

Center for Economic Democracy
PO Box 64, Olympia, WA 98507.
CED is researching economic democracy in order to build sustainable economies & communities. Research topics include alternative currencies, credit unions, CSA's, farmers markets, consumer co-ops and local media. In adition to publishing *The Boycott Quarterly*, CED is developing a consumer co-op library, information network and computer bulletin board.

Center for Living Democracy
RR 1, Black Fox Rd., Brattleboro, VT 05301, 802-245-1234.
Francis Moore Lappe's new organization works to transform the practice of democracy into a rewarding way of life.

Center for Neighborhood Technology
2125 W. North Ave, Chicago, IL 60647, 312-278-4800.
Community-based economic development, focus on urban issues, community reinvestment, sustainable manufacturing, community and neighborhood empowerment. Publishes *The Neighborhood Works*, highly recommended magazine for community activists.

Center for Popular Economics
PO Box 785, Amherst, MA 01004, 413-545-0743.
Demystifies economics. Workshops, books, speakers' bureau.

CERES (Coalition for Environmentally Responsible Economies)
711 Atlantic Ave., Boston, MA 02111, 617-451-0927.
Promotes the CERES Principles. Publishes quarterly newsletter, *On Principle.*

Chicago Community Loan Fund
343 South Dearborn, Ste. 1001, Chicago, IL 60604, 312-922-1350.

CIKARD News
318 B Curtiss Hall, Iowa State Univ., Ames, Iowa 50010.
Quarterly newsletter published by the Center for Indigenous Knowledge for Agriculture and Rural Development.

Citizen Action
1120 19th St., NW, Ste. 630, Washington, DC 20036, 202-775-1580.

Citizen's Clearinghouse for Hazardous Waste
PO Box 6808, Falls Church, VA 22040, 703-237-2249.
National organization with over 7,000 grassroots groups fighting for a clean environment and local control in their communities. Publishes extensive activist materials as well as some company reports and the bi-monthly newsletter, *Everyone's Backyard.*

Citizens Trade Campaign
1025 Vermont Ave., NW # 300, Washington, DC 20024, 202-783-7400.
Educating people about the implications of free trade agreements.

Clean Yield Asset Management, Inc.
PO Box 6578, 67 Bow Street, Ste. 3, Portsmouth, NH 03802, 603-436-0820.
Socially responsible portfolio management. Also publishes quarterly newsletter, *The Clean Yield.*

Clearinghouse on Environmental Advocacy & Research
1718 Connecticut Ave., NW, #300, Washington, DC 20009, 202-667-6982.
Information on corporate front groups.

Co-op America
1850 M Street NW, Ste. 700, Washington, DC 20036, 800-424-2667.
Membership organization promoting a sustainable economy based on justice, cooperation and a healthy environment. Its many services include alternative health insurance, SRI money management (through First Affirmative Financial Network), *Co-op America Quarterly* (a publication that incorporates Boycott Action News), annual *National Green Pages* and Co-op America's *Socially Responsible Financial Planning Handbook.* If you can join only one organization, this is the one.

Co-op Directory Services
919-21st Ave., S, Minneapolis, MN 55404.
Provides info on food co-ops and food buying clubs. Send SASE.

Co-op News Network
Box 583, Spencer, WA 25276, 304-927-5173.
Publishes *The National Co-op Directory.*

Co-op Resources & Service Project (CRSP)
3551 White House Place, Los Angeles, CA 90004, 213-738-1254.
Education, training and development for all kinds of cooperatives. Sponors local LETS system, revolving fund, book and video library. Los Angeles Eco-Village demonstration project. Newsletter.

Coalition for Justice in the Maquiladoras
3120 W. Ashby, San Antonia, TX 78228, 210-732-8957.
Coalition of labor, religious, environmental, investor and justice organizations and individuals organizing for change in the Maquiladoras—United States—owned companies operating just over the border in Mexico.

Coalition for Women's Economic Development
315 West 9th St., Los Angeles, CA 90014, 213-489-4995.
Provides information, technical assistance, and loans to women to promote economic independence through self-employment.

CoHousing Company
1250 Addison St., #113, Berkeley, CA 94702, 510-549-9980.
Design firm of the authors of *CoHousing* (Kathryn McCamant and Charles Durrett) offers various levels of assistance to cohousing groups.

Cohousing Network
PO Box 2584, Berkeley, CA 94702, 510-526-6124.
Cohousing clearinghouse and quarterly newsletter.

CoHousing Newsletter
2169 E. San Francisco Blvd., Ste. E, San Rafael, CA 94901, 510-528-2212.
National newsletter.

Common Harvest Farm
2406 31st Ave., South, Minneapolis, MN 55406, 612-729-8695.
Common Harvest Farm is a CSA project that produces organic produce for about 120 families in the Minneapolis area.

Common Wealth Revolving Loan Fund
1221 Elm Street, Youngstown, OH 44505, 216-744-2667.

Communities Magazine
Rt. 1, Box 155, Rutledge, MO 63563, 816-883-5543.
Forum for exploration of ideas and issues about cooperative living. Publisher of *Directory of Intentional Communities* with more than 400 communities listed.

Community Capital Bank
111 Livingston Street, Brooklyn, NY 11201, 718-802-1212.
Community-based development bank founded in 1990 serving New York City.

Community Economic and Ecological Development Institute (CEED)
1807 Second St., Studio #2, Santa Fe, NM 87501, 505-986-1401.
Clearinghouse on CED.

Community Information Exchange
1029 Vermont Ave., NW, Ste. 710, Washington, DC 20005, 202-628-2981.
Provides information and technical assistance for community-based economic development. Many publications available including a quarterly newsletter, *Strategy Alert.*

Community Jobs
50 Beacon St., Boston, MA 02108, 617-720-5627.
Job listing and personal computerized job search services.

Community Loan Fund of SW PA
48 South 14th St., Pittsburgh, PA 15203, 412-381-9965.

Community Service, Inc.
PO Box 243, Yellow Springs, OH 45387, 513-767-2161.
Fifty year old organization helping people improve their communities. Mail order book service, newsletter, conferences on simple living and land trust consultation.

Community Workshop on Economic Development
100 Morgan St., Chicago, IL 60607, 312-243-0249.
Chicago coaliton of over 60 organizations. Promotes CBE planning, job creation, community enterprise and youth entrepreneurship.

Community-Supported Agriculture of North America (CSANA)
Indian Line Farm, RR 3, Box 85, Great Barrington, MA 01230.
Resources about CSA. Send SASE for information.

Cooperative Fund of New England
108 Kenyon St., Hartford, CT 06105, 203-523-4305.

Cooperative Housing Foundation
PO Box 91280, Washington, DC 20090, 301-587-4700.

Cornerstone-Homesource Regional Loan Fund
PO Box 6842, Cincinnati, OH 45206, 513-651-1505.

Corporate Crime Campaign
989 Sixth Ave., 8th Fl., New York, NY 10018, 212-967-3180.

Council on Economic Priorities
30 Irving Place, New York, NY 10003, 212-420-1133.
Non-profit public interest corporate research organization. Publishes 10–12 Research Reports annually and an edition of *Shopping for a Better World*. Also provides a corporate environmental data Base.

Covenant Investment Management
309 W. Washington St., Ste. 1300, Chicago, IL 60606, 312-443-8472.
Mutual fund plus individual and institutional portfolios.

Crocus Investment Fund
303-275 Broadway Ave., Winnipeg, Manitoba R3C 4M6, Canada, 204-925-2401.
Canadian investor-supported venture capital fund created to support small and medium sized businesses in Manitoba with good long-term prospects and ethical business practices. Investors' return depends on value of Fund's portfolio when shares are redeemed after a minimum of seven years.

Cultural Suvival
46 Brattle St., Cambridge, MA 02138, 617-441-5400.
Provides sources for Brazil nuts from forest-based communities (used in Rainforest Crunch) and other non-timber forest products. Promotes indigenous peoples around the world. Many publications including *Cultural Survival Quarterly*.

Data Center
464 19th St., Oakland, CA 94612, 510-835-4692.
User-supported library and research center. Offers customized research services.

Daybreak Magazine
PO Box 315, Williamsville, NY 14231.
Magazine that explores and promotes Native American and indigenous peoples' worldviews. Quarterly. Edited by John Mohawk.

Delaware Valley Community Reinvestment Fund
924 Cherry St., 3rd Floor, Philadelphia, PA 19107, 215-925-1130.

Dine CARE
Dilkon Chapter Office, HC-61, PO Box 272, Winslow, AZ 86047, 602-657-3376.
First Native American environmental group to defeat a toxic incinerator proposed for their land.

Domini Social Index Trust
Six St. James St., Boston, MA 02116, 800-762-6814.
Open-end, equity fund designed to replicate the performance of the Domini 400 Social Index, which is made up of 400 companies that have passed multiple screens.

Drum, Inc.
381 Chestnut St., Manchester, NH 03101, 603-644-3777.
Provides social services and community economic development programs to Native Americans in New Hampshire and other parts of Nortj American Indian Country. Social services include crisis intervention, cultural and educational programs, help for Native Americans seeking to identify their heritage and substance abuse counseling. Economic development includes Native Starts, a Native American Micro Business Incubator.

Dwelling House Savings & Loan
501 Herron Ave., Pittsburg, PA 15219, 412-683-5116.

E. F. Schumacher Society
Box 76A, RD 3, Great Barrington, MA 01230, 413-528-1737.
Committed to the vision of "small is beautiful." Focuses on community land trusts, the development of practical economic alternatives including forms of community currency, loan funds, affordable housing that are of, by and for local people. Offers publications, a resource center and library, annual lecture series, and technical assistance.

Eagle
Eagle Wing Press, PO Box 579MD, Naugatuck, CT 06770.
"New England's American Indian Journal", bi-monthly.

Earth Island Institute
300 Broadway, Ste. 28, San Francisco, CA xxxxx.
Founded by David Brower, develops innovative projects to protect and conserve the environment. Publishes quarterly *Earth Island Journal*.

Earth Island Journal
(see Earth Island Institute)
From the "front lines of environmental journalism; local news from around the world". Recommended.

Eco-Home Network
4344 Russell Ave., Los Angeles, CA 90027, 213-662-5207.
Offers: tours of an eco-home in Los Angeles, a newsletter, a mail-order bookstore and information packets.

Ecoforestry Institute
PO Box 12543, Portland, OR 97212, 503-231-0576.

Ecoforestry Institute Canada
PO Box 5783 Stn B, Victoria, BC V8R 6S8, Canada, 604-598-2363.

The Ecologist
Distributed by MIT Press, 55 Hayward St., Cambridge, MA   02142, 617-253-2889.
Highly recommended.

Ecology Action/Common Ground
5798 Ridgewood Rd., Willits, CA 95490.

EcoVillage at Ithaca
Anabel Taylor Hall, Cornell University, Ithaca, NY 14853, 607-255-8276.
Creating a "model village" in Ithaca on 165 acres of land. Envisions a "pedestrian, multi-use village. Whole-systems approach encompasses permaculture; housing integrated into a food-producing landscape of gardens, ponds, orchards and farms; renewable energy/energy efficiency and the preservation and restoration of wetlands and natural areas." Planning process is on-going with building scheduled to begin in 1995.

Elk Horn Bank & Trust Co.
Box 258, Arkadelphia, AK 71923.

Enterprise Jobs Network/Enterprise Foundation
500 American City Building, Columbia, MD 21044, 410-964-1230.
Training, technical assistance and information sharing in operating a job search.

Environmental Choice Program
107 Sparks St., Ste. 200, Ottawa, ONT K1A 0H3, Canada, 613-952-9440.
Canada's government-sponsored, voluntary certification program established in 1988. Over 700 products and services carry the EcoLogo, the program's "seal of approval." including batteries, diapers, energy-efficient lamps, laundry detergents, major household appliances, recycled products, water heaters, and dry cleaners.

Environmental Research Foundation
PO Box 5036, Annappolis, MD 21403-7036, 410-263-1584.
ERF offers "Rachel" (Remote Access Chemical Hazards Electronic Library), a computerized database of information about hazardous materials. ERF also publishes "Environmental & Health Weekly", a short report "providing news and resources for environmental justice."

Equal Exchange
101 Tosca Dr., Stoughton, MA 02072, 617-344-7227.

Ethical Growth Fund
Vancouver City Savings Credit Union, 515 West Tenth Ave., Vancouver, BC V5Z 4A8, Canada, 604-877-7613.
Largest ethical fund in Canada.

Ethical Investments, Inc.
430 First Ave. No., Ste. 204, Minneapolis, MN 55401, 612-339-3939.
Investment management firm specializing in publicly traded securities. Particularly active in working with clients new to SRI.

Ethicscan Canada
Box 165, Postal Station S, Toronto, ON M5M 4L7, Canada, 416-783-6776.
Prepares independent research reports on the social performance of 1500 Canadian companies.

Fair Trade Foundation
  65 Landing Rd., Hagganum, CT 06441, 203-345-3374.
  A new organization designed to change the way the United States does business with the Third World started by Co-op America founder Paul Freundlich. Crafts, technical assistance.

Federation of Appalachian Housing Enterprises
  Drawer B, Berea, KY 40403, 606-986-3283.

Federation of Southern Cooperatives
  PO Box 95, Epes, AL 35460, 205-652-9676.
  Assistance in community-based development to rural and urban poor people, generally in the South.

First Affirmative Financial Network
  1040 South 8th St., Ste. 200, Colorado Springs, CO 80909, 800-422-7284.
  Nationwide network of investment professionals specializing in SRI. Call for location nearest you.

First Environment
  266 Blackman Hill Rd., Berkshire, NY 13736, 607-657-8438.
  Joint international project of Plenty Canada and Center for Community Change, established by Mohawk midwife Katsi Cook to provide appropriate health information to Native women. Biannual newsletter.

First Nations Financial Project
  69 Kelley Rd., Falmouth, VA 22405, 703-371-5615.
  Economic development in context of Native culture and traditions. Provides technical and financial assistance.

Food & Allied Service Trade Department/AFL-CIO
  815 16th St., NW, #408, Washington, DC 20006, 202-737-7200.
  Makes available two excellent corporate research guides: *Manual of Corporate Investigation and Basic Organizing Research for Private Companies.*

Food and Water
  RR 1, Box 30, Old Schoolhouse Common, Marshfield, VT 05658.
  Grassroots food safety organization. Corporate campaigns, neighborhood networks, direct action and trustworthy information. Publishes quarterly newsletter. Membership: $25/year.

Forest Partnership
  PO Box 426, Burlington, VT 05402, 802-865-1111.
  Supports and promotes sustainable forestry, certification and marketing of certified wood products.

Forest Stewardship Council
  RR1, Box 188, Richmond, VT 05477, 802-434-3101.
  Accreditation organization for sustainable forestry certifiers.

Forest Trust
  PO Box 519, Santa Fe, NM 87504, 505-983-8992.
  Supports programs in the areas of community forestry, national forest policy, land trusts and land stewardship services.

FORGE
  Rt. 6, Box 134-1, Tahlequah, OK 74464, 918-456-1615.

Franklin Management Corporation
217 Lewis Warf, Boston, MA 02110, 617-367-1270.
Registered investment advisory firm providing customized investment management services.

Franklin Research & Development
711 Atlantic Ave., Boston, MA 02111, 617-423-6655.
Employee owned investment advisory firm managing funds exclusively for social investors. Publishes the newsletter, *Insight*.

Friends of the Third World
611 W. Wayne St., Fort Wayne, IN 46802, 219-422-6821.

Fund for an OPEN Society
311 S. Juniper St., Ste. 1127, Boston, MA 02116, 617-338-0010.

Funding Exhange
666 Broadway, 5th Fl., New York, NY 10012, 212-260-8500.
National organization of 14 community-based public foundations that fund grassroots and activist organizations.

Gardener's Supply Company
128 Intervale Rd., Burlington, VT 05401, 802-863-1700.
Catalog offering garden and composting supplies, etc. Promotes sustainable agriculture and organic gardening.

Genesis Fund
14618 NE 178th, Woodinville, WA 98072, 206-483-1258.
Provides capital and technical assistance to small businesses owned and operated by low-income people, women and people of color in Washington State.

GEO **(Grassroots Economic Organizing Newsletter)**
PO Box 5065, New Haven, CT 06525, 203-389-6194.
Bi-monthly publication focusing on sustainable community economics: jobs, currency, money, education, resources, and projects.

Global Education Associates
475 Riverside Drive, Rm. 570, New York, NY 10115, 212-870-3290.
Working to create a "more humane world order." Publications and newsletter.

Good Money **Publications, Inc.**
PO Box 363, Worcester, VT 05682, 800-535-3551.
Publishes a newsletter for socially concerned investors and *Social Funds Guide*. This annual comprehensive guide to mutual and money market SRI funds includes detailed information on screens, investments, performance, and social audits of the funds. Materials for workshops also available.

Government Accountability Project (GAP)
25 E Street, NW, Ste. 700, Washington, DC 20001, 202-347-0460.
Provides legal assistance to corporate whistleblowers, works with grassroots groups to help them make the most effective use of information from whistleblowers. Publications, newsletter, technical assistance.

Greater New Haven Community Loan Fund
5 Elm St., New Haven, CT 06510, 203-789-8690.

Green Alternatives
  38 Montgomery St., Rhinebeck, NY 12572, 914-876-6525.
  Bimonthly magazine for consumers seeking ecological alternatives to mainstream products.

Green Builder Program
  206 East Ninth St., Ste. 17.102, Austin, TX 78701, 512-499-3506.

Green Century Funds
  29 Temple Place, Boston, MA 02111, 800-93-GREEN.
  Family of environmentally responsible mutual funds. Fund is advised and administered by Green Centry Capital Management, which distributes 100 percent of its net profits to non-profit environmental organizations. Minimum investment: $2,000.

Green Consumer Letter
  1526 Connecticut Ave., NW, Washington, DC 20036, 800-955-GREEN.
  Monthly newsletter.

Green Motor Works
  5228 Vineland Ave., N., Hollywood, CA 91601, 818-766-3800.
  Only full-service electric vehicle dealership in United States.

Green Seal
  30 Irving Place, 9th Fl., New York, NY 10003, 212-533-SEAL.
  Founded in 1990, assesses the environmental desirability of some products from manufacture through disposal.

Green Seal
  1250 23rd St., NW, Ste. 275, Washington, DC 20037, 202-331-7337.
  Independent, environmental certification organization.

Greenmoney Journal
  West 608 Glass Ave., Spokane, WA 99205, 509-328-1741.
  Quarterly newsletter focusing on SRI resources.

Greenpeace
  1436 U Street, NW, Washington, DC 20009, 202-462-1177.
  Contact address for national office. Call for information on current campaigns and regional contact persons. Quarterly newsletter.

Habitat for Humanity
  Habitat and Church Streets, Americus, GA 31709, 912-924-6935.

Hartford Food System
  509 Wethersfield Ave., Hartford, CT 06114, 203-296-9325.
  Creating food systems that work for low-income neighborhoods in Hartford. Resources available, information on projects that can serve as models.

Harvest Times
  PO Box 1399, Kingston, NY 12401, 914-688-5030.
  Quarterly newsletter on CSA, edited by CSA farmer. Database can connect you to CSA in your area.

HEAD Corporation Revolving Loan Fund
  PO Box 504, Berea, KY 40403, 606-9486-3283.

HFG Expansion Fund
PO Box 81367, Wellesley, MA 02181, 617-431-2322.
Venture capital fund with social/environmental goals.

Highlander Center - Economy/Environment Program
1959 Highlander Way, New Market, TN 37820, 615-933-3443.
The Highlander Center helps and inspires community organizing through training, workshops, networking. The Economy/Environment Program was initiated to "help active citizen groups redefine and replace false trade-offs (jobs vs the environment, for example) in a practical and effective way."

Ikwe Marketing Collective
Rt. 1, Box 286, Ponsford, MN 56575, 218-573-3411.
Nonprofit organization run by Native American women. Certified organic natural lake wild rice, baskets, beadwork, quilts. Catalog available.

Illinois Facilities Fund
300 West Adams St., Chicago, IL 60606, 312-629-0060.

Impact Project
21 Linwood St., Arlington, MA 02174, 617-648-0776.
Counsels people with inherited money about taking charge financially, handling family money issues, finding meaningful work and fulfilling dreams.

In Business
Box 323, Emmaus, PA 18049, 215-967-4135.
"Magazine for Eco-Entrepreneurs."

In Context
PO Box 11470, Bainbridge Island, WA 98110.
"Quarterly of Humane Sustainable Culture." Full of practical and inspiring articles focusing on actual projects as well as visions and ways of thinking. Highly recommended.

Indian Treaty Rights Center
4554 N. Broadway #258, Chicago, IL 60640.

Indigenous Environmental Network
PO Box 485, Bemidji, MN 56601, 218-751-4967.
Alliance of Native groups working on sovereignty, government accountability issues, related.

Indigenous Thought
6802 SW 13th St, Gainsville, FL 32608.
Bi-monthly, activist oriented newsletter.

Industrial Cooperative Association (ICA)
20 Park Plaza, Ste. 1127, Boston, MA 02116, 617-338-0010.
Committed to creating and strengthening employee-owned and other community-based enterprises. Offers workshops and technical assistance to new businesses as well as to employees seeking to buy their company.

Industrial Cooperative Association RLF
20 Park Plaza, Ste. 1127, Boston, MA 02116, 617-338-0010.

INFACT
256 Hanover St., Boston, MA 02113, 617-742-4583.

Insitute for Community Economics (ICE)
57 School St., Springfield, MA 01105, 413-746-8660.
In addition to its revolving loan fund, ICE is a clearinghouse as well as a technical assistance provider for land trusts. Publications include: *Community Land Trust Handbook* and *Profiles of Community Land Trusts.*

Institute for Bau-Biologie and Ecology, Inc.
PO Box 681468, Park City, UT 84068, 801-783-2579.
Healthy, non-allergenic design and construction. Resources.

Institute for Local Self-Reliance
2425 18th St., NW, Washington, DC 2009, 202-232-4108.
Non-profit organization using waste as a tool for community-based economic development (waste is a resource). Publications, books, technical assistance.

Institute for Social Ecology
PO Box 89, Plainfield, VT 05667, 802-454-8493.

Institute for Sustainable Forestry
PO Box 1580, Redway, CA 95560, 707-923-4719.
Sustainable, community-based forestry.

Interfaith Center on Corporate Responsibility (ICCR)
475 Riverside Drive, Room 566, New York, NY 10115, 212-870-2936.

International Alliance for Sustainable Agriculture
1701 University Ave., SE, Minneapolis, MN 55414, 612-331-1099.

Investor Responsibility Research Center (IRRC)
1755 Massachusetts Ave., NW, Ste. 600, Washinton, DC 20036, 202-234-7500.

Ithaca Money
Box 6578, Ithaca, NY 14851, 607-273-8025.

Job Seeker
Rt. 2, Box 16, Warrens, WI 54666.
Newsletter specializing in environmental and natural resource vacancies nationwide. Published twice monthly.

Jubilee Community Loan Fund
55 Tree Haven Rd., Buffalo, NY 14215, 716-836-83559.

Kinder, Lydenberg, Domini & Co, Inc.
129 Mount Auburn St., Cambridge, MA 02138, 617-547-7479.
Full service SRI research house. Various publications and data base services for investors.

Kokopelli Notes: Transportation Choices for a Greener Planet
PO Box 8186, Asheville, NC 28814, 704-683-4844.
Magazine that encourages transportation alternatives.

Label Letter. **Union Label & Trades Department, AFL-CIO**
815 16th St., NW, Washington, DC 20006.
Bimonthly publication maintains on-going list of labor boycotts sanctioned by AFL-CIO.

Lakota Fund
PO Box 340, Kyle, SD 57752, 605-455-2500.

Land Stewardship Project
14758 Ostlund Trail North, Marine, MN 55047, 612-433-2770.
Works to develop "a sound stewardship ethic toward our nation's farmland and for public policy changes that will lead to a development of a sustainable agriculture system." Information on community supported agriculture, sustainable agriculture initiatives, etc. Quarterly newsletter.

Land Trust Alliance
900 17th St., NW #410, Washington, DC 20006, 202-785-1410.
A national organization of land trusts. Publishes newsletter and other information including handbook, *Starting a Land Trust*.

Landsman Community Services/LETS
600 Embleton Crescent, Courtenay, BC V9N 6N8, Canada, 604-338-0213/0214.

Latino Economic Development Corporation
1789 Columbia Road, NW, Ste. 3, Washington, DC 20009, 202-588-5102.
Community development organization. Programs include community controlled credit union, a microenterprise loan fund, and insurance partnerships.

Leviticus 25:23 Alternative Fund
299 North Highland Ave., Ossining, NY 10562, 914-941-9422.

Local Initiatives Support Corps
733 Third Ave., New York, NY 10017, 212-455-9800.
Offers grants and low-interest loans to community development corporations in areas of neighborhood renewal, job creation, low-income housing.

Los Angeles EcoVillage/Cooperative Resources & Services Project (CRSP)
3551 White House Pl., Los Angeles, CA 90004, 213-738-1254.
The Los Angeles EcoVillage is a two block area three miles west of downtown Los Angeles utilizing an "approach in which physical, social and economic systems" are planned and developed on a collaborative basis. CRSP operates a LETS system, the L.A. Shared Housing Network, the ELF revolving loan fund for sustainable enterprise development and a library of over 3,000 books, publications and audio-visual materials on cooperatives, CED, planning, etc.

Low Income Housing Fund
605 Market St., Ste. 709, San Francisco, CA 94105, 415-777-9804.

McAuley Housing Fund
1650 Farnum St., Omaha, NE 68102, 402-346-6000 ext. 344.

McAuley Institute
8300 Colesville Rd., Ste. 310, Silver Spring, MD 20910, 301-588-8110.

Menominee Tribal Enterprises
PO Box 10, Neopit, WI 54135, 715-756-2311.
Practicing sustainable forestry since 1854. Wholesaler of certified sustainable wood.

Michigan Housing Trust Fund
3401 E. Saginaw, Ste. 212, Lansing, MI 48912, 517-336-9919.

MICRO
802 East 46th St., Tucson, AZ 85713, 602-622-35539.

Montreal Community Loan Association
914 Rachel East St., Montreal, QUE H2J 2J1, Canada, 514-525-6628.

Multinational Monitor
PO Box 19405, Washington, DC 20036, 202-387-8030.
Newsmagazine founded by Ralph Nader, dedicated to tracking and exposing the illegal, abusive and deceptive activities of multinational corporations. Recommended.

National Association of Community Development Loan Funds
924 Cherry St., Philadelphia, PA 19107, 215-923-4754.
Member organization of community development revolving loan funds of the type discussed in this book. Contact for general information on RLFs, technical assistance and information on individual RLFs.

National Bank of Boyertown
Reading & Philadelphia Avenues, Boyertown, PA 19512, 215-369-6236.
Large community bank serving southeastern Pennsylvania. Developed SHARE account in 1989. Funds are used to make no interest second mortages or outright grants to prospective homeowners.

National Business Incubation
One President St., Athens, OH 45701, 614-593-4331.
Trade association for developers and managers of small business incubators.

National Center for Appropriate Technology
PO Box 3838, Butte, MT 59702, 800-428-2525.
Clearinghouse for information on appropriate technology. Free technical assistance on energy efficiency, sustainable agriculture and economic development for rural communities.

National Center for Economic Alternatives
1000 Connecticut Ave., NW, Ste. 9, Washington, DC 20036, 202-483-6667.

National Center for Employee Ownership
2201 Broadway, Ste. 807, Oakland, CA 94612, 510-272-9461.
Publications, consulting and conferences on employee-ownership.

National Committee for Responsive Philanthropy
2001 S St., NW, #620, Washington, DC 20009, 202-387-9177.

National Congress for Community Economic Development
1875 Connecticut Ave., NW, Ste. 524, Washington, DC 20009, 202-234-5009.

National Cooperative Bank
140 I St., NW, Washington, DC 20005, 202-336-7655.
Financial services to cooperatively structured, democratically owned and controlled enterprises.

National Cooperative Business Association
1401 New York Ave., NW, Ste. 1100, Washington, DC 20005, 202-638-1374.
Mission is to represent, strengthen and expand the cooperative form of business and link members.

National Council for Urban Economic Development
1730 K St., NW, # 915, Washington, DC 20006, 202-223-4735.

National Federation of Community Development Credit Unions
120 Wall Street, 10th Floor, New York, NY 10005, 212-809-1850.
Can help you find a credit union near you. Also assists community-based organizations form new credit unions.

Native Action
PO Box 316, Lame Deer, MT 59043, 406-477-6390.
Works on social justice and environmental issues on the Northern Cheyenne reservation.

Native Americans for a Clean Environment (NACE)
PO Box 1671, Tahlequah, OK 74456, 918-458-4322.
Grassroots action primarily on local issues including nuclear waste and economic conversion.

Native Forest Network (NFN)
PO Box 57, Burlington, VT 05402, 802-863-0571.
International network of forest activists committed to protecting and defending temperate forests worldwide and the indigenous and forest-based peoples that live in them. NFN has contacts in various regions in the United States, Canada, Australia, Chile, Argentina, Europe and Japan.

Native Self-Sufficiency
See Seventh Generation Fund.
News concerning Native peoples, appropriate technology, Native rights, and economic development. Published quarterly.

Natural Cotton Colours, Inc.
PO Box 66, 67 No. Tegner St., Wickenburg, AZ 85390, 602-684-7199.
Information about FoxFibre cotton (cotton grown in colors that requires no dyes.)

Natural Rights Center
PO Box 90, Summertown, TN 39483, 615-964-2334.
Protects the natural rights of those often ignored: indigenous peoples, non-human species, the land ,and the water in the courts.

NCB Development Corporation
1401 Eye Street, NW, Washington, DC 20005, 202-336-7680.
Affiliate of the National Cooperative Bank providing specialized financial services to cooperatives nationwide. Special initiatives in areas of community economic development, affordable and specialized needs in housing and healthcare.

Neighbor to Neighbor
135 West 4th St., New York, NY 10012, 212-505-2185.

Neighborhood Enterprise Center
80 Boylston St., Ste. 1207, Boston, MA 02116, 617-565-8240.
Peer group lending, enterprise training and peer group support programs targeting economicaly disadvantaged people, especially minorities and women.

Neighborhood Works
Center for Neighborhood Technology, 2125 W. North Ave., Chicago, IL 60647, 312-278-4800.
Focuses on organizing city neighborhoods around energy, environment, transportation, housing, jobs, manufacturing, and economics. Excellent for resources, contacts and inspiration.

New Alternatives Fund
295 Northern Blvd., Great Neck, NY 11021, 516-466-0808.
Founded in 1982, mutual fund that invests in companies involved in alternative energy and that do not harm the environment. Includes investments in solar cell production, resource recovery plants, recycling and co-generation. Excludes nuclear energy and petroleum resources.

New Consumer Institute
PO Box 51, Wauconda, IL 60084, 708-526-0522.
Information on green and socially responsible products and services. Newsletters, reports.

New Dimensions Radio
PO Box 410510, San Francisco, CA 94141, 415-563-8899.
National public radio series dedicated to personal and social transformation through in-depth interviews with innovative thinkers in politics, health, ecology, and spirituality.

New Hampshire Community Loan Fund
Box 666, Concord, NH 03302, 603-224-6669.

New Jersey Community Loan Fund
PO Box 1655, Trenton, NJ 08607, 609-989-7766.

New Mexico Community Development Loan Fund
PO Box 705, Albuquerque, NM 87103, 505-243-3196.

New Roadmap Foundation
PO Box 15981, Seattle, WA 98115, 206-527-0437.
Organization that teaches how to achieve financial independence and live more consciously and frugally through alternative life and work choices.

Nonprofit Facilities Fund
12 West 31st St., New York, NY 10001, 212-868-6710.

Northcountry Cooperative Development Fund
400 19th Avenue South, Ste. 202, Minneapolis, MN 55104, 612-339-1553.

Northeast CoHousing Quarterly
155 Pine St., Amherst, MA 01002, 413-549-3616.
Regional newsletter.

Northern California Community Loan Fund
14 Precita Ave., San Francisco, CA 94110, 415-285-3909.

Northwest Policy Center
University of Washington, 327 Parrington Hall DC-14, Seattle, WA 98195, 206-543-7900.
Strategies to maintaini a vital economy and a healthy environment in the Northwest. Publications, newsletter, conferences, and technical assistance.

Ohio Hempery, Inc.
14 N. Court St., #361, Athens, OH 45701, 614-593-5826.
Hemp products including fabric, tree-free paper, body products, oil and seeds, twine, rope, books. Catalog and fabric samples, $2, refundable with first order.

OMB Watch
1731 Connecticut Ave., NW, Washington, DC 20009, 202-234-8494.
Free database: RTK Net (Right to Know Network).

One World Trading
1 DeSoto St., Pittsburgh, PA 15205, 412-921-7208.
Handcrafted jewelry, clothing, crafts directly from artisans in Central and South America and Indonesia. Catalog available.

Oxfam America Trading
PO Box 821, Lewiston, ME 04240, 800-639-2141.

Parnassus Fund
244 California Street, San Francisco, CA 94111, 800-999-3505.
Founded in 1985, mutual fund that makes use of a "contrarian" investment policy of going against the "established wisdom" of Wall Street. Invests in companies that "practice corporate social responsibility."

Partners for the Common Good Loan Fund
Our Lady of the Lake University, 411 SW 24th St., San Antonio, TX 78207, 210-431-0616.

Partnerships for Self-Sufficiency/SEEDCO
915 Broadway, New York, NY 10010, 212-473-0255.
Support for forming partnerships and developing community-based businesses.

Paul Terry & Associates
185 Arkansas St., San Francisco, CA 94107, 415-255-0131.
Small and micro business advisory services.

Pax World Fund
224 State St., Portsmouth, NH 03801, 800-767-1729.
Founded in 1970. "Invests in those companies whose products and services enhance the quality of life." The affiliated Pax World Foundation works for the world's poor and world peace.

Peacework. **American Friends Service Committee (AFSC)**
2161 Massachusetts Ave., Cambridge, MA 02140.

People for the Ethical Treatment of Animals
PO Box 42516, Washington, DC 20015, 202-726-0156.
Offers cruelty-free shopping guide with list of products and companies that do and don't test products and ingredients on animals.

Piedmont Peace Project
406 Jackson Park Rd., Kannapolis, NC 28038, 704-938-5090.
For description, see section on "Community Organizing."

Pioneer Valley Cohousing Group
116 Depot Road, Hatfield, MA 01038.

Planet Drum Foundation
Box 31251, San Francisco, CA 94131, 415-285-6556.

Focuses on bioregionalism, urban and rural. Publishes membership newsletter, *Raise the Stakes*.

Plenty, USA
PO Box 2306, Davis, CA 95617, 906-753-0731.

PR Watch
3318 Gregory St., Madison, WI 53711, 608-233-3346.
Uncovers behind-the-scenes manipulation of media by large corporate interests.

Progressive Asset Managment, Inc.
1814 Franklin Street, Ste. 710, Oakland, CA 94612, 800-786-2998.
Full service investment broker/dealer specializing in socially and environmentally responsible investing.

Public Citizen
2000 P St., NW, Washington, DC 20036, 202-833-3000.
Founded by Ralph Nader, fights for government and corporate accountability, safe products, etc. Magazine, health letter, books.

Pueblo to People
PO Box 2545, Houston, TX 77252, 713-956-1172.
Catalog of clothing and gifts from Latin American craft cooperatives.

Rainforest Action Network
450 Sansome, #700, San Francisco, CA 94111, 415-398-4404.
Action on behalf of the world's rainforests and indigenous communities who live in them. Publishes "Action Alerts", the "World Rainforest Report" and extensive information on corporate, institutional and governmental destroyers. Supports direct action.

Rainforest Alliance/Smart Wood Program
65 Bleeker St., New York, NY 10012, 212-677-1900.
Certifier of well-managed and sustainable forestry in tropics and temperate and boreal forests of North America.

Real Goods
966 Mazzoni St., Ukiah, CA 95482-3471, 800-762-7325.
Catalog offers products for "intelligent, sustainable living" including energy, tools, power systems, solar, appliances, composting toilets, non-toxic cleaners, and natural fiber clothing.

Regional Economic Justice Network
PO Box 240, Durham, NC 27702, 919-683-1361.
Multiracial grassroots association of union and nonunion worker and community groups grappling with economic survival.

Revision
1319 Eighteenth St., N.W., Washington, DC 20036-1802.
Quarterly "Journal of consciousness and transformation."

Rocky Mountain CoHousing Quarterly
1705 14th St., #317, Boulder, CO 80302, 303-442-3280.
Regional newsletter.

Rocky Mountain Institute/Economic Renewal Program
1739 Old Snowmass Creek Rd., Snowmass, CO 81654, 303-927-3851.

Rogue Institute for Ecology and Economy
PO Box 3213, Ashland, OR 97520, 503-482-6031.
Certifier of sustainable forestry in pacific northwest. Focus is on "community forestry" which includes both forest communities and the communities of people that live in and with them.

Rural Community Assistance Corporation
2125 19th St., Ste. 203, Sacramento, CA 95818, 916-447-2854.
Information, networking, training, conferences and excellent publications. *Pacific Mountain Network News* and *Pacific Mountain Reveiw* both publish regularly on issues relating to community-based economic development.

Rural Enterprise Assistance Project (REAP)
PO Box 406, Walthill, NB 68067, 402-846-5428.
Project of Center for Rural Affairs that supports microenterprise with technical assistance and loans.

S.U.R.E. Exchange/Grassroots Resources, Inc.
PO Box 11343, Takoma Park, MD 20913, 301-588-7227.
Quarterly newsletter focuses on sustainable communities and fostering partnerships for sharing information and resources between cities and rural areas.

Save America's Forests
4 Liberty Court, SE, Washington, DC 20003, 202-544-9219.
"Nationwide campaign to protect and restore America's wild and natural forests. Lobbies, informs, and campaigns. Offers newsletter and fax alerts. Membership includes most grassroots forest organizations in United States.

Scientific Certification Systems (SCS)
1611 Telegraph Ave., Ste. 1111, Oakland, CA 94612, 510-832-1415.

Seeds of Change
621 Old Santa Fe Trail, #10, Santa Fe, NM 87501, 505-983-8956.
Sells certified organic, open-pollinated seeds for gardeners. Heirloom and traditional varieties. Catalog costs $3.00, refundable with first order.

Self-Help Credit Union
PO Box 3619, Durham, NC 27702, 800-476-7428.
Founded in 1984, focuses on economic development for disadvantaged communities.

Self-Help Ventures Fund
413 East Chapel Hill Street, Durham, NC 27701, 919-683-3016.

Seventh Generation
49 Hercules Dr., Colchester, VT 05446, 800-456-1177.
"Products for a healthy planet" catalog.

Seventh Generation Fund
PO Box 2550, McKinleyville, CA 95521, 707-839-1178.
Funds and provides technical support to small grassroots oriented Native economic development projects.

Silva Forest Foundation
PO Box 9, Slocan Park, BC V0G 2E0, Canada, 604-226-7222.

Supports a cooperative, consensus-based decision-making process in local communities to plan the use of forests.

Social Equity Group
5900 Hollis Street, Ste. H, Emeryville, CA 94608, 510-596-9960.
Specializes in personalized portfolio managment, low-income housing and social research.

Social Investment Forum
PO Box 57216, Washington, DC 20037, 202-833-5522.
The Social Investment Forum, founded in 1981, is a national organization dedicated to promoting the concept and practice of SRI. Publishes annual *Social Investment Services Guid* listing funds, advisors, brokers, research organizations, and others involved in SRI. Excellent resource to find out who's doing what, and to locate advisors/brokers in your state.

Social Investment Organization
336 Adelaide St., E #447, Toronto, Ontario M5A 3X9, Canada, 416-861-0403.
Canada's national network of socially responsible investors—individuals, institutions and businesses.

Social Responsibility Investment Group, Inc.
The Chandler Bldg., Ste. 662, 127 Peachtree Street NE, Atlanta, GA 30303, 404-577-3635.
Money management firm and registered investment advisor.

Social Trust Network
1586 S. 21st St., Ste. B, Colorado Springs, CO 80904, 800-279-4944.
Socially responsible financial and estate planning.

South Shore Bank of Chicago
71st and Jeffery Blvd., Chicago, IL 60649, 800-NOW-SSBK.
Mnodel for community development banking.

Southeastern Reinvestment Ventures
159 Ralph McGill Blvd., NE, Rm. 505, Atlanta, GA 30308, 404-659-0002 ext. 3240.

Southside Bank
2023 Eastern S.E., Grand Rapids, MI 49507, 616-241-0288.
Community development bank in Formation.

Stop Junk Mail Associatioin
c/o 3020 Bridgeway, St. 150A, Sausalito, CA , 800-827-5549.
Gets member's names removed from junk mail lists. Free brochure.

Task Force on Multinational Corporations/Inst. on Trade Policy
PO Box 389, Seattle, WA 98111, 206-783-5009.

Time Dollars
PO Box 19405, Washington, DC 20036, 202-686-5200.
Resources for starting a Time Dollars Program, including the book, *Time Dollars* by Edgar Cahn and *The Complete Time Dollar Kit* (manual and computer program) .

Toward Freedom
209 College St., Burlington, VT 05401, 802-658-2523.

Tracking Project
PO Box 266, Corrales, NM 87048.
Dedicated to community education by helping people gain an experience of the natural world through music, storytelling, dance, martial arts, tracking and traditional survival skills. Programs actively support cultural and community revival.

Tranet
PO Box 567, Rangeley, ME 04970, 207-864-2252.
A bi-monthly newsletter of, by and for people participating in the social paradigm shift in all parts of the world. A digest of all aspects of the Alternative & Transformational (A & T) movements. Numerous contacts in a wide variety of diciplines.

Tree People
12601 Mulholland Drive, Beverly Hills, CA 90210, 818-753-4600.
Urban forestry programs.

UNC Ventures
711 Atlantic Ave., Boston, MA 02111, 617-482-7070.
Venture capital firm that invests in minority enterprises.

United States Trust Company
40 Court Street, Boston, MA 02108, 800-441-8782 ext. 7250.
Asset management.

Urban Ecologist
PO Box 10144, Berkeley, CA 94709, 510-549-1724.
Publishication of Urban Ecology (see below).

Urban Ecology
PO Box 10144, Berkeley, CA 94709, 510-549-1724.
Non-profit organization working to create sustainable urban environments. Sponsors conferences, develops resources and publishes a quarterly journal, *The Urban Ecologist*.

Urban Habitat Program
300 Broadway, Ste. 28, San Francisco, CA 94133, 415-788-3666.
A project of the Earth Island Institute, focuses on developing multicultural urban environmental leadership. Publishes bi-monthly newsletter, *Race, Poverty and the Environment*.

Urban Institute
2100 M St., NW, Washington, DC 20037, 202-833-7200.
Non-profit research organization that investigates social and economic problems in U.S. cities and assesses government policies and programs, including global warming, ground water, energy and population.

Urban Land Institute
625 Indiana Ave., NW, Washington, DC 20004, 202-624-7000.

Vermont Community Loan Fund
PO Box 827, Montpelier, VT 05601, 802-223-1448.

Vermont National Bank, SRB Fund
PO Box 804, Brattleboro, VT 05302, 800-772-3863.

Socially Responsible Banking Fund offers depositors opportunity to support affordable housing, environmental and conservation projects, agriculture, education and small business.

Vermonters Organized for Clean-up
PO Box 120, East Calais, VT 05650, 802-472-6996.

Washington Area Community Investment Fund
2201 P Street, NW, Washington, DC 20037, 202-462-4727.

Western Shoshone Defense Project
PO Box 211106, Crescent Valley, NV 89821, 702-468-0230.

White Earth Land Recovery Project
PO Box 327, White Earth, MN 56591, 218-473-3110.
Rebuilding land-base of White Earth reservation in northwestern Minnesota. Tribal organic wild rice marketing collective (available directly or in various catalogs and "green" stores such as Co-op America).

Wild Forest Review
3758 SE Milwaukie, Portland, OR 97202, 503-234-0093.
The forest activist's publication isn't afraid to tell it like it is, nor does it avoid opinions that differ from the editor's. Irreverant, fun, accurate and radical. Recommended highly.

Wild Iris Forestry
PO Box 1423, Redway, CA 95560, 707-923-2344.
Leaders in setting standards of sustainable forestry in California. Small mill operation, research, information, and contacts.

WOMONEY
76 Townsend Rd., Belmont, MA 02178, 617-489-3601.
Financial education and planning for women (and men).

Woodstock Institute
407 South Dearborn, Ste. 550, Chicago, IL 60605, 312-427-8070.
Non-profit organization works in a technical assistance capacity with non-profits and in a consulting capacity with financial institutions, philanthropic organizations and government agencies to increase investment in disadvantaged communities.

Worcester Community Loan Fund
PO Box 271, Mid Town Mall, Worcester, MA 01614, 508-799-6108.

Workbook
Southwest Research & Information Center, PO Box 4524, Albuquerque, NM 87106, 505-262-1862.
Resources about environmental, social and consumer issues.

Working Assets Common Holdings
111 Pine Street, San Francisco, CA 94111, 800-223-7010.
Offers Working Assets Money Market Portfolio and Citizen's Portfolios.

Working Capital
2500 N. River Rd., Manchester, NH 03106, 603-644-3124.
Supports microenterprise in New England.

Worldwatch Institute

1776 Massachusetts Ave., NW, Washington, DC 20036, 202-452-1999.

Worldwatch's mission is to "foster a sustainable society." It publishes the annual *State of the World*, *Vital Signs*, Environmental Alert book series, *World Watch Magazine* and *Worldwatch Papers*.

Z Magazine

18 Millfield St., Woods Hole, MA 02543, 508-548-9063.

Index

D

E

F

H

I

M

T

U

About the Author

SUSAN MEEKER-LOWRY first became involved in economic alternatives in 1981 when she co-founded (with Ritchie P. Lowry and Peter R. Lowry) *Good Money*, the nation's first newsletter for socially concerned investors. In 1983 she began publishing *Catalyst: Investing in Social Change*, later changed to *Catalyst: Economics for the Living Earth*, which was published until 1993. She also co-founded the nonprofit organization, Catalyst, in 1986 to promote economic alternatives in the context of the whole earth community. Susan's first book, *Economics as If the Earth Really Mattered*, was published in 1988.

Today, Susan is the managing editor of Food & Water's quarterly newsletter, where she also researches and writes special reports. She also works with the Dawnland Center, an intertribal, nonprofit organization based in Montpelier committed to community healing and renewal in the Native communities of New England. She serves on the board of directors of *Toward Freedom* newsletter in Burlington, Vermont. Even though the organization Catalyst no longer exists, Susan continues to be active locally and helps organize conferences and events in the region where she lives. Her articles have appeared in publications such as *Z Magazine*, *Earth Island Journal*, *Sojourners*, *Vermont Woodlands*, *In Business*, *Talking Leaves*, *Woman of Power*, and other journals, newsletters, and local papers. She also offers workshops and presentations. Contact Susan at P.O. Box 734, Montpelier, Vermont or through New Society Publishers.

Susan lives with her three sons and four cats in Montpelier, Vermont.

New Society Publishers

NEW SOCIETY PUBLISHERS is a not-for-profit, worker-controlled publishing house. We are proud to be the only publishing house in the North America committed to fundamental social change through nonviolent action.

We are connected to a growing worldwide network of peace, feminist, religious, environmental, and human rights activists, of which we are an active part. We are proud to offer powerful nonviolent alternatives to the harsh and violent industrial and social systems in which we all participate. And we deeply appreciate that so many of you continue to look to us for resources in these challenging and promising times.

New Society Publishers is a project of the New Society Educational Foundation and the Catalyst Education Society. We are not the subsidiary of any transnational corporation; we are not beholden to any other organization; and we have neither stockholders nor owners in any traditional business sense. We hold this publishing house in trust for you, our readers and supporters, and we appreciate your contributions and feedback.

New Society Publishers
4527 Springfield Avenue
Philadelphia, Pennsylvania
19143

New Society Publishers
P.O. Box 189
Gabriola Island, British Columbia
V0R 1X0